Joe Alsop's Cold War

Edwin M. Yoder, Jr.

The
University of
North Carolina
Press
Chapel Hill &
London

Joe Alsop's Cold War

A Study of

Journalistic

Influence and

Intrigue

Library of Congress Cataloging-in-Publication Data

Yoder, Edwin.

Joe Alsop's cold war : a study of journalistic influence

and intrigue / Edwin M. Yoder, Jr.

p.   cm.

Includes bibliographical references (p.   ) and index.

ISBN 0-8078-2190-x (cloth : alk. paper)

1. Alsop, Joseph, 1910–89.   2. Alsop, Stewart.

3. Journalists — United States — Biography.   4. Press

and politics — United States — History — 20th

century.   5. United States — Foreign relations —

1945–1989.   6. Cold war.   I. Title.

PN4874.A43Y63   1995

070'.92 — dc20   94-33793

[B]   CIP

99 98 97 96 95   5 4 3 2 1

FOR WILLIE MORRIS

and other American Oxonians, 1956–58

One profession alone seemed possible—the Press . . . still the last resource of the educated poor who could not be artists and would not be tutors. Any man who was fit for nothing else could write an editorial or criticism. The enormous mass of misinformation accumulated in ten years of nomad life could always be worked off on a helpless public, in diluted doses, if one could but secure a table in the corner of a newspaper office.

—Henry Adams, *The Education of Henry Adams*

Being a newspaper columnist is a little like being a Greek chorus. . . . You describe the parts of the drama that do not take place on the open stage.

—Joseph and Stewart Alsop, 1958

Contents

A section of photographs can be found following page 94.

Acknowledgments

I n Washington, there exists an informal Joe Alsop club, consisting of friends who enjoyed his company and who still relish tales about an American original. I have interviewed many of its members; from others, I have gleaned valuable incidental insights. My understanding of Joe Alsop owes much to them. Many were also friends of Stewart Alsop, but he had vanished from the Washington scene before I arrived and is not present to me as a personal memory. His distinguished columns for the *Saturday Evening Post* and *Newsweek* were must reading for me, however, and there was no American journalist whose writing I admired more.

No writer could wish such a project to receive a more open-hearted welcome than this one received from members of the Alsop family, many of whom I am fortunate to count as friends. Joe's niece Teeny (Corinne Chubb) Zimmermann and her husband Warren, for instance. We go back a long way. I first met Joe Alsop in the flesh at one of their Sunday lunches in Great Falls. Warren and Teeny nurtured the friendship on other enjoyable occasions. Their son Timothy, a schoolboy at the time of that first encounter, has followed his great-uncles into journalism and, as a diplomatic correspondent for *U.S. News & World Report*, carries on their tradition in style.

Susan Mary Alsop and Tish Alsop, good friends both, reminisced candidly and vividly about the brothers they married. Corinne Alsop Chubb, a keen and urbane presence, warmed a brisk March afternoon and evening at her hospitable New Jersey farm with recollections of her brothers. Though we were not able to arrange a formal interview, John Alsop extended friendly help—especially by providing a copy of his written comments on the draft manuscript of Joe's recent memoirs. Others of the Alsop connection, as well, were warmly encouraging.

Several friends and colleagues read drafts of the manuscript, in whole or in part, and made valuable suggestions. They are Jeffrey Frank, Frank A. Sieverts, John Maurice Evans, Truman Schwartz, Hampden Smith III, and Jonathan Yardley. My thanks to them all.

I wish also to acknowledge by name a few of the persons who helped in other ways: Robert Barnett, Luke Battle, Michael Beschloss, Sir Isaiah Berlin, James Billington, Evangeline Bruce, Art Buchwald, McGeorge Bundy, Edward Burlingame, Douglass Cater, John Milton Cooper, Jr., W. Robert Connor, Aida Donald, Alfred and Pie Friendly, Clayton and Polly Fritchey, Phil and Sherry Geyelin, Lewis Gould, Katharine Graham, Meg Greenfield, Richard Helms, Sir Nicholas Henderson, Gerald Holton, Alistair Horne, Peter Jay, Margaret Jay (now the Baroness Jay of Paddington), George F. Kennan, Henry A. Kissinger, Andrew Knight, Nelson Lankford, John Lukacs, James B. Meriwether, Edmund Morris, The Honorable Daniel Patrick Moynihan, Paul Nitze, Don Oberdorfer, Sir Peter Ramsbotham, James Reston, Arthur M. Schlesinger, Jr., Godfrey Sperling, Roger Stevens, Athan Theoharis, Bill Van Alstyne, Sam and Sherry Wells, David Wigdor, George F. Will, and Sir Edgar Williams. My thanks, as well, to the staff of the Manuscript Division of the Library of Congress, friendly and efficient custodians of the Alsop Papers.

And finally, a word about the dedication. On a gray October day in 1956, the *Flandre* sailed for England from New York with most of the 1956 crop of American Oxonians aboard. Willie Morris, to whom I have dedicated this book, was one of them. Our common embroilment in the college newspaper wars of that time had made us correspondents even before we ended up, by happy coincidence, on this voyage into the future. Our friendship ripened as we toasted the Statue of Liberty from the ship rails, and it has never flagged. As a constant friend and brilliant editor he has done me more good turns by far than this gesture can repay. From the camaraderie of that transatlantic voyage grew other lasting friendships. To none of those friends who embarked that day for Plymouth (including Mark Ball, Mike Hammond, Ed Selig, Neil Rudenstine, John D'Arms, Rocky Suddarth, Van Ooms, Carey Parker, and Dick Baker, and others) were the persons and issues explored in this book strange. They were, in the words of the title Murray Kempton gave to a much-admired work of that period, "part of our time," as some are now "ruins and monuments" (Kempton, *Part of Our Time: Some Ruins and Monuments of the Thirties* [New York: Simon & Schuster, 1955]). This book is dedicated to Willie and the other American Oxonians of that vintage in the belief that it reflects in significant ways what the fifties taught our generation about this country and its responsibilities. For others, it may serve as a modest guide to what is too quickly becoming—as someone elsewhere has said of the past—"another country." As always, I must thank the very closest friend who saw me off on the *Flandre*, though happily not forever—Jane Warwick Yoder, the most astute of mentors on the great subject of human character.

Joe Alsop's Cold War

Prologue

his is a book about two Washington newspapermen, Joseph and Stewart Alsop, brothers and, from 1946 to 1958, partners in a widely read column. Of the two, Joe, the elder by four years, was much the better known and more celebrated. He was also a more assiduous keeper of records than his younger brother and junior partner, with the result that the present examination of the archives they jointly left behind is tilted heavily in Joe Alsop's direction—to the point, indeed, that Stewart, who died a tragically early death in 1974, often appears to be a shadow by comparison.

This book is also about the 1950s, the decade in which the influence of the Alsops' column and of their reporting for the *Saturday Evening Post* stood at its height. It was also the decade in which my own interest in journalism and national security affairs ripened; and national security, in both its overseas and domestic aspects, was their specialty.

I did not know the Alsops personally then. But as a junior journalist, first at college and later professionally, I read their writing avidly from a distance—always with interest, often with admiration, sometimes with wonder at the senior partner's erudition. Joe Alsop seemed to be as much at ease in the distant past as in the present; he was as likely to hang a column on the otherwise prosaic subject of farm subsidies upon a passage from the Roman historian Livy or Edward Gibbon's speculations on the decline and fall of the Roman Empire as upon the headline story of the day before.

By the time I moved to Washington in June 1975 to edit the editorial page of its fine old afternoon paper, the *Star*, Joe Alsop had retired to write *The Rare Art Traditions*, his huge book on the history of art collecting.[1] His younger brother Stewart had been dead for two years of a mysterious strain of leukemia. In the final gallant exercise of his exceptional reportorial capacities, Stewart Alsop had gazed death in the eye with the humor and aplomb of the former OSS liaison to the French maquis he once had been. He called his memoir *Stay of Execution*, and its bravery and gallows humor were universally admired.

The present book is an inquiry into a question that haunts anyone who makes a career of commenting on the news. Does journalistic commentary, written on the wing and often qualifying for the dismissive label "instant analysis," really matter? If so, how much? How risky is it to follow history—in the memorable words of Sir Walter Raleigh—so close at the heels that it may kick out all one's teeth? Does one write disinterestedly in the public interest, or is the exercise, as the ever-candid George Orwell might have said, a form of self-diversion publicly exercised so that others, if they care to, may look casually over the shoulder of an otherwise self-absorbed observer?

Now and then the words "influential" and even "powerful" are applied to journalists. Both adjectives were freely used, in their time, of both the Alsop brothers. But such adjectives are now more usually reserved for television anchormen or investigative reporters like Seymour Hersh of the *New York Times* and Bob Woodward of the *Washington Post*, who with his partner, Carl Bernstein, helped crack the Watergate conspiracy. The Alsops thought of themselves primarily as investigative reporters and only secondarily as pundits. Their game, they insisted, was revelation—the fresher the better. One of their many rules was that every column they wrote must offer at least one "new" fact that no one else had reported; no stand-alone opinionizing was allowed.

In the great age of the Washington column, they were rivaled—if at all—only by Walter Lippmann, the mainstay of the *New York Herald Tribune* syndicate, which distributed their work as well, and by Arthur Krock and James (Scotty) Reston of the *New York Times*. That age might be dated from September 1931, when Lippmann departed from the *New York World* to write his "Today and Tomorrow" column, to 1974, when Joe Alsop decided, not long after Stewart's death, to withdraw from columnizing. In those years, syndicated columnists held a roving license to patrol and occasionally cross the unmapped boundaries between reporting and editorializing. Such promiscuity was strictly forbidden in the news columns, which were in theory consecrated to the "who-what-where-when-how" relation of fact—fact that was sometimes barren of its indispensable context. Today, commentary, thinly disguised as analysis, is a fixed constituent of news pages in almost every newspaper; and this reality, together with the pervasiveness of television, has clearly devalued the opinion columnist's wares.

Still, it was an important and eagerly read journalistic form in its heyday, attentively followed by the political cognoscenti, high and low. At the 1964 Republican National Convention, for example, Dwight D. Eisenhower denounced "sensation-seeking" columnists for what they were saying about Senator Barry Goldwater, the eventual Republican nominee; the former president did not identify his targets by name, but the roar of the crowd suggested that he hardly needed to.

One of the principal aims of this book, which aims to be history with a biographical flavor, is to examine how the Alsops worked, where they got their information (which was often surprising), and how their columns came to be thought of—not very accurately—as an outlet for leaks. Leaking in Washington is not widely understood, even in the capital city itself. It is basically an equalizing weapon for outsiders, potential losers, and underlings. The leak may be used, for instance, to reveal and thus undermine some policy initiative when untimely revelation may have the effect of a well-aimed torpedo. It may also be used selectively, by powerful and influential figures, to try out an idea or appointment before announcing it formally. The Alsops' most important sources, it would appear, were often too important to be accurately classified as mere leakers. At best, Joe Alsop took a somewhat toplofty attitude toward leaks and leakers, especially if they concerned intricate or sensitive national security secrets, and maintained for the record that journalists were citizens first and journalists second.

As for influence or power, its existence in journalism is elusive and difficult to measure objectively. Most newspapermen, most of the time, are pretty sure that the revelation of hard fact—novel, astonishing, timely, untimely, disconcerting, or embarrassing—is likelier to make waves than someone's utterance of a mere unadorned view, unless the utterer happens to be a president, a chief justice, or a congressional magnate of a now-vanishing breed. The Alsops certainly thought so and geared their workdays to the discovery and publication of fact. Besides, journalistic influence, like political influence, is in the eye of the beholder; it is a matter of perception. Those who are regarded as having influence have it by virtue of the very supposition. Sometimes, also, it can be conferred. Joe Alsop could not have been unhappy to learn, in a letter from his friend Paul Hyde Bonner, then in Rome, that Clare Boothe Luce had pronounced him at someone's dinner table "the best political analyst now writing in America." "I heard no dissent," Bonner added.[2] For the most part, influence would have to be measured by asking what happened—or failed to happen—because of something a columnist wrote. Of the two possibilities, the veto power of publicity is probably the more likely. But even that test is often hard to apply, because, as many have observed, history does not disclose its alternatives. Perhaps the closest Joe Alsop ever came to wielding influence of the kind that makes waves and jars the eyeteeth was when he and his brother took up one of their many crusades to head off what they saw as approaching strategic weapons inferiority—the so-called "missile gap" controversy of the late 1950s, which is examined in chapter 12 of this book. Even there, the threads of cause and effect are hard to disentangle, inasmuch as Joe Alsop was apparently unaware of the secret surveillance of Soviet missile deployments by the U-2 overflights, whose findings in part contradicted his fears but were known to President Eisenhower and a few others. Here, it could be argued, the Alsopian influence was a bit perverse. It surely helped Kennedy's campaign for the presidency. But once in office, Kennedy lost little time in announcing that a study by Paul Nitze had dispelled apprehensions about a missile gap.

BY THE TIME I came to know him, Joe Alsop enjoyed an enviable celebrity in Washington. Its elements were not wholly flattering. Tales of his bullying and rhetorical excesses (even at his own dinner table, and certainly at others) swirled about him. In his evocative description of the cast of characters attending the funeral of John Paul Vann, the flawed hero of America's attempt to preserve a non-Communist Vietnam, Neil Sheehan captures the aura of Joe Alsop two years before his retirement:

> Joe Alsop, the newspaper columnist and journalist of the American establishment . . . was sitting in one of the center pews on the left, dressed in a sober blue suit made by his English tailor, with a matching polka-dot bow tie and white shirt. John Kennedy had once displayed his esteem for Alsop's advice and friendship by stopping at Alsop's Georgetown home for a bowl of turtle [actually, terrapin] soup on the night of his inauguration in 1961. . . . Alsop was a scion of the Anglo-Saxon elite of the Northeast that had determined the standards of taste, morality and intellectual respectability for the rest of the country. . . . At sixty-one he remained the man of contrasts he had always been . . . an aesthete who collected French furniture and antique Chinese porcelain and Japanese lacquer; an accomplished amateur historian of art and archaeology . . . a man of kindness, loyalty and consideration to his friends and relatives—the godfather of nearly thirty of their children. In his professional life, however, he was the ferocious combatant. . . . He did not see those who disagreed with him as merely incorrect or misguided. He depicted them as stupid men who acted from petty or selfish motives.[3]

This was the Joe Alsop of 1971—by then, in a way, one of the countless casualties of America's ferocious debate over the war in Vietnam, which he had supported from the first—indeed, as an ensuing chapter will show, as early as 1954, when the Indochina cause was still exclusively French—and which he advocated ever more shrilly as prospects of victory in Southeast Asia seemed to recede. But it rings true. Joe Alsop in his later years was respected by many, loathed by some, pitied by a few and, as Sheehan notes, held in genuine affection by those who had seen him in private, vulnerable and disarmed. Discerning friends had long since come to understand that he was a lonely, yearning man who, for all his great adventures, his worldliness and accomplishments, was saddened by roads not taken and eager to recapture some of the lost idealism and certainties of his youth. He camouflaged this vulnerability with brusqueness and insult, even at times under his own roof: a place where, braving the risks of personal insult and inquisition, caste-conscious

Washingtonians very much liked to be seen. He could be autocratic and peremptory, and sometimes morose. He could also be the soul of consideration and kindness, especially to younger colleagues in the "trade" (as he insisted it be called) of reporting.[4]

I saw him fairly often in his last fifteen years, and few of my visits with him fail now to register sharply in the memory. My last visit was typical. I had found a copy of his brilliantly original 1964 book on the archaeology of the Greek Bronze Age, *From the Silent Past*,[5] and telephoned to ask if he would sign it for me. It was a cool late-autumn night in 1988, a few months before the onset of his final illness. He had been visibly failing for a couple of years, but the spark and spirit still flared on occasion, and he remained defiant of his doctors' edicts against cigarettes and Scotch whisky. Unless he expected a number of people for dinner, Joe often answered his own doorbell at the elegant old N Street townhouse in Georgetown he had leased for life as his retirement residence. By 1988 he had noticeably slowed, and his hunched-over walk, the posture that an old professor of mine used to call "the card-catalogue stoop," had become a bit tottery. Yet, as usual, the Benson & Hedges cigarettes followed one upon another, their filter-tips ritually broken off, into his cigarette holder. I mixed us both a drink at the bar that stood across the room from his reading chair. On this last of our private visits, the talk turned for some reason to Bill Moyers, the former Lyndon Johnson press secretary. Joe, who refused to own a television set (or at least to acknowledge that he owned one), had never seen Moyers perform as an interviewer and seemed interested when I told him that Moyers struck me as superb in the role.

"He tried to use me once," Joe said. "I once asked him [Joe would have said *awsk*, in the English manner] what his favorite reading was. I quite expected him to say Holy Writ. But not at all! He said it was Machiavelli's *Prince*, a strange choice for a holy man. Uh?" Here, Joe paused to punctuate the interrogative, as he often did, with a growling half-laugh in his deep, rumbling baritone voice.

"A good thing I did ask. One day when I was looking for a column subject, Moyers called me to say that the president was going to announce an important appointment I'd been interested in the next morning. He gave me the man's name. I decided to write about it, and was halfway along when I remembered that Lyndon Johnson hated nothing more than being tipped in the papers. It was one way to be sure the man wasn't appointed at all. Moyers obviously didn't want this man in. He was using me! A good thing I remembered his interest in Machiavelli!"

When I said I was surprised at this "trait" in Moyers, Joe growled again. "Not a *trait*, dear boy, it's quite the wrong word." "Habit, then," I ventured; and the conversation moved on. Even about such details, even in casual conversation, Joe could be exacting. This and perhaps a dozen other private conversations stick in my memory, because, while I had become very fond of Joe, I was also intensely curious, fascinated by him as a living relic of a great era in Washington and Washington journalism. I was a later, more modest, practitioner of the trade in which he had been a star of the first magnitude. For me, even at his prickliest, he embodied the romance of that "visitable past" of which Henry James writes in the preface to one of his best tales—the past to which we may be connected by a living presence, "the marks and signs of a world we may reach over to as by making a long arm we grasp an object at the other end of our own table."[6] In large part, the following pages were written to gratify that personal curiosity and to probe the works and days of the man and, to a lesser degree, his partner/brother. And the great national security issues of the 1950s, which engaged them almost to the point of obsession, seem to me to form the natural vehicle for seeing them at work at their best.

AT THE HEART of this inquiry is a paradox—some would doubtless say a contradiction. The Alsop brothers, especially Joe, wrote in often alarmist terms about the threat to American national security and freedom posed by Communist aggression. Like many others of their generation, they initially supposed—incorrectly, as we now may say with perfect hindsight—that world communism was a menacing monolith, reflecting and manipulated by a conspiratorial Kremlin. When writing about what he took to be the errors and misjudgments of the past (for instance, about the 1949 Maoist takeover in China), Joe Alsop did not spare even his friends and former associates if he regarded them as wrong or mistaken. To be sure, his judgments on them differed in emphasis, depth, precision, and candor from the venomous slanders that demagogues in those days were also offering in the guise of domestic debate. Yet the Alsops, while sounding the alarm, abhorred the ex post facto inquests and inquisitions to which the general anxiety gave rise in domestic politics— the stupidities and cruelties of the Truman and Eisenhower "loyalty" and "security" programs; the rampages of Senator Joe McCarthy; the ghastly misconceptions and misjudgments that underlay the J. Robert Oppenheimer security case; the often-savage congressional investigations that served no larger purpose than to blacken the reputations of those who could be portrayed as "soft on communism," or who had shared the Popular Front mentality of the 1930s. The interplay of these apparently contradictory strands of the Alsops' journalism—militant anticommunism in foreign policy, equally militant insistence on civility and fair play in domestic politics—is the central thread of the following story. Indeed, it is perhaps the key thematic question: Did the two aspects of the Alsops' reporting and advocacy—the noisy tocsin-ringing regarding the world threat, the gallant defense of political civility and civil liberties at home—work at cross-purposes? Were they fighting a fire that they themselves had helped to set?

For the Alsops, the example and influence of their great-uncle Theodore Roosevelt, whose portrait was prominently displayed in Joe Alsop's entrance hall on N Street, was an anchorage in history. Distinguished historians and biographers of their Uncle Teddy have pointed me to books in which, they said, useful parallels might be found—for TR also had believed both in strength abroad and civility at home.[7] A diligent search has revealed no exact parallels. The issues and the political ethos of the two eras are too different. For instance, it would be interesting to know what Theodore Roosevelt, had he survived World War I, would have had to say about the great Red Scare—the Mitchell Palmer raids and all that—which swept the nation. By the time the post–World War I inquisition was at its height, the former president was dead. But Theodore Roosevelt, like his journalizing grand-nephews, undoubtedly believed in both American involvement in the world and the liberal spirit in domestic politics and saw no inconsistency between them. This was perhaps the American equivalent of the so-called liberal imperialism of Lord Rosebery and others in England. It was a short-lived political style, very "Anglo-Saxon" in its way and reinforced by personal transatlantic ties, which combined an unblushing exercise of military power with a tutelary mission (as in the Philippines) to the world's native peoples. The terms of the arrangement were, of course, defined by the tutelary power.

Though Joe's writings could at times take on a faintly apocalyptic tone, both Alsop brothers had an urbane understanding of the theory and practice of Soviet power. Their personal friendships with two formative figures, Charles Bohlen and George F. Kennan, the State Department's two great "Soviet experts" of the 1950s, assured an informing and tempering influence. Long before the implications of Tito's defection from the Comintern were clear to others, they had begun to modify the Alsopian assessment of events. Yet within the Alsops' column, anxiety frequently got the better of urbanity, and a tone of clammy fretfulness crept in. One spring afternoon in Princeton, George Kennan kindly talked with me about his friendship with Joe Alsop and allowed me to peruse a thick file of personal correspondence, stretching over many years. I was struck, as I read through the Kennan-Alsop correspondence, by Joe's tendency to break into hectic, hand-wringing worry about the forthcoming Russian extinction of freedom. Kennan invariably took the longer, more reassuring view of the historian. In one exchange, Kennan was moved by Joe's worries to cite Winston Churchill's admonition that in much anxiety about the unfathomable future it is merely "old man death" we mortals seek to elude.

Which leads, naturally, to the ultimate question—the effect of temperament and personality on outlook. Stewart Alsop, by the testimony of those who knew him, was far less flamboyant than his older brother, though he was an equally good reporter and writer. It was Joe Alsop who seemed at times almost to relish gloom for gloom's sake, as he did in a notable address to the Signet Society at Harvard in the late 1940s. Even in his thirties, he assumed the mantle of an aging prophet and compared the fate of Western man to that of the Spartans at Thermopylae. The journalist Douglass Cater, who was present for the occasion, recalls that "he urged free men today, like the ancient Greeks, to 'comb their golden hair in the sunlight and prepare to die bravely.'"[8]

In his soberer and less hectic moments, Joe Alsop was a superb political observer. It was when he unleashed the fretful Jeremiah in himself that gross exaggeration and misjudgment got the upper hand. He remained from start to finish a fount of dire predictions and forecasts that, fortunately, often failed to pan out. As one got to know him, one began to see that Joe Alsop was a theatrical personality with a strongly developed aesthetic side and a tendency to measure men and events by aesthetic and emotional criteria. In that respect, he was less self-contradictory than he appears in Neil Sheehan's portrait of him at the Vann funeral. The collector of fine old furniture, lacquer, and porcelain was a man of taste in his political judgments as well.

Moreover, in ways I cannot pretend to analyze, Joe's outlook and manner may have reflected a troubling secret of which I began to hear only after undertaking to write this book. That he was homosexual was known to many of his close friends and some, though apparently not all, of his family. In an age when it was far more dangerous than it is today to flout sexual taboos, his vulnerability in this regard could have been a source of occasional worry and insecurity; and this may suggest a key to Joe Alsop's baroque personality. A distinguished historian of science articulated it best for me when we were discussing Joe's heroic labors in behalf of the great nuclear physicist J. Robert Oppenheimer. I reported, as I had been told by more than one observer of that alliance, that Joe "couldn't stand" Oppenheimer, on whose behalf he performed prodigies of advocacy—a fact which, if true, could scarcely be inferred from any surviving document. He himself had known Robert Oppenheimer, he said, as well as Joe Alsop, and "both of these very strange men was, each in his own way, deeply insecure and both masked that insecurity by very elaborate and artificial personalities."[9] I did not know Oppenheimer, who certainly did not share Joe Alsop's concealed sexual orientation. But the observation rings true. In Joe's case, there is an explanation for the insecurity, though whether it is the right one I cannot say. Whatever life of sexual adventure Joe led, he was very discreet about it.

In any case, it is not my purpose here to delve beyond my competence into psychoanalytic explanation. It does seem to me that without some endeavor to trace the most obvious sources and features of his flamboyant personality, this could become a dry tale, one that would thus be less than true to its subject. In a subsequent chapter, accordingly, I probe a bit into the world, and the family, out of which the Alsop brothers came, and of which they were certainly very proud. They had what the French call *race*. Both Stewart, in *Stay of Execution*, and Joe, in his posthumous memoirs, have left delightful evocations of their childhood world, which I shall not try to duplicate. Those accounts should be read and savored independently, in the original and not in thinly diluted form. But there are many things which can be known that are not touched on in the brilliant early chapters of *"I've Seen the Best of It."*[10] I have tried, also, to describe the setting and working habits of the Alsop partnership.

The story really comes to a natural conclusion with the dissolution of that partnership, after twelve eventful years, in 1958. The junior partner had discovered that he had outgrown the junior role and was ready to move on into a specialty, magazine journalism at the *Saturday Evening Post* and later at *Newsweek*, which he enjoyed more. Except for a brief glimpse at Joe Alsop's idyllic (and now, as the Sheehan quote again indicates, also legendary) relationship with John F. Kennedy, the end of the collaboration is the end of this story. With the turn of *that* decade, America turned a corner, of which the most calamitous consequence would be the deepening of that "commitment" in Indochina which Joe had so long advocated. The full story of Joe Alsop and Indochina is a story that should be told, for it largely determined the view—false in so many vital respects— that would be taken after 1963 of Joe Alsop and his journalism. It was a story from which he himself shied in later years. One warm spring night in his Georgetown garden, the conversation had turned to Dean Acheson. I said that I, too, was a great Acheson admirer but had been disappointed in him on one occasion.

"When was that?" Joe demanded. "It was," I said, "when he was being interviewed on public television by a panel of high school students and tried to maintain that Vietnam and Korea were indistinguishable."

"They were indistinguishable!" Joe roared, with all the peremptory assurance he could muster. "No, Joe," I said, "let me offer you a few distinctions between the two wars and you can shoot them down."

"*I never discuss Vietnam,*" he roared with finality; and that was that. That, also, was Joe, one of those who usually had to have the last word, even if it was inconclusive or even—in view of the passion he had long invested in the Indochina issue—patently absurd.

Though they are not without their darkness and mystery, the chapters of his life related in the following pages fell in the time before Vietnam turned into a national calamity. It was, for Joe, a time of challenge but of relative and uncharacteristic optimism.

Chapter One Baldwin's Ghost

One supreme peril stood out among many facing the United States in the postwar world of 1946, when the Alsop brothers began writing their four-times-weekly "Matter of Fact" column for the *New York Herald Tribune* and some four dozen other initial subscribers. That peril was Russian aggressiveness; and it ranked among the great stories of the century. Now as in the age of Uncle Teddy Roosevelt, the Alsops believed, the United States must discard its traditional isolationist impulses. It must rearm and prepare once again to stand at Armageddon and battle for the Lord.

Americans might be weary of war, they might still long to bask in the victory of 1945. But now for the first time in the nation's history, the country was menaced by the possibility of devastating attack from an enemy thousands of miles away—an enemy that was meanwhile subverting, or attempting to subvert, sovereign states on its periphery, especially Poland and Czechoslovakia. And the threat could only intensify.

The crisis constituted, above all, a good story, and like all good reporters, the Alsops were storytellers at heart—English majors (Joe at Harvard, Stewart at Yale) who had a command of the language and literature and who knew that journalists must tell an arresting tale. If the story required some dramatic simplification, if it demanded some rounding of the rough edges of complex events for the sake of an intelligible and exciting narrative, the challenge was rarely refused.

Josef Stalin's Soviet Union, the source and presumed coordinator of this global threat, had entered a period of what seemed from a Washington perspective to be aggression tinged with paranoia. Still heavily armed, the Russians were probing at all points—not only in Europe but in East Asia and the Middle East—where vital United States and Western European interests might be found ill-defended. The postwar Big Four conferences on the future of Germany, now under joint occupation, were getting nowhere. They seemed, in fact, to be increasing the sense of strain and hostility. Even Joe Alsop's friend George F. Kennan, the most distinguished and imaginative of the State Department's corps of Sovietologists, shared the general sense that the Russians were very dangerous. In later years, Kennan would modify and qualify his earliest postwar warnings. But in September 1945, when the echoes of the last cannon-fire and bombings had hardly died in the ruins of central Europe, Kennan was writing to warn of the implications of a Soviet atomic weapon "or any other radical and far-reaching means of destruction . . . against which we might be defenseless if taken by surprise." In Kennan's rather grim view, to which Joe Alsop then and later attached extraordinary importance, "nothing in the history of the Soviet regime . . . could justify us in assuming that the men who are now in power . . . would hesitate for a moment to apply this power against us if by doing so they thought that they would materially improve their own power position in the world."[1]

Eventually, Kennan's gloomy assessment would be softened and nuanced, as the dawning Cold War took on a life and momentum of its own. But the bleak realism of his memorable "long telegram" of 1947 from Moscow to the State Department would set the tone and theme of American policy for many years to come.[2] It would become an integral part of the story the Alsop brothers told their readers about the dangerous world Americans suddenly, and involuntarily, found themselves in. But Kennan's lofty historicism was not the only ingredient. The Alsops' narrative drew on other elements as well—above all, on their vivid memory of the failure of the Stanley Baldwin and Neville Chamberlain governments, barely a decade earlier, to warn and rearm Britain in the face of the Hitler menace in Nazi Germany. Again and again, in newspaper columns and in special *Saturday Evening Post* articles, this analogy—which would have a very long life in the national security debates of the forties, fifties, and sixties—would be invoked.

An early example was "Must America Save the World?," the cosmic-sounding question the Alsops posed for *Saturday Evening Post* readers in the issue of February 21, 1948. Their answer was emphatic and affirmative. "The biggest story on earth," they wrote, "is the story of the new world role of the United States." If Americans did not play up to that challenging role, the future would "hardly bear thinking about."[3]

The article grew out of a jarring incident that had suddenly forced official Washington to rethink whatever complacent assumptions it had entertained about the postwar world. Greece and Turkey, whose security against Russian expansionism had been for more than a century the traditional, often exclusive, concern of the British Foreign Office, were now to be turned over to the United States by their exhausted protectors at Westminster. Suddenly, for the first time in history, the United States found itself with European client states, thousands of miles away.

The British note informing Washington of this pressing need brought with it no ready solution. The sudden demand for a program of economic and military aid so far from American shores presented a political problem of the first magnitude, and President Truman was bluntly warned by the leaders of the Senate—Majority Leader Arthur Vandenberg and others—that this unprecedented role would only be accepted by the American people if he, the president, "scared the hell" out of them. That meant speaking to Congress and the public in sweeping terms. It meant a departure from customary policy that came to be labeled the "Truman Doctrine" and was disconcerting even to internationalists like Walter Lippmann.

The Alsops, relishing a good scrap—especially for a cause they strongly believed in—were not reluctant to amplify Truman's high rhetoric. Whatever scary things Harry Truman could say, they could say doubly. But a geopolitical framework was lacking. What would the American people say of a proposal that required them to become the guardians of Greek and Turkish security? How would it fit the American vision of the world, where for the most part people were supposed to tend to their own local knitting?

Then and there, in the heat of the debate over Greek and Turkish aid, what eventually would come to be known as the "domino theory" came into play. It figures prominently in the *Saturday Evening Post* piece of February 1948—not for the first time, perhaps, but with a strident emphasis. Years later, Joe Alsop boasted to a London newspaperman, Peter Jay of the *Times*, that he had been the originator of the theory. "You speak as if you believe in the domino theory," Jay had said to Alsop one evening at a Washington party where the two had just met for the first time. "Dear boy," said Joe, "I invented it."[4] Whether that was true or not, the domino theory applied a version of the lawyer's "slippery slope" to strategic issues and, more important, to the question of whether America must save the world. As the Alsops put it in the February 1948 article: "In plain language, if the Soviets gain Greece, Turkey will be open. If they gain Turkey, the Middle East will be open. If they gain the Middle East they will hold the crossroads between Europe and Asia, and control the oil which is Europe's lifeblood and America's last great reserve. *And this is their real objective.*"

The piece bore Joe Alsop's unmistakable touch. "We cannot meet the tests [of the new world responsibilities] in our present manner of a somnambulistic giant holding up the western world in his uneasy sleep." Stewart was the cosigner of the article, in keeping with their usual practice. But the lines about the somnambulistic giant, with their buried image of Hercules, bore Joe's stamp. If the advice was that Americans must surrender their isolationist habits, though, it was softened by a nostalgic tribute to the way things had been: "The scenes of that America before the First World War now float before our eyes like pictures in a dream. We seem almost to smell the sweet dust of summer raised in the air by the passing surry; our passions are tenderly engaged in the arguments around the cracker barrel, where men disputed political issues so small they seem almost cozy." The nostalgia was rhetorical, designed to point out the antithesis between the old and comfortable ways and the new ways to which the country would now have to adapt itself. Joe Alsop had grown up in the Connecticut countryside, and he had been four years old when the First World War began—that much was authentic. But he had spent more time in elegant European and American drawing rooms than around a country-store cracker barrel.

The Alsops clearly knew that they were up against two powerful American traditions. One was the tendency to draw sharp, bright lines between war and peace, to treat both as absolutes. Americans, disliking the historical ambiguities of the old world, might find it hard to conceive that they now lived in a limbo-land world suspended between the two. Americans thought of war as an all-out condition: you were in it or you were not. As some of the policies and decisions of World War II suggested, its absolute and sweeping demands all but excluded diplomacy. There had been, for instance, the argument about the wisdom of the "unconditional surrender" demand announced by President Roosevelt in the midst of the war. In the views of its critics, the formula left little or no space for the 1944 conspiracy to depose Hitler, which came so near succeeding. Peace, similarly, was also seen as a sort of sacred absolute. Perhaps it could be "waged," as a cliché of the day had it, with the weapons of diplomacy, sloganeering, and propaganda. The basic reality, however, was that from the vast twelve-million-man army of 1945 the United States had pared its armed forces down to a token level, and they were mostly engaged in occupation duties in Germany and Japan. The Alsops' opinion was that President Truman, faced with a fierce struggle over budget priorities within his own administration, had abjectly surrendered to the pinchpenny view of his conservative secretary of the treasury, John W. Snyder, Jr., a Kansas City banker and one of Truman's old friends from mid-America.[5]

The Alsops had issued their grim *Saturday Evening Post* warning of the hardships ahead in early 1948, before President Truman's stunning upset victory over the Republican candidate, Governor Thomas E. Dewey of New York. As that critical year waned and startling events clarified the new challenges abroad, the Alsops began to fear that while the Truman administration had finally stirred itself to take up the standard of internationalism from the faltering British, the new policies would not be adequately financed.

On the last day of November, a month after Truman's surprise victory, Joe Alsop encountered Truman's chief aide, Clark Clifford, at a Washington party. Apparently inflamed by zeal and drink, as he often was — apologies for intemperate language abound in the correspondence of that era — Joe began lecturing Clifford on the desperate need to overcome Snyder's influence and pass a bigger defense budget. Clifford, who later became one of the capital's supreme lawyer-lobbyists and public servants, had been credited in part with Truman's successful election strategy and was obviously on the rise as a man of influence. As usual, Joe Alsop found himself apologizing the next day for his "vehemence" on a social occasion.[6] But he did not retreat from his argument and warned Clifford that the attack on Truman administration defense parsimony would be pursued in future newspaper columns. The choice, he confidently advised Clifford, "is the choice that confronted the British government in the early thirties," when Prime Minister Stanley Baldwin "chose business as usual" and "the chief advocates for Baldwin's policy, Neville Chamberlain and Sir John Symington [*sic*: a slip of the pen, no doubt, for "Simon"] used precisely the arguments that you now use, that the first essential was to sustain England's economic strength." Then and later, Joe and Stewart Alsop scoffed at the argument that excessive defense spending would draw critical resources away from, and weaken, the domestic economy. Offered the choice between being safe and broke or rich and vulnerable, Joe liked to say, he would unhesitatingly choose the former.

In every particular, Joe's December 1 letter to Clark Clifford anticipated the newspaper column he wrote two days later, to which Joe attached the irritating caption, "Enter Baldwin's Ghost, Mewing." The column argued that President Truman's $15-billion ceiling on defense outlays in the new budget for fiscal 1949 recalled Baldwin's blindness "when Winston Churchill and other British leaders visited him in solemn deputation to warn of Hitler's rearmament" and were rebuffed. The Truman budget ceiling meant virtually the same thing—that the seventy-group air force for which Secretary of Defense James Forrestal and others were pushing (the number seventy had taken on the same talismanic force as would the Reagan administration's six-hundred-ship navy many years later) would shrink to fifty groups. And this force, the brothers warned, would not be enough to safeguard the nation against the threat of Soviet air attack.[7]

The budget figures were disappointing, even alarming, the Alsops thought. But 1948 had been a memorable year, not without heroic moments. In June, the president had mounted the Berlin airlift to break a Soviet blockade of the Western sectors of the jointly occupied German capital. That spring, Truman had also signed into law a new Draft Act, which required the registration of all males eighteen to twenty-five years old. It was also late in the same year, even as the debate over the defense budget flared up, that the Alger Hiss espionage and perjury case entered the headlines. The young Representative Richard Nixon of California charged the Truman administration with a cover-up in the Hiss case, one of the most colorful and complicated of the postwar era. Hiss was accused of passing State Department documents to a Soviet spy ring during the war. His eventual conviction of perjury (in denying the underground ties his accuser Whittaker Chambers had alleged) would vastly sharpen the domestic dispute over the dangers of Communist penetration of government.

WHEN THEY TEAMED UP in late December 1945, the Alsops were young men with a glittering journalistic future before them. Their new column, called Matter of Fact, was to appear four times weekly in the *New York Herald Tribune*, Joe's prewar paper, and through its syndicate in some forty other client papers. The list would eventually climb into the two hundred range and include most major newspapers in the United States and several of consequence in Canada, Great Britain, and Western Europe.

The column's standing title described its journalistic orientation. Matter of Fact was designed to be just that—a reporting column, among whose rules two ranked as absolute. The first rule was that no column would be a mere expression of opinion unbuttressed by reporting. Joe had long since concluded that facts alone sway policy-makers and that no columnist's opinion as such, however cleverly or elegantly phrased, was of the slightest importance. Indeed, when a columnist began to suppose that his views as such mattered, it was time, Joe liked to say, for a visit to his psychiatrist.[8]

The other firm rule was that every column should report at least one new item of hard information no one else had reported. The two columnists stuck to their rules to a fault, as one painful incident illustrates. One day during the years haunted by Senator Joe McCarthy's inquisition into domestic Communism, the Alsops learned through a letter from Arthur Schlesinger, Jr., that their friend James Wechsler, the editorial page editor of the *New York Post*, was deeply hurt not to have their support in his battle with the Wisconsin senator. Wechsler was under interrogation by McCarthy's investigative committee because as a student editor at Columbia in the thirties, Wechsler had joined the Communist Party. Wechsler, like many of those who had drifted to the left in the thirties, had long since abandoned his tenuous Communist ties and become active in the anti-Communist wing of the Democratic Party, centered in the Americans for Democratic Action. The Alsops apologized for the oversight. They were sad to learn of Wechsler's distress, Joe explained, but their excuse was that, much as they sympathized with him, they had nothing new to report in his case.[9]

Another ironclad rule, especially in the reporting of overseas matters, was "Go and see for yourself." Joe Alsop dated this rule to his experience in China in the early days of the war. He had written about the situation there from a great distance yet "with lordly self-confidence." When he actually arrived on the scene in late 1940, he found himself at the British ambassador's dinner table. It was a few weeks before Pearl Harbor. "The chance remarks at the dinner table progressively showed up as purest drivel" all that he had been writing about the tangled affairs of China. That, as Joe explained it, was the beginning of his firm belief that you could not grasp the inwardness of a complex foreign situation except by taking a first-hand look at it.[10]

The immediate postwar years, the prime early years of the Alsop partnership, were a golden age for the Washington column. Not only did newspapers then retain their commanding position in politics and journalism, since television, as a mass medium, was in its infancy; but a vast accretion of power and influence had suddenly made Washington the capital of the world. The observations of writers such as Lippmann, Krock, Reston, Doris Fleeson, Marquis Childs, Drew Pearson, and, of course, Alsop would become familiar daily fare to every newspaper reader. In these years, reporters for the news pages were still bound by ironclad canons of "objectivity." Their function was to pursue and publish pure fact (and it was naively supposed that pure fact existed), unadorned by even the shadow of interpretive bias. All of this changed rapidly during the next twenty years, as reporters and editors, reflecting on the phenomenon of "McCarthyism," pondered their vulnerability to demagogues and headline hunters and found it rooted in the idea that journalism could serve the reading public adequately as a mere transmission belt of raw fact. Senator McCarthy and his fellow congressional inquisitors had thus influenced the ground rules of American journalism as few have done before or since. And what rules the experience of McCarthyism did not shake were soon to be shaken by the influence of television. Newspapers, sensing that they must furnish what the headline-service of television and radio could not, began to experiment with new interpretive forms, labeled "news analysis" or "commentary."

But in the prime years of the Alsop partnership, during the 1950s, columnists enjoyed an exclusive license to frame what they reported in some sort of interpretive context. They had the best of both worlds. Joe took it for granted that only the best information deserved to be reported. And he defined the best information as what could be carefully culled from well-placed officials who knew complex situations first-hand. The Alsop correspondence files are filled with pleas to friends like Paul Nitze, George F. Kennan, Charles Bohlen, and others for the kind of briefings that would admit columnists to the world in which high policy-making functioned.[11]

These pleas tended to be rebuffed on various grounds, as we shall see; but Joe Alsop was nothing if not imperious. Washington chuckled for years at the tale that Joe, having been summoned for an Atomic Energy Commission briefing which he found less than useful, had loftily informed Admiral Lewis Strauss, its chairman, that he had "wasted a half hour of our valuable time."[12] At times Joe even tried to tell the British Foreign Office how to conduct press policy—in the process offending a foreign secretary and a very old friend by refusing to conduct an interview in which the official proposed to have his press secretary present.[13]

The search for news demanded a constant struggle against government's incurable proneness to keep needless secrets—to say nothing of bureaucrats prone, as the Alsops wrote in *The Reporter's Trade*, "to classify everything but the toilet paper."[14] The Alsops' social relations with President Truman's courageous but unpopular secretary of state, Dean Acheson, were strained by demands for access to his thinking—demands that Acheson, no fan of the press, declined to grant. When the Alsops later reflected on their thirteen-year partnership, they singled out their friend Dean Acheson for special citation as an enemy of the press. He was "a great secretary of state," but he had committed a cardinal sin. He had inspired a cult of secrecy, "afflicted" as he was "with imitation English views about secrecy." Acheson, in their view, gave too little thought to "the peculiar nature of the national debate that makes our system work, and to the special role of the press in this vital debate." Acheson had set a bad example for lesser officials by ordering uncalled-for "security investigations" of reporters and of officials suspected of merely talking to reporters. The Alsops themselves boasted that they had "been honored with no less than six security investigations."[15]

Some of those inquiries resulted from comic mixups. In September 1949, Secretary of Defense Louis Johnson, a special Alsop target, spread a rumor on Capitol Hill that the Soviet atomic bomb test probably was a fake of some sort. Johnson's skepticism reflected President Truman's own and was soon echoed in a Senate speech by Owen Brewster of Maine. The Alsops, however, were convinced through their important sources in the world of science that the Russians indeed probably had the atomic bomb and the Truman administration's complacency was inane. But because they had no proof, they asked themselves, "How do we know it isn't a fake?" No official would or could say. One day Stewart Alsop had a bright idea. He rang Georgetown University and asked to speak to the head of the physics department. The unknown academic came on the line. Stewart posed the same question and found himself with an informative answer: Nuclear explosions could be detected at great distances by air sampling and seismic instruments. When the Alsops reported this finding in the column, they were soon visited by FBI agents. It turned out that President Truman himself had asked the same question. A briefing paper prepared for him happened to overlap, even in terminology, with what the Alsops had learned from their source at Georgetown University. In a capital addicted to suspicion, the conclusion seemed obvious: The Alsops had a leak. Indeed, Stewart later recalled that the FBI agents seemed only half-persuaded by their explanation and "left convinced . . . that we had some still-open pipeline into the 'secret places of the most high.'"[16]

A few years later, before the Soviet Union unsettled the assumption of American scientific and technological superiority by launching Sputnik, the first space satellite, a fantasy concocted by Stewart Alsop—"What if the United States woke up one day to find that the Russians had placed a satellite in orbit?"—found its way into a White House briefing paper prepared for President Eisenhower. Fond of this fantasy, Stewart decided to print it. An enraged Eisenhower concluded, not for the first time, that the Alsops were being leaked to. It wasn't so, but still another investigation was ordered.

The truth was that diligent journalistic legwork explained most, if not all, of the scoops the Alsops obtained. But myths and legends still abounded. On November 1, 1956, Charles Sergis, who was writing a master's thesis on the Alsops at the University of Missouri school of journalism, wrote to ask "if it is true that [Joe] has a rather unique method of interviewing news sources. . . . Does he rap on their desks with his cane (presuming it is true that he carries one)? Has it indeed been his resolution since his younger days to insult at least one person every day?" Sergis conceded that the questions perhaps sounded a bit silly, but he referred to recent profiles of the Alsops in *The Nation* and *The Reporter*. He wished to verify or "bury" the rumors. Joe responded that he had "always made it a practice to talk to officials as though they were citizens, as I am," not as if to a "superior race." But he assured Sergis that he had never carried a cane. As for the suggestion that he had a daily quota of insults to hand out, "I have never heard such nonsense in my life."[17]

It might have been nonsense; but a lot of people thought of Joe Alsop as a stuffed shirt. In 1968, when antipathies about Vietnam were at their height, the humor columnist Art Buchwald wrote a comedy called *Sheep on the Runway*. With Roger Stevens as producer, the farce ran for over one hundred performances on Broadway and, because of its topical satire, caused a considerable stir in Washington. The butt of the action is a pompous syndicated columnist, Joe Mayflower, who intrigues to transform the remote neutral Himalayan kingdom of Nonomura into a U.S. protectorate and bastion of anticommunism. Mayflower is identified as the author of the books *The Many Roads to War* and *Is Peace Inevitable?* He detects events "boiling under the surface" of Nonomura when no one else notices.

When Joe Alsop began to be teased by his friends about the play, he declared in the presence of a *Washington Post* gossip columnist that anyone who went to see Buchwald's play was no friend of his. Mediation efforts by mutual friends of the two Washington columnists, including such journalistic luminaries as Ben Bradlee and Phil Geyelin, failed. Buchwald feared that he had made an "enemy for life" of Alsop, whether or not he had intended to. Alsop refused to speak to Roger Stevens for several years. Stewart Alsop, reviewing the play in the *Washington Post*, wrote huffily that "Buchwald's Mayflower . . . lacks the qualities—notably the courage to be unfashionable—that have made Joe Mayflower [Joe Alsop] a great reporter."

Whether or not Buchwald modeled his Joe Mayflower on Joe Alsop—he claims that the "hysterical columnist" was based on his friend Joe Kraft, by then a distinguished Washington journalist—the satire is broad and distinctly simplistic. Joe Alsop, with his strong belief in the expertise of those who really knew foreign parts, would never have said, for instance, "Never trust a man who speaks the language of the country where he's stationed," or anything remotely like it. But as we shall see, Joe Alsop was not above foreign-policy intrigue. In fact, the figure of Joe Mayflower is a cartoonish caricature of what many of his Washington detractors (and even some of his would-be friends who didn't know him well) *imagined* Joe Alsop to be like. And while it has its moments, *Sheep on the Runway* is distinctly a period piece, a relic of a time when the divisive passions of the Vietnam issue not only impaired manners and friendships but occasionally dulled the comic spirit.[18]

Caricature certainly pursued Joe, and those who knew him understood why. In his days as a roving diplomatic correspondent for the *Wall Street Journal*, Phil Geyelin frequently teamed up with Joe. Geyelin remembers a festive evening in Cairo during the fifties when Sam Pope Brewer, the *New York Times* correspondent, told Joe as they were having convivial drinks in the bar of Shepherd's Hotel that he, Joe, obviously knew nothing about the Port of Latakia. "Joe said something scatological," Geyelin recalls. But the next day, as Joe and Geyelin rode through the city in a cab, Alsop remorsefully said that he had checked on the geography of Latakia and Brewer was right. "I shall have to correct it," he said, "but how? I can't send him flowers." Joe paused. "I know, I'll give him a party." And he did, Geyelin recalls, "complete with the French ambassador." Once, when he and Geyelin were detained at the Syrian border with Lebanon on a reporting trip, Joe lost his patience. "Put me through to the foreign minister," he shouted to the quailing border officials. He seized the telephone and, to the amazement of his companions, was soon talking to the foreign ministry. Within minutes, the party of reporters was waved on to Damascus. It was the Alsop touch.[19]

FOR THE ALSOPS, the heroic figure of the internal struggle for adequate defenses in the Truman years was James Forrestal, a former Wall Street investment banker and first occupant of the new post of Defense Secretary. Forrestal was one of the eminent Wall Streeters serving with distinction in the U.S. defense establishment. He was also a born worrier with disturbing nervous tendencies who had become the early and chief promoter of George Kennan's dark view of Soviet intentions. One day in May 1949, Forrestal would leap to his death from an upper-floor window at Bethesda Naval Hospital, the victim of acute clinical depression. In a tribute titled "Dark Lesson," Joe marked Forrestal's suicide by recalling "the almost precisely similar" suicide of Lord Castlereagh. That nineteenth-century British foreign secretary, one of the architects of Napoleon's defeat, had cut his throat with a penknife in a fit of what was then called melancholia. Like Castlereagh, Joe wrote, Forrestal had been overtaxed by crushing official duties and, at the same time, unappreciated. Americans had a habit of underrating the importance of government and "the habit has persisted of treating the best men in the government as a set of dubious payrollers and hacks." Joe was not explicit, but perhaps he was thinking back to his days as an English student at Harvard and to Shelley's angry poem on the so-called Peterloo massacre, "The Mask of Anarchy," which, three years before Castlereagh's suicide, identified him in its second stanza with "Murder": "He had a mask like Castlereagh — / Very smooth he looked, yet grim."[20] Forrestal was, as the Alsops would later write in their book *The Reporter's Trade,* the "tragic hero" of the immediate postwar era, "the only public man whom we had thought invariably right. . . . He was whipped onward by the fierce whip of an intense patriotism. He carried a burden of foresight, a vision of the dangers of the future, that gave him no rest by night or day."[21]

Forrestal's heroism lay, as the Alsops saw it, in his unyielding opposition to the defense budget ceilings imposed by the president. Truman took the view that the U.S. atomic weapon monopoly, shortly to be ended but then still intact, required less augmentation by bombers and aircraft carriers than the air force and the navy claimed. It was the germ of a strategic debate that would linger for decades. What, exactly, did effective deterrence consist of? When did one go beyond prudence and safety into mere redundancy, wasting the public's money, inciting the Soviet Union to follow the example ("apes on a treadmill," as one future arms negotiator would call it in a famous article)? Given their extravagant admiration for Forrestal, it was foreordained that the Alsops would regard his successor as an antihero, even if that successor had been a more distinguished figure than Louis Johnson.[22]

The Alsop-Johnson feud became one of the fixtures of Washington bureaucratic and journalistic struggle in the late 1940s; and it was not without its comedy. One day in 1950, two years after Johnson had succeeded Forrestal, Marquis Childs of the *St. Louis Post Dispatch* happened to be chatting with the cheerful, balding defense secretary in the latter's

Pentagon office. What, Childs asked, did Johnson have to say about the charges regularly made against him in the Alsop column—that he was misleading both the public and the president about American military strength?

"Johnson's reply," wrote a clearly amused Childs, "was to turn dramatically and pull aside a curtain, revealing a white telephone. 'When my predecessor Mr. Forrestal was in office, it was attached by a direct line to the Alsops' house. One of the first things I did was to have it disconnected. Naturally they do not like that.'"[23]

Joe Alsop did not find the story amusing. In a draft column which, apparently, he thought better of and decided to confine to his files, he denounced it as "pure invention." No such hotline between their office and the defense secretary's had existed, Joe wrote. Their relationship with Forrestal had been with "a wise high official, interested in honestly and honorably informing the public." In fact, Joe revealed, it was Louis Johnson, not Forrestal, who had promptly given the columnists his own private phone number and invited them to use it. The feud with Johnson continued until shortly after the outbreak of war in Korea in June 1950, when Johnson's position at the Pentagon became untenable and he left office—ironically, to lobby for higher defense spending! Thereafter, the Alsops frequently claimed to have helped drive Louis Johnson out of town. This claim was perhaps an exaggeration; but if they didn't do it, it was not for want of trying. Events, however, are usually more decisive than words. What actually brought Johnson down was a defense policy that, when the Korean War began, left the country in a state of unpreparedness. That much the Alsops had predicted. But until the Korean debacle, Johnson, more than any respectable government figure of those years, remained the great Alsop bête noire.

If the Alsop brothers were almost obsessed with Johnson and defense spending, the obsession was reciprocated. The defense secretary began to feel that he was the special target of a conspiracy. Johnson had become "religiously convinced," the Alsops later wrote, that the two columnists were being leaked to on key defense arguments within the Truman inner circle by Undersecretary of State Dean Acheson. (In fact, the very opposite was true; Acheson, though a social friend, flatly rebuffed the Alsops' attempts to see him on public business and did so with a flourish that rubbed in his haughtiness about mere reporters.) Another suspected leaker, Johnson thought, was Stuart Symington, then secretary of the air force. One day Joe was sitting in Symington's office at the Pentagon questioning the air force secretary on a technical matter—the total weight of air frames currently on order for his service.

The question was quickly answered from published data, when the corridor door of Symington's office opened and the bulky figure of Louis Johnson appeared. . . .

Johnson closed the door and stood there, saying nothing, nodding his huge bald head up and down with the air of a virtuous husband who has at last caught his erring wife in flagrante delictu. Symington broke the unhappy silence by attempting an introduction. . . . "Yes," Johnson replied, "I know MR. ALSOP," and he pronounced the hated name loud and clear. There was another long, uncomfortable pause, while Johnson continued to nod his head up and down, grinning horribly, before he turned and left. Symington and Alsop thereupon collapsed into undignified giggles.[24]

Johnson, a former national commander of the American Legion, made a perfect scapegoat for the depleted state of American forces at the outbreak of the Korean War. But his major fault was perhaps that, unlike Forrestal, who seems to have been torn between loyalty to Truman and an obsession with preparedness, Johnson was a wholly uncritical servant of the president. And it was President Truman, after all, who had imposed the supposedly dangerous ceilings on the defense budget and thereby, in the view of Joe and Stewart Alsop, exposed the nation to peril. This was not the only complaint registered in the Alsop column against the Truman administration—a memory that, years later, embarrassed Joe Alsop. Joe was not easily given to the revision of his emphatic views; but in this case, he decided in retrospect that he and his brother had been unjust to Truman and wrote the former president a letter of apology. Truman replied handsomely, and by then Joe Alsop was inclined to think that the man from Missouri had been almost up to the Alsop standard.

But what was that standard, and what were its origins and roots? Here we must suspend the story briefly and go back in search of the two Alsops—who they were, where they came from, and what their heritage taught them about the ideals of public responsibility that they so confidently set before their readers four days a week.

Chapter Two **A Public Heritage**

The evening of June 24, 1950, was radiant, one of those soft warm nights before the heat of the Washington summer sets in. Joe Alsop, a great party-giver, had thrown himself a homecoming party. The guest of honor was a great favorite, Justice Felix Frankfurter of the United States Supreme Court.

As the talk grew lively on the twilit terrace at 2720 Dumbarton Avenue in Georgetown, the phone rang. Joe's Filipino butler emerged from the house to announce "a telephone call for Mr. Rusk." Dean Rusk, the assistant secretary of state for Far Eastern affairs, vanished into the house. He soon returned "white as a sheet," as Joe recalled. He took two other guests aside, Secretary of the Army Frank Pace and Undersecretary of the Air Force John McCone. The three huddled and then quickly bid their goodbyes. As Rusk hastened off to the State Department, he explained that there had been "a rather serious border incident in Korea." In fact, thousands of miles away, on the Korean peninsula, where the United States held a United Nations protectorate over the southern half of a divided country, armed forces of Kim Il Sung's Communist North Korea had crossed the 38th Parallel and were driving toward Seoul, the South Korean capital. The Korean War had begun; the question was how the United States would react.[1]

None of Joe's guests—a distinguished company that also included George Kennan, the State Department's ranking Soviet analyst—forgot the hasty departure of Rusk, Pace, and McCone. Yet it was but one unusually dramatic instance of what might have happened on almost any evening in those eventful early years of the Cold War. Joe Alsop's dinners typically attracted high Truman administration officials, many of them old personal friends. Rival reporters, envying the access Joe and his brother Stewart seemed to enjoy, supposed that it was the allure of Joe's gourmet food and fine wines. Washington was, as one old saying had it, the only vessel that leaked from the top; and it sometimes seemed to leak most copiously when the Alsop brothers needed news.

In fact, the distinction of Joe's dinner-party guest lists was a bit misleading. The exclusive reports that sometimes appeared to be the yield of privileged access more often reflected systematic reporting, the energy spent in countless daily interviews. (Both brothers tried to do at least three every working day; it was one of their fixed rules.) They waged a relentless and aggressive struggle for news that sometimes strained social ties and what they called "tribal" connections. Nothing angered Joe more than intimations that he and his brother fed on the casually discarded conversational scraps of embassy-row cocktail parties and dinner-table gossip. The story was more complicated than that. Hearsay was discounted. Rule Number One of the Alsops' journalism was "Go and see for yourself." That rule included asking questions for yourself, as well. But the domestic setting was very much a part of this operating procedure.

JOE ALSOP'S HOUSE, furnishings, and garden in Georgetown were, in large part, tools of the trade. To his Chinese-red dining room came China specialists and diplomats, art historians and congressmen, fellow newspapermen, even a future president or two. There they sat under the gaze of the much-painted Alsop ancestors, whose portraits continued to the end of his life to crowd the walls of Joe's dining room. *Vogue* once pronounced this ambience "the talk of Washington." From the sunroom-atrium, with its lacquered Japanese utensils on the walls, one could look out into a cool, all-green garden, with its stepped levels and eight varieties of boxwood. After one visit in 1949, Arthur Schlesinger, Jr., wrote that he could not escape "certain H. G. Wellsian anxieties over the picture of yourself, watering those somewhat sinister plants day after day, until eventually they seize and strangle you." The almost-animate plants were a sort of household joke, apparently. In his recollections of the Kennedy years, Ben Bradlee, the longtime executive editor of the *Washington Post*, remembers a "landmark column" Joe had written on gardening, a favorite of President and Mrs. Kennedy. Joe wrote that "watching the new green cover a box bush is just as exciting as watching the progress of the anti-guerrilla effort in South Vietnam. But in the reporter's trade, alas, the anti-guerrilla efforts have to be covered more intensively than the old earth's annual effort of self-renewal." "No one but Joe Alsop," comments Bradlee, "could strike that metaphor and make it stick."[2]

Joe ascribed his fascination with the physical setting—house or box bushes, antique furniture, portraits and food—mainly to the Alsop family's "almost pathological fondness for giving parties," which he had inherited. He took care, also, to dress the part. In the memoir published after his death in August 1989, Joe disclosed that the model for his noon luncheon attire had always been the J. P. Morgan partner, circa 1929.[3] Achieving the desired effect was no casual matter. His shirts were tailored for him in Italy. Suits, jackets, trousers, and waistcoats came from his London tailors, Anderson & Sheppard of 30 Savile Row, who at times were tailors for John F. Kennedy and Prime Minister Harold Macmillan as well. His shoes were custom-made at the famous firm of Lobbs, in St. James, London, where at the time of his death custom-made shoes were selling at some £900 per pair, or approximately $1,800 at the prevailing exchange rate. (Economies of scale were possible if one bought more than one pair, as most Lobbs customers did.)

Joe Alsop's tastes in jackets could be as finicking as his taste in food. Once Anderson & Sheppard, in relining a favorite dinner jacket, failed to do so with just the right shade of pink silk, while extending the lining to the very edge of the vents. The jacket was returned with elaborate instructions for correction. Joe once instructed his London tailors to copy an old waistcoat of his grandfather's, except that "the lower edges . . . should be scooped out just a little more to make the points a bit sharper and to make the curve very slightly concave."[4] Douglass Cater, the Washington editor of *The Reporter*, had a drink one day with Joe when both men were covering a political campaign. Cater said that he was planning his first trip to the Soviet Union and asked what Joe would recommend in the way of travel clothes. Were drip-dry shirts useful? Joe stared. "Dear boy," he said, "nothing but silk ever touches my skin!"[5]

Similar care was taken over wine and book orders, especially the latter. Book orders regularly issued from Dumbarton Avenue on the grand scale. Once in the 1960s Joe Alsop's secretary ordered nearly one hundred books at once from Blackwell's, the Oxford booksellers, on subjects ranging from Elizabethan history, genetics, Oriental archaeology, and Italian history to early Muslim architecture, Turkish military history, art (Eastern and Western), Greek history and literature, and the origins of Icelandic sagas.[6]

WELL BEFORE PEARL HARBOR, when he was still in his twenties, Joe Alsop had established himself as one of the best reporters—and sprightliest writers—in Washington. But six months earlier, in June 1941, an embarrassing gaffe had lent the deepening conflicts in Europe and Asia a personal edge. Joe and his columnist-partner Robert Kintner (also a former reporter for the *Herald Tribune*, specializing in economics) reported in their "Capital Parade" column that a U.S. destroyer in the North Atlantic had attacked a German submarine with depth charges. The story happened to be true. Because the British Royal Navy was stretched to the snapping point keeping the transatlantic sea lanes and supply routes open, President Roosevelt had secretly assigned the U.S. Navy a far more aggressive role at sea than the American public knew. But administration officials did not regard truth as a sound defense. The Alsop-Kintner story alarmed the White House and infuriated Navy Secretary Frank Knox, the Chicago newspaper publisher FDR had recently recruited. Summoned to Knox's office in the War, Army, and Navy Building (now known as the Old Executive Office Building), Joe began to ask himself whether, with war threatening, he really ought to be putting journalism first. He and Kintner soon filed their last column, and Joe, having wheedled a navy commission, was off to India, where he expected to be attached to the U.S. embassy at Delhi. There he encountered the dashing Claire Chennault, the leader of Chiang Kai-shek's irregular air force; and that chance encounter led him eventually to China, where, as we will see, he would spend much of the war.

When peace came in 1945, Kintner joined the new world of electronic journalism—he would eventually become president of NBC—and Joe, now back in Washington, sought a new partner. His brother Stewart was a natural choice. Later they would joke about the origins of the partnership. After finishing at Yale in 1936, Stewart had worked as a book editor at Doubleday, a New York publisher, before enlisting in the British army. When he returned from the war to join his established and more experienced older brother in newspapering, he later wrote, "he had never entered a newspaper office in all his working life. A high-minded high school senior subsequently wrote him, to ask 'what was the best way to become a newspaper columnist . . . ' He probably disconcerted the high-minded senior a little by replying that 'the best way to become a columnist is to have a brother who is one already.'"[7] But of course the real story was deeper and richer than that. It went back to the Connecticut countryside and, even beyond that, to family traditions rooted in colonial America.

In a nation vain of its democratic and egalitarian ideals, the Alsop brothers were oddities; and Joseph Wright Alsop V was the oddest of the lot. As their excellent reporting won coveted reporting prizes from the Overseas Press Club and other organizations (though never a Pulitzer, despite the lobbying of friends), Joe's eccentricities and mannerisms attracted caricature. His weakness for dogmatic, violent, sometimes abusive after-dinner argument, his groans of ritual despair over the imminent doom of the world or the dimness of the city of Washington ("Oh, what a dreadful time our parents chose to bear us in!," he exclaimed in his typical manner in a letter to an English friend): all this was part of being Joe Alsop. From the Savile Row suits to the gourmet dinner table to the scholarly pursuit of art and archaeology flowed the ingredients of a Joe Alsop legend that was in some ways misleading.

Stewart, four years younger, was quieter, less ornate, his personality so much the antithesis of his older brother's that years later his friends would find it difficult to evoke him for others. He had been, they would say, "a regular fellow," warm and friendly, a fine and engaging companion. When friends compared the two, it was as if they spoke of the contrast between matter and antimatter. As a boy Stewart had been closer to his younger brother John; the two of them were known in family circles as "the boys." Stewart, severely asthmatic, had been nursed through childhood ailments by his Scottish nurse, Aggie Guthrie, who came to live at the Alsops' Connecticut tobacco farm when he was nine months old. He was very much the younger brother in every way. It was the colorful and eccentric Joe—fat, foppish, epicurean, bookish, loud, often aggressive—who evoked for old friends and fellow journalists so many vivid memories.

Joseph Wechsberg was typical of those fellow journalists. In March 1953, Wechsberg proposed to write a piece for *Reader's Digest* on a journey to East Germany that he and Joe and several companions had made two years earlier. Their announced purpose was to visit a Leipzig trade fair. In fact they meant to scope out the world beyond the iron curtain. Wechsberg told Joe in a letter that he planned to make "the great Alsop . . . the protagonist." In the satirical tones friends often adopted in describing Joe, Wechsberg pictured his arrival on the morning of their departure from Berlin, "followed by a couple of sturdy Teutons carrying two large suit cases, a cardboard box filled with candy bars and cigarettes, a case of canned beer and another box full of sandwiches." He was "impeccable in a Savile Row suit of brown gabardine . . . and carr[ying] Xenophon's *Anabasis* under his arm. He was going to Leipzig, he said, as 'a student of history.'"

Once the reader got past the props and wardrobe, the portrait of Joe —his daredevil teasing of the East German police, his defiance of arbitrary and oppressive police regulations in grim, gray Leipzig—had heroic overtones. No one ever questioned Joe Alsop's courage. But Joe was disgusted by Wechsberg's light-hearted reminiscence and protested irritably that "I am a reporter . . . not an itinerant comedy turn." He did not "talk like a character out of P. G. Wodehouse." (Joe was mistaken; his Anglicized vowels and inflections would not have been out of place at Bertie Wooster's Blandings Castle.) Later Joe decided that he had overreacted and that he rather liked Wechsberg's piece after all.[8]

Because others also enjoyed writing about him in this satirical way, Joe left a trail of stories behind him. Stewart would add some of the funnier tales in his memoir *Stay of Execution*. In particular, Stewart recalled a bitter winter's day in Wisconsin in 1960 when the two had been sampling opinion on the forthcoming presidential election. Joe, dressed in their grandfather's old coaching cloak and a big Russian fur hat, "looked like an angry, large-nosed, bespectacled animal peering out from behind a bush." In Wausau, an Irish-looking woman stared at the senior partner and cried, "Holy Mother of God!" Another, hearing Joe's accent, asked,

"Why you spik so broken?" Still another, who admitted that she could never vote for a Catholic for president, drew a wrathful response: "Madam," Joe roared, "I think you're a God-damned bigot."[9]

THE ALSOP BROTHERS grew up on a working farm in the Connecticut Valley. Woodford Farm, near the village of Avon, lay just over gentle hills from Hartford. The farm was anchored by an 1830s farmhouse, "no thing of beauty," Stewart recalled. Their father, Joseph Wright Alsop IV, after studying at Groton, in Germany, and at Yale's Sheffield School of Science, had become a gentleman farmer, raising tobacco and Ayreshire cattle. His Italian workers called him "Mr. Pockets," for as the perennial first selectman of Avon he would preside over town meetings with his hands thrust deep in his rear pants pockets, gently rocking to and fro. Like the English gentry, or southern cotton growers of an earlier day, "Pa" divided his time between private and public pursuits, farming and politics. He had sat for many terms in the Connecticut assembly, and he and his sons believed, as an article of family faith, that he would have been elected governor of the state but for the Bull Moose Revolt of 1912. He had followed his wife's uncle, the former president Theodore Roosevelt, into the Progressive defection. Later the prevailing Republican stalwarts punished his disloyalty; Bull Moosers thereafter were frozen out of state office.

"Pa" Alsop had indeed shown early Progressive tendencies. He had helped write the state's first utility regulations. But times change, putting once-adventurous views into new perspective, and his sons found his views crusty and reactionary. He was distinctly anti–New Deal. Stewart recalled years later that he regularly spoke of his in-law Franklin D. Roosevelt as "that crazy jack in the White House."

The senior Alsop had grown up in Middletown, where the family had flourished since colonial times, "barely keeping their noses above water," as Joe later wrote in his colorful last will and testament. By keeping their noses above water, he meant acquiring the financial means to live as gentlemen. Richard Alsop, an early sprig of the American family, had found his way into the history books as a minor member of a minor literary circle known as the "Connecticut wits." Joe took a perverse pleasure in saying that he had read the old gentleman's work and found it "not very witty at all." Like the Alsops, the family house in Middletown (now the arts center at Wesleyan University) was unusual to the point of eccentricity. Its early-nineteenth-century builder had run out of funds and could not pay for the planned plaster columns, so he had them painted on. The trompe l'oeil façade is preserved to this day. Joe himself would build an equally eccentric house at 2720 Dumbarton Avenue (later renamed Dumbarton Street) in Georgetown. Its homely cinder-block exterior, painted a dull yellow ochre because that was the cheapest color of paint, was regarded by neighbors as an eyesore. Soon after this house was finished, a municipal ordinance forbade the building of other cinder-block houses.

The Alsops often spoke and wrote of their family as a "tribe," and there was something tribal, perhaps clannish, about its habits, history, rituals, and celebrations. Old family albums show photographs of generations of children lined up uniformly in a sort of military pose, arranged in descending order of ages, and photographed front, side, and rear. None of the family memoirists seem to remember how the practice originated. It was one of the tribal things Alsops did.[10] Later, in the Washington houses of the two columnists, family portraits crowded the walls. "We Alsops are thing-oriented," Stewart wrote. "We like objects, especially if we inherited them, and more especially if they are valuable." Their father had once interested himself in the family's English origins and had commissioned two genealogists to explore them. Both researchers agreed that the Alsops had arisen from a village of that name in Derbyshire; but one thought "the original Alsop was one Alsop-le-dale, a knight who accompanied William the Conquerer," while the other concluded, disappointingly, that the name "derived from Ale-shop."

It was less the rather crusty Alsops than the Roosevelts, however, whose legacy mattered more politically to the future columnists. Their grandmother, Corinne Roosevelt Robinson, Theodore Roosevelt's adoring younger sister, gave them close connections with both the Oyster Bay and Hyde Park branches of that extensive clan. She was a vivid, influential character. Those who had known her often recognized the hereditary marks in her lively grandsons. Every summer the Alsop boys had been packed off in August to Henderson, a large country house built of huge stones in the Scottish baronial style, overlooking the Mohawk Valley in upstate New York. There Grandmother Robinson presided over "a rolling house party" that one reached, in those earlier days, by horse-drawn conveyance over steep, twisting roads, the approach heralded by a horn. At Henderson the boys and their sister, Corinne, rode fierce Shetland ponies (which the unathletic Joe hated) and swam under their grandmother's supervision in an icy pool. Corinne Robinson lived until February 1933, long enough to witness the election of another Roosevelt to the White House.[11] "Among her own large, loud, spirited family," David McCullough writes in *Mornings on Horseback*, "she thrived especially on talk and roars of laughter and huge dinner parties." One noted visitor advised another regarding survival at one of Corinne Robinson's dinners, "Talk as loudly as you possibly can and answer your own questions."

By later accounts, no doubt stylized in the telling, it was Grandmother Robinson who decreed that Joe would go into journalism, not law, and for severely practical reasons. Another three years at Harvard, where Joe had spent many happy and bibulous hours at Porcellian Club parties and dinners, threatened to make a permanent drunkard of him.[12] The sad memory of Eleanor Roosevelt's charming, dipsomaniacal father was the cautionary example: "If you get right down to it," the Alsops would write some years later, "Our uncle [Elliot] was the real reason why both of us became reporters." As each of them went off to college, the "vast tribe would fix its powerful collective eye on the new-fledged freshman, to see whether he too would choose the primrose path." When the "same sad pleasure-loving tendencies" were detected in Joe, Grandmother Robinson turned to her "old tribal friend" Mrs. Ogden Reid, publisher of the *New York Herald Tribune*. One day in 1932, Joe was simply informed that it was "all arranged" that he would become a reporter. His grandmother added that "it would be all for the best." All in all, insofar as political character is transmissible, the Roosevelt connection went far to explain the Alsop outlook. Like Uncle Teddy, Joe and Stewart Alsop believed in a strong America, a big navy (and later a big air force too), interventionism abroad, and progressivism at home.

Joe came to believe that the greatest political change in his lifetime was "the inclusion of the excluded," beginning with Franklin D. Roosevelt's New Deal. The Roosevelt reforms foreshadowed the decline of what Joe called the "WASP ascendancy," the historic domination of American society and politics by families very much like his own. Perhaps the opening shots of that social revolution might have been heard when Great-Uncle Teddy began to make anti-administration noises (he was acutely disappointed by his hand-picked successor in the White House, William Howard Taft) and stepped up his speeches against corporate monopoly, class greed and interest, and the fixed conservative doctrines peculiar to the Republican stalwarts.

In Joe Alsop's version of recent American history, the extension of the Progressive legacy by the second Roosevelt presidency was portrayed as a natural continuation of the first. A telling clue to Joe's fundamental outlook appears in the refracted light of what he wrote about FDR in his brilliant centennial reminiscence of 1982. FDR, he wrote, "was the unrelenting enemy of misery, poverty, oppression, cruelty, injustice, meanness, smallness, obscurantism, and every other form of nastiness and source of unhappiness . . . and he was the stout friend of plenty, generosity, decency, liberality, geniality, openness, justice and freedom. . . . He loved the light and loathed the darkness, and in hard and testing times he was also inspired and sustained . . . by a simple, rather old-fashioned, but deep and unshakeable Christian faith."[13]

Joe appended one note of reservation. He thought FDR, could he have seen into the future beyond 1945, would have lamented the fading of the old WASP values and the dimming of their influence in American life and politics. This was, to Joe, the only substantial minus of the political transformation that struck him as the essence of his time. America had shed its WASP virtues "like a lizard dropping its tail," but "no coherent view of the American historical identity" had replaced it.

The legacy of the two Roosevelt presidents and more than a hint of tribal pride may be read between the purplish lines of a piece Joe wrote in 1939 for *Life*. "A President's Family Album" offers explanatory captions for a collection of photographs of the Hyde Park branch of the family. Joe relished small touches. For instance, one in-law of the president's father had married a Frenchman, and her Paris salon had the great distinction—"a caste mark," as Joe put it—of being mentioned in Proust "as a special haunt of members of the Jockey Club." Not even John Quincy Adams "had so handsome a start in life as the first leader of an American popular front."[14]

At Woodford Farm in the Alsops' childhood, the cultivation of political argument was daily food and drink. Their mother, Corinne Robinson's daughter, was also a politician, one of the first women elected to the Connecticut senate. A future daughter-in-law observed in her "that special Roosevelt quality"—a gift of solicitude and riveted attentiveness, especially for children, that could sometimes be almost cloying. Philip Geyelin, a friend who later edited the *Washington Post*'s editorial page and was a traveling companion of both brothers, remembered Ma Alsop as "the only person who could tell Joe to shut up and get away with it." She had the same instinct for seizing events by the throat that had made her eminent uncle a fabled maelstrom of energy and drive. Like her husband, she found the White House policies of her distant cousin Franklin deplorable. She had strongly supported his 1936 Republican challenger, Kansas governor Alf Landon—in fact, had seconded Landon's nomination. "It took a certain brass for her to ask favors of the president," Stewart remembered, "but it never bothered her at all." She would ask the president for "a little chat" in the Oval Office, usually to promote the interests of her sons, and often won her way. She was an aggressive Republican. Joe and Stewart, who maintained their voter registration at Avon for years after moving to Washington, suspected her of tampering with their heretical Democratic ballots.[15]

She supervised her children's early education, teaching them to read, then sending them over the hill to Hartford, where Joe studied in a private school in Mark Twain's old house. She took the future columnist to enroll at Groton School in the fall of 1924, and her exchange on that occasion with the famous headmaster Endicott Peabody soon took its place in family legend.

"Now Endicott," she said—she was, of course, on a first-name basis with the formidable educator and muscular Christian—"Joe is a bookish boy and likes to read."

"Don't worry, Corinne," Peabody jovially replied, "we'll get that out of him soon enough." He failed. On the English exam for Harvard, Joe Alsop scored a perfect 100, the highest grade recorded at that time, and Peabody declared a holiday at Groton. Yet the boy's Groton years, though academically successful, had not been entirely happy. Joe's sister, Corinne Chubb, thought it was probably because Joe's clothing was dowdy and old-fashioned, and not from Brooks Brothers. She couldn't imagine why "Ma" had sent Joe to Groton without the right clothes.[16]

And there was the weight problem. For the first twenty-seven years of his life he was (or thought of himself as) very fat. Even after he took stern measures to shed weight and keep it off, the struggle never stopped. He became a keen student of diet theories and fads and, with his usual combativeness, once declared war on the nutrition editors of the *New York Times* because they spoke dismissively of the Air Force diet, a low-carbohydrate system that finally—in the 1970s—enabled him to get into his clothes. But then again, the food he liked was never plain. In 1956, as he prepared to lease his house to a friend from Alabama, "Oatsie" Leiter, he listed a few of his chef's specialties. They included oyster-crab soup, shrimp risotto, sweetbreads with financière sauce, beef à la mode in jelly, and chocolate mousse.[17]

But the crisis had come years earlier, when Joe, as a convivial Washington bachelor with excellent family connections, found himself most evenings at lavish dinner tables. His weight soared. One day in 1937, at the time he was reporting the great Supreme Court "court-packing" battle between FDR and congressional conservatives, he tipped the scales at 247 pounds (on a five-foot, nine-inch frame). His doctor warned that if this trend continued he would die within months. Joe retreated, with his typewriter, to a room at the Johns Hopkins Medical Center in Baltimore, where under the direction of Dr. John Eager Howard he lost nearly a hundred pounds. He would strive to keep it off, more or less, for the rest of his life. In a reflection on the experience, called "How It Feels to Look Like Everybody Else," he wrote that suddenly his "excavated" nose resembled a pyramid, while his chin, "bereft of its pendent cascades of brother chins," had turned out "ignobly small." He thought of growing a beard to strengthen it but decided not to. But there was no longer "a nice suggestion of one of the later Roman emperors" about his physique.[18]

No one has left a more vivid portrait of the prewar Joe Alsop, in his twenties already a rising star in New York and Washington journalism, than the famous Stanley Walker, his former city editor at the *New York Herald Tribune*. "It is well to remember a salient point," Walker wrote to a correspondent almost thirty years later:

> He was reeking with Roosevelt blood. . . . You asked if the other men on the staff did not regard him as "arrogant." That is not quite the word, though it may be close. He merely had that Harvard manner, that peculiar self-assurance, or brashness, which characterizes all Roosevelts, Teddy and FDR and Eleanor and all the rest. Alsop's impact on his comrades on the paper was similar to that of old Teddy on the cattlemen and others of the Bad Lands when he went there to ranch. In neither case did the new-found associates laugh very long. . . . One night I was about to take a cab up to see Alex Woollcott about something or other. I had been struck by a strange similarity between [them]. . . . He and Woollcott became great friends, and for a time saw

a deal of each other. It was a wonderful thing to see these two fat showoffs spouting poetry to each other, talking of Proust, etc. etc. Each of them liked to give parties . . . and each presided with great unction and effervescence. They reminded me of two Buddhas, except they were much more lively.[19]

As war clouds gathered in the late 1930s and early 1940s, Joe Alsop plunged headlong into the interventionist cause. He had soon outgrown his brief flirtation with Senator Nye's isolationist theories, which explained U.S. involvement in World War I as the work of a munitions and bond lobby, the so-called merchants of death. Joe had given isolationist views an airing at the dinner table at Woodford Farm when he was covering the Nye hearings. Pa Alsop had scoffed and assured Joe that he didn't know what he was talking about, and apparently he shortly came to agree. The New York Century group and William Allen White's Committee to Defend America by Aiding the Allies, both of which were lobbying quietly to involve the neutral United States more deeply in the destiny of beleaguered Britain, had Joe's enthusiastic support.

One day in the spring of 1940, his friend John Foster at the British embassy told him about a then-secret Churchill initiative. The Royal Navy needed more destroyers, and Churchill had set his eye on the mothballed "four-pipers" of World War I vintage that were now idling at anchor in U.S. naval ports. Roosevelt's initial response was cool. In a foretaste of his zeal for backstage intrigue, Joe plunged into active support of the cause. Eventually, in one of the major emergences from thirties isolationism, FDR agreed to swap fifty of the "overaged" destroyers for ninety-nine-year leases on British bases in the Western Hemisphere. General Pershing's crucial speech in support of the swap was written, Joe claimed, by Joe and Walter Lippmann. Joe's unfolding career as a reporter-activist was thus launched. It would be resumed five years later, after many adventures, when the war was over.

Chapter Three **Under Fire**

Two days after the sudden outbreak of war in Korea had disrupted his dinner party, Joe Alsop set off for the front lines—not merely to follow his "see for yourself" rule but also to test his response to battle. He had never before been under fire, even in wartime China, and wondered how he would react.

The Korean War, which began while the famous sixty-six-page state paper known as NSC-68 was circulating at the highest levels in Washington, came as a godsend for those, including the Alsops, who were pressing for a larger defense budget. Drafted under the supervision of Paul Nitze, George Kennan's successor as chief of policy planning at the State Department, NSC-68 had initially been inspired by the daunting news of the Soviet atomic bomb test—and by Chiang Kai-shek's forced abandonment of mainland China.

The document viewed the Communist challenge to American security as worldwide and as extending to the most peripheral theaters and conflicts. Moreover, that challenge was believed to be psychological as well as military and political. And while the analysis of NSC-68 was more flexible and subtle than its ultimate reputation would suggest, Nitze's assessment tended to boost precisely the view which the Alsops had been putting forward in their fervent comparisons between the complacency of Truman-Johnson defense preparedness and the Baldwin-Chamberlain period in prewar England.

The North Korean incursion whose anticipated repulse Joe was traveling out to watch had surprised almost everyone but the Alsops. It gave them meager satisfaction to recall that they had warned, two years earlier, of just such an attack. In late August 1948, in a column that their anchor paper, the *Herald Tribune*, titled "How Not to Make Policy," they reported the Truman administration's decision to withdraw American troops from the peninsula. The planned withdrawal, they conceded, would meet the terms of the United Nations mandate. But the hidden premise of the withdrawal, in their view, was the Truman administration penny-pinching which they had condemned in other manifestations — another effort to tailor worldwide security policy to the narrow dimensions of the Treasury Department spending ceilings imposed by John W. Snyder.

"After the American evacuation," the Alsops wrote, "the Kremlin can take South Korea when and if it chooses, without moving a single Russian soldier." As usual, their argument for keeping U.S. ground troops in South Korea drew on the domino theory, the all-purpose hypothesis that aggressors prospered on the conciliations and concessions natural to democracies. American "abandonment" of South Korea would have "an immediate disastrous psychological and political effect on all the forces of resistance to Communist expansion through Asia." This was especially true in China, they said, where Chiang Kai-shek's Nationalist government at the time still clung precariously to its foothold on the mainland. (By June 1950, Chiang had been expelled to his exile on Formosa.)[1]

In any case, NSC-68, with its closely held arguments (the paper would not be declassified or published until 1975) was now at hand to fortify policy-makers who argued for a greatly augmented defense effort in the post-Korea summer of 1950. "The Korean War," as John Lewis Gaddis has observed, "appeared to validate several of NSC-68's most important conclusions . . . [including] the argument that all interests had become equally vital; that any further shift in the balance of power, no matter how small, could upset the entire structure of postwar international relations." The budgetary effects were dramatic, and very much to the Alsops' liking: With various supplements, in fiscal 1951 Congress authorized the spending of $48.2 billion for defense, a 257 percent increase over the prior Truman ceiling of $13.5 billion. The Kansas City bankers had lost the argument.

However persuasive or unpersuasive such arguments sound four decades later, the message propounded by NSC-68 was textbook strategic orthodoxy in Washington in the late 1940s, at the outset of what John F. Kennedy would call a "long, twilight struggle" against world communism. Most Washington analysts, not the Alsops alone, assumed that a ripple effect would follow any break in the anticommunist front in Asia. They also assumed—and this belief was perhaps decisive in prompting President Truman to respond—that the attack on South Korea had been part of a coordinated Soviet plan, which appeared even more sinister following the ouster of Chiang from China by the forces of Mao Tse-tung.

The Alsops would lay out this thesis for the American reading public, in all its electric detail, within a few weeks of the North Korean attack. "The Lesson of Korea" elaborated for *Saturday Evening Post* readers the theme of recent columns; it pronounced that lesson "grimly simple." The Kremlin would probe for any soft spot in the Western flank and exploit it at any opportunity. Korea should be viewed as "only the first episode of an attempt to bring all Asia and all Europe within the Soviet empire . . . [making] the living death of the slave society the universal condition of mankind, from the shores of the Atlantic to the islands of Japan." Indeed, the Alsops assured their no doubt frazzled readers, "expert observers"—not then identified—had already discovered the broad lines of this "world strategy."

The plan to attack Korea had been expounded, they believed, at a meeting that took place nine months before the actual incident, at a secret conclave of Communist leaders in Peking. Again, the Alsops deployed the Baldwin-Chamberlain analogy from prewar Britain. With every passing month, it was suggested, American military power was waning. If the trend continued, "we shall have to choose between launching a war of desperation or surrendering in our turn." The root of the trouble lay in the postelection decisions of November 1948, when James Forrestal, "gray-faced, exhausted by his burdens, already in the last phase before his tragedy," warned against the Soviet military buildup but lost the argument in President Truman's inner circle. The immediate result was a $3-billion cut in the defense budget. Thus "American foreign policy was radically changed . . . to save $3 billion." In other words, the "lesson of Korea" was ultimately that Joe and Stewart Alsop had been prophetic, both in what Joe had told Clark Clifford in the noisy argument a few nights after the election and in what they had written about the "mewing" ghosts of Baldwin and Chamberlain.[2]

Might Joe Alsop have suspected that he was exaggerating a danger just a bit for psychological effect, "scaring the hell" out of people much as President Truman had done three years earlier when he had to sell an unprecedented degree of American assistance to Greece and Turkey? Some of his expert correspondents—notably, the British air marshal, Sir John Slessor—admonished Joe that the prospects that freedom would be submerged or another world war would break out were far less dismal than he made them out to be.[3] Yet it was an alarming time, and no one in the summer of 1950 had the gift of foresight. Not even the most optimistic observers then foresaw such turning points as the breach between the Soviet Union and Maoist China, which would reach a point of armed hostility within a decade. Nor did anyone whose influence counted in Washington seem to suspect, in the summer of 1950, that the attack in Korea was less carefully calculated, its origins and impulses more tangled, than official, conventional strategic wisdom supposed. The alternative press was skeptical at the time. In his *Hidden History of the Korean War*, which appeared before the eventual truce, the independent journalist I. F. Stone cited several clues which indicated to him that Stalin and the Soviet Union were less solidly behind the Korean adventure than was officially assumed.

In his memoirs twenty years later, the revisionist and anti-Stalinist Soviet premier Nikita Khrushchev would offer a starkly different account. As Khrushchev told it, Stalin had been bewitched by the North Korean dictator Kim Il Sung's prediction that a mere prod from the North Korean bayonet would make South Korea crumple. A fifth column who hated Syngman Rhee, the autocratic U.S.-installed president of the Republic of Korea, would collaborate with the invaders. But these facile predictions misfired. When the United States unexpectedly resisted, Stalin, according to Khrushchev's account, quickly jerked his Soviet advisers out of Korea. Khrushchev recalled Stalin's words: "We don't want there to be any evidence for accusing us of taking part in this business. It's Kim Il Sung's affair." Khrushchev's account may be false or self-serving (though there is no apparent reason for doubting his version of the story), but the picture of muddled intentions seems more plausible than the Alsop theory, shared by most of the influential sources they talked with, of an encompassing and unified Kremlin conspiracy.[4]

PUTTING THESE OFFICIAL Washington quarrels over money and strategic priorities behind him, Joe Alsop flew off to Japan and then Korea on June 27 for a first-hand look at the war. In his grubby combat fatigues, he soon became an eyewitness on a battlefield which, within a year, was to see dramatic ups and downs in American fortunes.[5] From first shot to last, the Korean War was fought in oscillating extremes of heat and frost over the mountainous and inhospitable North Asian peninsula; and the war, like the terrain and the weather, was a teeter-totter affair. In June and July, the invading North Koreans routed the small, unwarned South Korean army and came near driving the small U.S. expeditionary force (composed chiefly of unseasoned occupation troops from Japan) into the sea. MacArthur's bold counterattack, which featured a brilliant and dangerous amphibious landing at Inchon that virtually all his advisers had opposed, in turn routed the North Koreans. The pell-mell North Korean retreat to the Chinese border, with UN forces in hot pursuit, would eventually bring vast Chinese armies into play and utterly change the character of the war.

In early August, though, all of this lay in the future; that month found Joe Alsop following the campaign on the southwest Korean coast, along the approaches to "the dirty little town of Chinju." The terrain struck him as a blend of Maine and, he wrote, drawing on his gift for evocative travelogue, "Chinese romantic landscape—precipitous pine-clad mountain slopes, luminous blue bays among green cliffs, and narrow, terraced valleys, where the thatched mud villages seem to grow like mushrooms from the brilliant green rice paddies . . . better country to look at than to fight over in heat above ninety degrees."

The fight at Chinju was keyed to the defense of the fragile UN perimeter at the southeastern tip of the peninsula; the foe was the North Korean Sixth Division. Most of the fighting occurred in darkness, under the garish light of flares. In the presence of military professionals, Joe's usual impulse to second-guess seasoned experts was, for once, muted. He described himself frankly as an "inexperienced observer" for whom the first experience of battle seemed to consist of "isolated scenes and incidents." It was quite unlike traditional fixed-front warfare, where thrust and parry were easier to define.

Joe was impressed with the patience with which the commanding officer pushed green, easily discouraged troops toward their objective and out of the way of the aggressively advancing marines who were coming up behind them. By August 11, after two days of costly fighting, Task Force Kean, the unit Joe had attached himself to, had won its objective—the high ground commanding Chinju. Joe, meanwhile, had learned something about himself. The experience of being in a battle zone was more exhilarating than frightening, he found. But what did it mean? When he paused for a backward glance at the experience a week later, Joe found himself condemning the stark contrast between GI heroism at Chinju and the "business as usual" attitude that seemed to him to prevail in the rear echelons. He was astonished to find that ground transport was still largely absorbed by commerce and even tourism. As for the fight for the Chinju heights, "while well conducted as an exercise . . . in outcome this tough and painful American effort seems to have served no visible military purpose whatever." No sooner had the task force gained the high ground than "they were recalled and with bitter anger retraced their steps to the old positions where they had jumped off." Joe thought of the obvious literary tag; he was reminded of the brave old Duke of York in the poem, marching his ten thousand men up the hill and then marching them down again. But the literary allusion did not mask his indignation as he quoted "one of the highest possible authorities" as admitting "that the real motive . . . was that we 'needed a victory.'"[6]

THE WAR IN Korea was, for Americans, a military novelty in almost every sense. For a doubting public, the discrepancy between the bitter sacrifice of life in small, detailed, and sometimes isolated engagements and the obscure and shifting strategic objectives became a constant of reporting and comment. Joe had noticed the difference at Chinju, in his first experience under fire. What he also saw then was the extreme contrast, hardly exceptional in any war, between the dedication and peril of everyday frontline soldiers and the fecklessness of their ultimate leadership in the "snake pit of Washington."

Chinju had been a powerful experience, as future references would certify. After more eyewitness reporting of another late-August engagement—this time of the Twenty-seventh Regiment, First Battalion, in the

Valley of Chanpyongdong—Joe Alsop found himself moved by the fighting spirit and patriotism of the GIs. But again, it was a Tolstoyan situation—the fog of war compounded in impossibly difficult terrain by darkness and the confusion of night fighting. The new unit to which he had attached himself as a correspondent had set up an ambush for North Korean tanks in the tunnel-like neck of a valley. The operation was pronounced militarily successful. Even so, "not even the wisest," Joe wrote, "was sure what was happening" as the battle raged. "In night fighting an infantry battalion is like an organist [*sic*: surely "organism" was what Joe originally wrote] with an inadequate central nervous system, which survives because all its well-trained members rapidly and correctly react to local stimuli."[7]

In a September 11 dispatch from Tokyo, Joe once again reflected on what he called the odd rule of warfare—"that all the good people are at the front and all the odious people are at higher headquarters." This was cliché, of course, but Joe was saying his thank-yous and goodbyes to his hosts of the First Battalion, "a fighting team that will go forward without counting costs; will hold an exposed position against heavy odds; will uncomplainingly endure great hardships." His thoughts turned to the Spartans, yet American soldiers were not "drilled, beautiful and unthinking" like Spartans. "They were Americans fighting not for iron laws but for a good life and a good society . . . in this now-darkening world."[8]

One further adventure awaited Joe Alsop before he packed his bags and returned from this baptism of fire: landing with the marines at Inchon and joining their victorious march back to Seoul. It was a "stirring, almost exhilarating experience." Joe tried to capture the essence of it, in his observation of Captain Sam Jasklika's Easy Company, and to express why it seemed to him to represent "so much of meaning and so much of goodness." He was impressed by the small band of marines, no more than twenty years old on average, whose grasp of what they were fighting for seemed to him strikingly unlike that of "academic-minded people at home." Their leader, an officer of Ukrainian ancestry from Connecticut, Joe's home state, had reached his rank by intelligence and courage. "Far from transforming the men of this company into the sarcastic or self-pitying cardboard cutouts of the war novelists, their harsh experience seems almost to have enlarged and amplified them." Their fighting virtues, "simple sentiment reinforced by stern training," had rekindled Joe's faith in the "hidden yet always present virtue of everyday Americans."[9]

JOE ALSOP, as references and allusions to the Korean experience would continue to suggest for years, had been deeply stricken with the romance of war—with its power to strip away mask and pretense, to expose the bedrock of character. He was proud that he had not been frightened under fire. He had discovered in the first-hand observation of combat some deeply satisfying intimations of the possibility of self-renewal and faith in ordinary people. In his war reportage there was less rhetoric than usual, and more direct personal observation—the reportorial virtues at which he had originally excelled as a writer, just as his old boss Stanley Walker had seen at the *Herald Tribune* fifteen years earlier.

The home-front reception of his columns from Korea was enthusiastic and at times almost delirious. Letters from readers as well as from the fighting units he had been with filled his mailbox. Some faithful readers felt that Joe Alsop, the pundit and prophet of doom, had found his métier in the ultimate exercise of his "go and see for yourself" rule. Lincoln Kirstein, an old friend from college days, had been "moved to tears" by at least two of the Korean pieces. He saw what Joe did not at first see— the essentially aesthetic vision that lay at the core of Joe's better writing:

It seems to me that your tone, your humanity, sweetness, anger and historical sense are exceptional, and I only hope one day you will write some sort of permanent book of memoirs. . . . Actually, it is a religious question: Do you believe in what you have seen up to the intensity of trying to fix it into some sort of order which is a candidate for whatever permanence we can think of, this side of immortality . . . something like "The Seven Pillars of Wisdom" . . . which at least can be read for its ferocity, its love of people and its beautiful anger.[10]

From George Kennan, now at the Institute for Advanced Study in Princeton, came more praise of the dispatches from Korea, couched in terms that must have pleased Joe immensely. They were, Kennan said, "like Tolstoy's passages from 'War and Peace.' Like Tolstoy, you are an artist and should write about what you see and perceive rather than what you think. For the latter I have respect, too, but not as much."[11] These two perceptive friends, Kirstein and Kennan, both men of sensibility, had seen to the heart of the matter: Joe was better at portraiture than punditry; he found his true note in feeling rather than analysis. The Korean experience had put him among young men facing death. For once the obsessively pessimistic think-pieces receded into the background.

None of the Korean dispatches showed the contrast more clearly than a late-September dispatch from Pusan, in which he once again weighed into the developing argument over high strategy. And the contrast was not favorable to his powers of prediction or judgment.

The reconquest of South Korea, now complete, raised an inescapable question: Should the United Nations allies halt their victorious drive at the 38th Parallel, the former de facto "border" between North and South Korea, or push on and unify the peninsula? The issue reactivated Joe's dogmatism. Joe was certain that Douglas MacArthur, who was known to be pushing hard for unification, was right. If only the strategists in Western capitals and at the UN would listen to MacArthur, they would choose "the bold course" and order the full occupation of North Korea. The risks, Joe pronounced in what proved to be a disastrously inaccurate forecast, were "infinitely less than they may appear to the policy makers." The clinching argument for the "bold course," Joe wrote, was that the Kremlin, which was still assumed to be quarterbacking the show on the other side, had passed up its best chance to aid the North Koreans. It had not sent its pilots into the war to fly planes with North Korean insignia. Soviet intervention now seemed far less probable. But "in crude terms," he wrote, "if the Kremlin is ready to risk a general war now, it is because the Kremlin expects to win a general war [and] . . . we must expect an early general war anyway." Nothing was said of China, which was assumed to be Stalin's obedient vassal.[12]

"You should write about what you see and perceive, not what you think," his friend George Kennan had said. Kennan's observation, and his admonition to trust perceptions, were both acute. In the end it was neither Kremlin intervention nor a general war that transformed the Korean situation from hope to despair by the grim winter of 1951; it was massive Chinese intervention. Together with the other shocks of that pivotal year, and Chiang Kai-shek's final defeat and exile less than a year earlier, Chinese intervention in Korea would wholly alter American strategic perceptions and would create a storm of anger and recrimination at home.

However alarming it was for others, for Joe this development was nothing less than opportune. Joe Alsop thought of himself as an old "China Hand." That central midcentury preoccupation would increasingly absorb the time and energies of the returning war correspondent.

Chapter Four China Hand

Joe Alsop's fascination with China—not necessarily his earliest entrancement with that unfathomable land—could be traced at least to mid-1941 and his chance pre–Pearl Harbor encounter with Claire Chennault, the maverick ex–U.S. Army Air Corps colonel whose American Volunteer Group ("Flying Tigers") served as Chiang Kai-shek's air force. The stone-deaf Chennault was one of those far-sighted military misfits whose services the peacetime army had found it could do without. His old force, Joe would write in a reminiscence at the time of Chennault's death in 1958, had laughed at the colonel's pioneering theories of airborne operations, "for cavalry was still more popular than airplanes in the 1920s."

By the time Joe began serving as a Chennault aide in wartime Kunming, in the early 1940s, "you would have called [Chennault] an old man —the skin of the deep-lined face was like the surface of long-aged oak— but the tremendous, telling jut of the jaw was still there. He needed what that jutting jaw implied for his bitter wartime battles with the air staff, and that brave old fool, Gen. Joe Stilwell, and with a lot of people." Indeed, Chennault's bitter contests with Stilwell were, from Joe Alsop's perspective, the central drama of the war years.

Pearl Harbor Day—December 7, 1941—found Joe in Hong Kong on a mission for Chennault. When the British crown colony fell on Christmas Day to the invading Japanese, he was marched off to the Stanley internment camp, where he devoted the six months of internment to the study of classical Chinese. He would later claim that he had forgotten most of the classical ideograms; but his fascination with classical Chinese civilization remained. From that time on the flavor of China lingered in Joe's life, together with impassioned views on the civil war between China's Nationalists, led by Chiang Kai-shek, and the Communists, led by Mao and Chou En-lai.

In fact, China dominated the decor of Joe's Georgetown houses. His shirts, hand-sewn of Chinese silk, were made in Milan. China silks covered the chairs and sofas, and vapors of Oriental potpourri perfumed the air. Vases, both Chinese and Japanese, peered from specially built alcoves, and silk hangings alternated with the Alsop family portraits and photographs on his walls. Joe patronized many of the Chinese restaurants in Washington and on occasion kept dinner companions waiting on the sidewalk while he gave jovial parting advice to a maître d'hôtel about recipes for honeyed ham and other dishes.

A PASSIONATE DISPUTE over American strategy in China turned bitter and partisan in 1949, when Mao's Communist forces defeated Chiang's armies after some two decades of civil war and consolidated their rule on the Chinese mainland. Secretary of State Dean Acheson resolved, however, that the Republicans and their "China Lobby" friends would not be permitted to write a one-dimensional version of the "fall" of China. Acheson ordered the study that grew into a thousand-page "white paper" known as *United States Relations with China*. Its central argument was that for all the American effort, and the billions in military aid extended to the Nationalist forces, and the many attempts at U.S. diplomatic mediation, China had all along been the mistress of her own fate, never America's to keep or to "lose." As Acheson wrote in his transmittal letter to President Truman, "The unfortunate but inescapable fact is that the civil war in China was beyond the control of the United States. Nothing that this country did or could have done within the reasonable bounds of its capabilities would have changed the result; nothing that was left undone by this country has contributed to it. It was the product of internal Chinese forces."[1]

The Acheson argument would someday make unassailable historical sense, but it was a hard sell in the summer of 1949. A scent of treason was in the air, and Joe Alsop, while he emphatically did not believe that betrayal was at issue, was one of those who declined to swallow the official State Department attempt at historical distancing. The official stance was also rejected by the angry legions of Chiang supporters—the Nationalist government's friends in Protestant missionary circles, the textile import trade, and elsewhere. The Republican Party had long been the natural political home of the Asia-Firsters, those who thought the United States should look west rather than east in search of its geopolitical interests and who had thought all along that the war in the Pacific should have taken precedence over the war in Europe. The debate over the revolution in China, the search for accountable parties, would come to assume a fierce edge. It would also inspire a round of witch-hunting to rival that of colonial Salem, Massachusetts.

The impending appearance of Acheson's white paper, no less than the events themselves, stirred Joe to undertake his own assessment. The two brothers had followed the developing China story in the column. But Joe would need more than the usual eight hundred words to expound his own eyewitness account of why the American effort to maintain Chiang in power had failed. Joe believed that the draftsmen of the white paper had been too cautious, "too fearful of Congress to tell the China story with forthright frankness."[2]

For him the story was primarily historical, not political—a question of accountability, indeed, but much more than that. In any case, given what he knew and the part he had played in the wartime years, he could not sit by in silence as the China dispute played itself out. As a minor but important player, he had occupied a ringside seat and had sometimes far exceeded the usual functions of a junior military officer. In time, Joe's personal perspective would weigh heavily in the heated competition to shape the China story. By midsummer he had dusted off his China files and was hard at work on a three-part series for the *Saturday Evening Post* called "How We Lost China." The general label, by the way, was apparently the invention of the magazine's layout department; but it inspired the notion that Alsop's views paralleled those of the China Lobby, as

Chiang's last-ditch defenders came to be called, more closely than they actually did.

Not that his views, then or later, were mild or tentative. Early drafts brimmed with fury at Joe's designated villain, "that brave old fool" General Joseph Stilwell, the U.S. military deputy to Chiang and the Generalissimo's nominal chief of staff as well until late 1944. Stilwell had been an authentic American folk hero, a people's general, admired for his democratic manner and bluntness. In early 1942, when the Japanese drove the Allies headlong from Burma, Stilwell, who led the famous "walkout," or retreat, declined to offer the usual excuses. A reporter later asked him what he "claimed" had happened. "I claim," said Stilwell, "that we got a hell of a beating. We got run out of Burma and it's humiliating as hell. I think we ought to find out what caused it, go back and retake it."[3]

Vinegar Joe Stilwell's determination to "go back and retake" Burma and to rebuild an overland supply route—the storied Burma Road—to connect the British foothold in India with the Allied forces in China struck Joe Alsop as the key to the eventual failure of Chiang's cause. In his view, the heart of the matter lay in Stilwell's unconcealed scorn for Chiang, which rendered a successful collaboration impossible.

The evidence was easy to come by, depending on what one selected and emphasized from an abundant but often contradictory and murky record. In their first interview, Stilwell had told Theodore White, then a young reporter for *Time*, that "the trouble in China is simple: We are allied to an ignorant, illiterate, superstitious, peasant son of a bitch." He meant Chiang Kai-shek. Stilwell's tragedy, as Alsop saw it, was that he had been given the wrong job, an assignment unfitted to his talents. "He was a fine combat soldier, brave, tough, energetic, utterly indifferent to hardship"; he also knew China, its culture and language—he had been an embassy military attaché there before the war. Yet "the complex political-military-strategic functions of a theater commander were quite beyond Stilwell's range. . . . He was as narrow as life in an old-fashioned army camp, and as prone to feuds as a Kentucky mountaineer." All these deficiencies were worsened by his "intense personal hatred of Chiang Kai-shek," whom Stilwell contemptuously called "Peanut" in diaries, letters, and private conversations.[4]

Ultimately, the story of the revolution in China as Joe recounted it for his *Saturday Evening Post* audience boiled down to historical melodrama, thick with stark contrasts of light and shadow, heroes and villains. Yet there was a distinction. Joe did not dream of characterizing the misjudgments of Stilwell and others, including General George C. Marshall, as "treason," as the McCarthyite right soon would be doing. But in later years, after American involvement in Vietnam became as bitterly disputed as policy in wartime China had been, Joe's *Saturday Evening Post* series became a touchstone of reference for those who thought he had been instrumental in defining the China debate in conspiratorial terms. The series was then resurrected by the young *New York Times* reporter David Halberstam, who thought that Joe Alsop in his *Saturday Evening Post* account had been "looking for conspiratorial answers" and had found them. Twenty years after they originally appeared, the three articles seemed to Halberstam, writing in *Harper's* and in his book *The Best and the Brightest*, to have "set the tone, though slightly loftier than some successors, for the *conspiracy view* [my italics] of the fall of China: the blame was placed on the State Department. . . . China was ours, and it was something to lose . . . an assumption which was to haunt foreign policy makers for years to come."[5]

There was some slight truth in Halberstam's evaluation, but it grossly misconceived the attitude of the *Post*'s editors and of Joe Alsop's partial but more subtle argument. In speaking of China as "lost," Alsop—or his headline writers—seemed to echo the cry of the China Lobby. These embittered partisans, led and largely financed by the New York silk importer Alfred Kohlberg, darkened the political scene with their scapegoat hunting. But their cause held no charm for Joe. As he beavered away at the *Post* series, he could hardly foresee the ironic twists that time and events would impart to his words, and he would have been dismayed to learn that his views and those of Kohlberg (with whom he exchanged acid letters about the China question) resembled one another in any respect. Joe's villain was Stilwell, not the State Department China Hands who would soon bear the brunt of right-wing anger.

As Joe worked at the series during the steamy summer months of 1949, the debate over Chiang's fate was gradually rising to a pitch of ugliness. In this unwholesome political climate, Joe Alsop was bearing witness to history he had personally experienced, not, he thought, promoting a partisan vendetta.

The editors of the *Saturday Evening Post* had no axes to grind. In fact, Joe's preliminary drafts aroused the resistance of his *Post* editors, Martin Sommers and Ben Hibbs. The pieces were beginning to sprawl beyond the space the *Post* could afford to give them. Sommers and Hibbs also were troubled by Joe's tendency to sprinkle the account with scorching adjectives, applied not only to Stilwell but even to such revered figures as General Marshall, who had undertaken one of President Truman's mediating missions to China and would soon become the target of venomous attacks by Senator Joe McCarthy and others. Sommers, the *Post*'s foreign editor, pressed Joe to squeeze the "rancor" from his early drafts. "Some of the adjectives you pile up on Stilwell," he wrote on October 21, "have got to come out. . . . The facts speak for themselves . . . [and] we do not believe that you ought to . . . tell the reader exactly what Stilwell's motives were. . . . That is to read Stilwell's mind."[6]

Hibbs, the *Post*'s editor in chief, felt the same way; the draft articles struck him as "shrill and rancorous," and he urged Joe to "lean over backwards . . . in an attempt to be somewhat more charitable to Vinegar Joe." Marshall, too, should be written about "in a little more charitable light. Marshall is my friend, and I also happen to think that he was a really great soldier." Hibbs, for his part, viewed the China debacle as "part of the leftist sweep that is going on all over the world where peoples have been oppressed and kicked around for generations." He thought American blunders might have hastened the Communist victory, "but I suspect it would have come eventually even if we had acted more wisely."[7]

Opinionated though he was, Joe as a rule cheerfully accepted editors' advice. He pruned and polished. Insulting and overheated adjectives fell away by dozens. By November, the articles—tempered, tightened, and toned down—were ready for the *Post* editions of January 7, 14, and 21 of 1950, just as the national postmortem on China began.

HOW PERSUASIVE WAS Joe's version of the China story? He had made a considerable effort to sound out those who he thought would question his interpretation; he had even sought to enlist the help of George Kennan and Kennan's deputy, John Paton Davies, who had served as Stilwell's chief State Department adviser during the war. On September 21 Joe wrote to ask Kennan to preview the China series confidentially before publication, "with a view to getting any suggestions you may have for making what I have written as fair as possible. I am equally anxious to avoid the faintest appearance of personal animus or persecution."[8]

Kennan thought the offer was motivated by a praiseworthy intent to be fair. But Joe's articles were sure to be critical of U.S. policy, and he and Davies, as government servants, preferred not to be accessories before the fact. Besides, Kennan wrote (a bit less plausibly), he and Davies found that their memories had grown dim four to seven years after the war. Kennan reminded Joe that every attempt the two of them had made to discuss the China issue "seems inevitably to draw us both into considerable acrimony." He would read the articles when the *Post* published them, but not before. Thus the tempering influence of Kennan and Davies, both of whom were capable of bringing an alternative perspective to bear, was withheld.[9] When the articles appeared in January, their most striking feature was Joe's dramatic attempt to reduce a great policy dispute to a clash of personalities—Stilwell's, Chiang's, and Claire Chennault's. The effort made for exciting journalism but questionable history.

The policy dispute was complex enough to begin with, even before the effect of powerful personalities was stirred into the mix. Alsop and his boss Chennault had vehemently opposed Stilwell's strategy, which was to train a large Chinese army and then lead it in the restoration of the land-supply route across Burma that the Japanese had captured and closed in 1942. For those like Chennault, who favored an air-power strategy in the China-Burma theater, the army plan was a wasteful obsession—General Stilwell's great white whale. This was the essence of Joe's explanation of the failure in China. But of course the "China tangle," as a later historian would call it, defied simplifications, including this one.[10] Even as one sought to understand it, it changed kaleidoscopically. From the time of the Japanese invasion of Manchuria in 1931, the Chinese had fought back after a fashion. As viewed sentimentally from Washington, China's ordeal superficially resembled that of the European "democracies," equally beleaguered by totalitarian enemies. Americans tended to project upon the sprawling and diverse land a coherent political structure that was alien to Chinese traditions and Chinese political history.

In truth, China was less a nation than an intricate mosaic of feudatory relationships. Chiang Kai-shek had fought to subdue and organize the warlords. But many of them still flourished, thinly disguised as "Chinese army" commanders and only nominally under Chiang's command. China had vast pools of young men of fighting age—forty million by one estimate. On paper, Chiang's army numbered more than three hundred divisions. Yet no one, certainly not Chiang himself, knew what China's fighting potential really amounted to. His forces were largely untrained, undisciplined, starved by the system of graft and corruption known as "squeeze," which their officers freely participated in. Stilwell deemed it his assignment to whip this force into fighting shape and carry the war to the Japanese. He seems, though, to have underestimated the difficulty. Stilwell's diplomatic adviser, Davies, writes in his memoir *Dragon by the Tail* that making Chiang's army combat-ready would have required wholesale executions and purges; and "confronted with a purge, most Chinese generals would have ceased to take orders and either have turned on the Generalissimo or simply assumed the character of war-lords, their troops staying with them."[11]

THOSE WHO EXPLOITED the China issue in domestic politics be-lieved, or professed to believe, that the choices in wartime China had been clear-cut. But they weren't—perhaps chiefly because of the strange relationship between Nationalists and Communists. Between Chiang's southern capital at Kunming and Mao's northern stronghold at Yenan stretched an elaborate web of personal and political ties that were baf-fling to the categorical Western mind. Just to keep track of the relation-ships was a challenge. Mao's deputy Chou En-lai, for instance, had served as political officer at the Whampoa Military Academy when Chiang was its commandant. Whampoa, in turn, had been created by a Stalinist op-erative in China in the early 1920s, when the Kuomintang and the Chi-nese Communist Party were still allied against the fading defenders of the old imperial China. But the fighting of 1927–28 had resulted in Mao's ex-pulsion from the Kuomintang and the beginning of Chiang's collabora-tion with the bankers and street thugs of Shanghai. In December 1936, Chou had rescued Chiang from a humiliating and life-threatening ab-duction by zealous young Communist officers.[12]

After the American contingent came to Kunming, Chiang's wartime capital, there was little military cooperation and great mutual suspicion among China's political factions. Most of the old enmity was suppressed so long as the Japanese invaders held much of northwest China, and on the surface there was less to distinguish the Nationalist from the Com-munist cause than conspiracy theorists would later imagine. Moreover, all the American proconsuls—from Stilwell to Patrick Hurley to General Albert Wedemeyer—encouraged collaboration, although in the end the efforts to coax the rivals into cooperation foundered on Chiang's demand that the Communist armies, veterans of the Long March, submit to his command. Mao and Chou believed that would be the end of their movement. Early in their struggle, they had formed the firm conviction that a Chinese political faction without its own army was helpless. Chinese history certainly supported that belief.

Then there was the issue of Stilwell's young advisers from the State Department—the China Hands, as they came to be called. The nature of their influence would become a central issue in the American anti-Communist inquisition of the 1950s. In his *Saturday Evening Post* series, Joe depicted John Davies and other U.S. diplomats as spellbound by the colorful Stilwell, and too much swayed by his personal contempt for Chiang. Actually, Davies and others seem to have been no more influenced by Stilwell than he was by them. Stilwell was above all a fighting general, preoccupied with the campaign to drive the Japanese out of Burma. Davies had Stilwell's permission to explore a possible Nationalist alliance with the Communists, but for military reasons, not political. By 1944— the critical year in the China-Burma theater, as Joe Alsop and everyone else agreed—a massive Japanese offense in eastern China (the Ichigo campaign) threatened to slice the country in two, adding new urgency to the quest for Nationalist-Communist cooperation.

Chennault, however, had his own ideas about the rescue of China, to which Joe Alsop was rigidly attached. His plan was air attack and bombing—the harassment of the Japanese army and the interdiction of its supply routes. He had personally boasted to President Roosevelt that air power alone, if properly supplied and supported, could defeat Japan. Stilwell, with the backing of Marshall in Washington, predicted—accurately —that without coordinated ground forces to consolidate the ground gained, Chennault's bombing campaign would only irritate the Japanese and sting them to drive against the air bases—as they finally did in the Ichigo operation.

All through the war, at high levels, the most Americanized of the famous Soong siblings kept the Nationalist cause alive in Washington. Mei-ling (Madame Chiang Kai-shek) and her Harvard-educated brother T. V., who functioned as Chiang's de facto prime minister, served as more than eyes and ears for Chiang, who spoke no English. At every opportunity, they fanned the flames of romance, portraying China as a plucky ally of Big Four dimensions. Joe's friendship and wartime correspondence with T. V. Soong and with Harry Hopkins, the key FDR aide who unofficially held the China portfolio, made him an important influence in the anti-Stilwell maneuvering.

In the Alsop Papers at the Library of Congress, for instance, there is a thirteen-page "Dear T. V." letter from Joe, dated July 12, 1943, and marked "Secret," full of gossipy derision about the state of Stilwell's command, of which the following is a typical example: "At Chungking . . . his personal Hq, which is, in effect, no more than a small nest of private cronies—the skeleton of a skeleton staff for such a theater as Stilwell commands, with its infinite complexity and diversity. . . . As an illustration of its inadequacy, its intelligence section still consists solely of Lt. Col. J. Stilwell Jr. (that master brain) and one warrant officer, with a sergeant stenographer to handle files and maps."[13]

T. V. Soong apparently forwarded a copy of Joe's letter directly to Harry Hopkins at the White House with a covering note dated September 25, calling the missive "an objective statement of facts that is positively alarming. Have the patience," Soong added, "to read it over and then destroy it." At the time Joe was between his navy and army commissions; and as he later admitted, it was more than a bit irregular for a junior aide or a mere U.S. Army captain attached to Chennault's headquarters to function behind the scenes as a lobbyist and high strategist. But Joe Alsop never worried about that.

JOE'S JANUARY 1950 *Saturday Evening Post* series on China recapitulated the great Stilwell-Chennault dispute and was at bottom an impassioned brief for Chennault's view. That view continued to be reinforced by Chennault's insistence, long after the war, that had he had his way, Chiang's defeat and collapse would have been averted. The practical significance of the argument, however, was that Stilwell's mulish obsession with recapturing Burma could be blamed for a revolutionary outcome that surely grew out of far more sweeping and historic forces.

Even today, with most of the principals long dead and the details of the argument remembered for the most part only by historians, its merits are hard to judge. Probably no strategy available to the United States during World War II could have yielded a unified "Free China" resembling Churchill's Britain or even Stalin's Russia. And irony of ironies, the reconquest of Burma, and even China itself, turned out to matter far less than the antagonists on both sides supposed it would. Both MacArthur's hopping across the Pacific islands and the arrival of the B-29s, which were especially designed for the long-range bombing of Japan's home islands, increasingly limited China's centrality as a base of air operations. By 1945, Stilwell's monumental effort had reopened the Burma Road and its parallel pipeline, and tons of supplies, including fuel and lubricants, were pouring into China. But meanwhile, the Allies had rapidly lost interest in China as a strategic theater. As the war neared its end, China had become a bit beside the point—a sideshow.[14]

By the time Joe wrote his *Saturday Evening Post* series, four summers after the end of the war, events had forced him to modify, if not change, his underlying historical thesis. The 1947 defection of Marshal Tito's Yugoslavia from the Stalinist Comintern had shown that it was possible for countries with forms of "national" communism not to be unfriendly to Western security interests. The developments in the Balkans seemed to Joe to throw a new light on John Paton Davies's wartime interest in the Communists, which now looked farsighted. Mao and Chou had sought American friendship during the war; that now was clear. It was Chiang's friendship they didn't want. In any case, an honest inquest into the "loss" of China was being crowded out by a raucous witch-hunt. Within months of Chiang's ouster, it was becoming evident that what America wanted was not diligent historical inquiry but surrogate treason trials.

Joe had begun by tending to agree with Alfred Kohlberg and other China Lobby stalwarts about the China issue. But the vicious quarrel over the past that broke out after Chiang's collapse—with its partisan jockeying, its hired and sometimes perjurious witnesses, its abuses of congressional investigative power, its tendency to portray misjudgment as treason—began to seem to Joe a greater threat to the national interest than the China calamity itself.

Within months of the appearance of the *Saturday Evening Post* series, a reversal of political alliances commenced: Joe found himself defending those whose judgments he had previously condemned. The first omen of the impending witch-hunt came in midsummer 1951, more than a year after the *Post* series. John Paton Davies, Jr., Stilwell's diplomatic adviser, was summoned by a State Department loyalty board. Under the Truman loyalty program—a response to political necessity which seems in retrospect to have planted the seeds of far worse proceedings—these boards were to certify the reliability of government servants.

The investigation of Davies, now Kennan's deputy at the State Department Policy Planning Council, began (as Kennan viewed the matter) with a bizarre misunderstanding. Davies had made some casual remarks at an interdepartmental meeting. They had been misinterpreted.[15] Such things happened during those years, in a Washington made jittery by the perjury conviction of Alger Hiss, the arrest and trials of atom bomb spies in both the United States and Canada, and, beginning in the winter of 1950, by Senator Joe McCarthy's wild but widely credited charges that the State Department and other agencies of the American government were riddled with concealed traitors.

The China Hands at the State Department were being generically condemned for hastening Chiang's collapse. Their wary observations about his slippery political footing were now being read, in hindsight, as outright advocacy of his overthrow. There had been the unfortunate *"Amerasia* affair" as well: John Stewart Service had indiscreetly given copies of his own confidential State Department memoranda to a stodgy left-wing publication of that name. A highly publicized grand jury investigation followed. The grand jury unanimously declined to indict Service, but his indiscretion had done substantial damage. It was just such follies that Joe Alsop had in mind when he described a couple of the China Hands, one of them Service, as "remarkably silly."[16]

JOE CERTAINLY DID NOT consider Davies "silly," and he admired Davies's command of Chinese politics. The loyalty board hearing seemed to Joe to mask the real purpose—an inquisition into Davies's role as political adviser to Stilwell and chief emissary to the Communist headquarters at Yenan. The congressional inquisitors had given currency to a certain phrase or tag—"agrarian reformers." That was supposedly what the State Department's naive China experts had thought Mao Tse-tung and his people were. The phrase implied that, as neither undemocratic nor menacing, Mao's followers were not quite to be taken seriously—they represented a Chinese version of midwestern populist insurgency, or something equally democratic and innocuous.

When he learned that Davies had been summoned for a hearing, Joe immediately wrote to the loyalty board chairman, General Conrad Snow, to offer himself as a witness.[17] Having played "a leading part in the events in China which have now caused [Davies] to be called," he could offer first-hand testimony. And "since I knew Mr. Davies very well, and at that time opposed the policy which he advocated, I feel that my judgment of his motives and loyalty may be of some value." Snow welcomed Joe's intervention. When the Davies hearing came, one day in mid-August 1951, Joe told his story. A few days later, in an unusually personal column, he tried to convey the flavor of the hearing—rather humdrum, he had found it, with "the three-man board, headed by a shrewd, dry-spoken New Englander," meeting in an ordinary State Department office borrowed for the occasion.

While he credited the loyalty board with doing its duty, Joe was more caustic about the forces and fears that had hauled Davies before it. Davies's suspension from his State Department duties, Joe wrote, was calculated "to make a burnt offering with a sweet savor in the peculiar nostrils of [Senators] McCarthy and . . . McCarran," the two emerging kingpins of the China inquisition. Joe by now had perhaps begun to wonder whether his own attempt to explain the "loss of China" for *Saturday Evening Post* readers some months earlier had unintentionally added thrust to the congressional witch-hunt. At a quick or superficial glance, the charges against the State Department China specialists sounded a bit like the charges he himself had made in the *Post* series. Joe now sought to distance himself from that misimpression. He told the Snow board, and repeated in his column, that in retrospect Davies looked remarkably far-sighted. He had "made what must now be accounted an extremely brilliant deduction—that Titoism was possible, before Titoism had been heard of." (Tito's defection from the Stalinist orbit offered a striking example of a "national" communism that remained on correct and even cordial terms with the West. Perhaps, Joe suggested, Davies's courtship of the Communists in China might have worked to the same effect.) The wartime circumstances had offered a difficult choice between "two perfectly logical and defensible American policies in China, and you could take your choice between them."[18]

An earlier column in defense of Davies had drawn a quick and admiring response from Kennan, who wired Joe that his column "could have been written only by a person of great distinction of mind and character and it makes me proud of your friendship." Davies himself was equally pleased; the piece struck him as "an eminently decent expression of opinion—a rare thing these days."[19]

Predictably, however, Joe's nemesis—the "China Lobby man" Alfred Kohlberg, a New York importer of Chinese laces and linens—thought that Joe had now trimmed his view to support an opportunistic defense of Davies. The column on Davies, Kohlberg wrote, "does credit to your

bigness of heart . . . [but] it plays hob with your record for consistency."
Hadn't Joe in his *Saturday Evening Post* series blamed the China calamity
squarely on Stilwell and his advisers, and hadn't Davies been one of those
advisers? Now Joe seemed to be claiming that the Communists could
have been won over "by love and kisses."[20]

The caustic letter from Kohlberg marked a turning point in the volu-
minous Alsop-Kohlberg correspondence. He and Joe had exchanged
amiable expressions of sympathy with Chiang for some time. In one of
their earlier letters, Joe had even asked Kohlberg for a favor: he needed,
he said, to replenish his silk supply for shirts and pajamas. But Joe now
stood his ground. He insisted that he had said exactly the same thing
about Davies in the *Saturday Evening Post* series that he was now saying in
the column and before the loyalty board. (He had, though the emphasis
had shifted.) To argue that "Chinese Titoism might have been encouraged by a well-calculated American wartime effort" was not the same as
trying to win converts "by love and kisses."

The sudden cooling of Joe's correspondence with Kohlberg was the
signal of big changes to come. Kohlberg soon became a lavish contribu-
tor to McCarthyite causes, and a close reader could track in his and Joe's
letters the developing quarrel in postwar America over the Chinese revolution. With their conspiratorial turn of mind, Kohlberg and his friends
seemed blind to a vital distinction—between a wartime alliance of con-
venience between Nationalists and Communists, which Davies had indeed advocated when the Japanese seemed on the verge of cutting China
in two, and a long-term alliance based on common political goals and
values, which no one from top to bottom of the American chain of command really believed to be possible. Moreover, Kohlberg recognized only
slight differences between a policy debate and treason and seemed to believe that the monumental failure of the American effort in China had to
be linked to a sinister design of equal magnitude.

The Davies loyalty case dragged on into the Eisenhower years; it finally ended in 1954, when the new administration's secretary of state,
John Foster Dulles, officially cleared Davies of "disloyalty" but fired him
from the Foreign Service for unspecified "weakness of judgment." Joe
warned Dulles that a decision to throw Davies to the wolves would make
it certain that "you and the president will be the next victims."[21] Dulles
ignored the warning. The comparatively sedate Davies affair, played out
bureaucratically at the State Department, was soon dwarfed by the brou-

haha that broke out in the Senate when Louis Budenz, a former Communist Party functionary and ex-editor of the *New York Daily Worker*, flatly accused two of the China Hands of having been under Communist discipline during the war—stirring a controversy into which Joe would hurl himself with his usual zeal. But the growing hysteria of those years over the China issue cannot be understood without a preliminary glimpse at the senator from Wisconsin whose Red-hunting would disrupt American government, spread panic through its ranks, and give his name to an "-ism": Senator Joseph R. McCarthy. It is time to turn to McCarthy and the Alsops' battle against him.

Chapter Five Senator Joe McCarthy

One day in the early summer of 1950, amid lingering echoes of Joe's *Saturday Evening Post* series on China, Stewart Alsop ventured to Capitol Hill for a first-hand look at the brothers' bête noire of the hour. Senator Joe McCarthy of Wisconsin was a burly, dark-browed young man of Irish extraction. He had the look of a brawler about him, and the sound of his importunate baritone voice would soon become all too familiar. Beginning with a couple of Lincoln's Birthday orations in February, he had made sensational charges that Communists were still at large in the State Department. In no time at all McCarthy had established himself as Washington's premier Red-hunter. He had produced no proof and, under challenge, had altered the details almost hourly. But in the nation's jittery and suspicious mood —galvanized by the recent conviction of Alger Hiss for lying about his own ties with Washington's Communist underground during the thirties and forties—proof seemed almost beside the point. Already it was being said that even if Joe McCarthy was a bit careless about evidence, it hardly mattered, because he was on the right track. This was a view with which the Alsops emphatically disagreed, and they had said so from the first.

McCarthy's Senate lair struck Stewart as the set for a minor Hollywood thriller. "Furtive-looking" figures darted to and fro, and in his inner office the senator himself looked like "the Hollywood version of a strong-jawed private eye." He cradled a telephone in "huge hands" and shouted instructions to a "mysterious ally" at the other end. As he barked into the phone he kept tapping it with a pencil. It was the standard method for thwarting bugging or wiretapping devices, then assumed to be widespread in Washington.[1]

Nothing in the brothers' developing career was more predictable than that they would become relentless critics of Joe McCarthy. Even if the Alsops had agreed with McCarthy about the nature of the Communist threat, they differed in almost every other respect. The Alsops were Yankee progressives from old Republican families. McCarthy was a renegade Democrat whose propensity to find conspiracies against the public interest echoed familiar midwestern populist themes. They were from colonial families in New York and New England; he was the son of recent immigrants. They had been taught to think of government as a profession for gentlemen, with complex unwritten rules. McCarthy repeatedly proved himself to be a political bruiser who acknowledged no known rule book.

When they took on McCarthy, the Alsops risked no exposure on the right. Even the blandest tincture of left-wing views in the past left a critic of McCarthy vulnerable to the suggestion that, of course, the critic was acting as a tool of the universal Communist conspiracy. To this retaliation the Alsops enjoyed an absolute immunity. Not only had they strenuously supported all the major postwar "containment" measures. They had exposed and criticized the Communist penetration of labor unions, of the Army commands in occupied Japan and Germany, and, more recently, of the Progressive Party campaign waged in the 1948 election by their old "tribal" friend Henry A. Wallace. They had been exposing these influences, in fact, when Joe McCarthy was wooing Communist voters in his Senate campaign against Robert LaFollette, Jr., asserting that "Communists have the same right to vote as everyone else."[2]

They also had long doubted, privately and in print, that congressional inquisitions of the sort McCarthy planned would produce useful re-

65
Senator Joe
McCarthy

sults. In an acid scrutiny of J. Parnell Thomas and his House Committee on Un-American Activities in August 1948, they had noted that Thomas's frenetic inquiries had resulted in little but unwarranted harassment of witnesses. The big security cases had never been touched. The *Chicago Tribune* had not been disciplined for revealing "the Navy's success in breaking the Japanese codes"; nor, at that point, had testimony from former Communists like Whittaker Chambers and Elizabeth Bentley led to arrests or prosecutions. (Alger Hiss had not yet been tried and convicted of perjury.)

The Alsops favored what they described as the Forrestal Plan—a blue-ribbon panel, something like a British royal commission, to look into the internal security problem, if there was one, in an orderly and systematic way. They had proposed, as members, eminent figures like former Supreme Court justice Owen Roberts, who had led the special investigation of Pearl Harbor, and Judge Learned Hand, the bench's most eminent civil libertarian. "We might get results, not headlines," the Alsops concluded. For Thomas, who was trying to define acceptable "Americanism" in politics, they reserved a special scorn. His zeal, they suggested, sprang from his own insecure identity. They noted that Thomas had been christened Feeney but had changed his name to something "more American." He had "magically evolved a great impersonation of a male member of the Daughters of the American Revolution."[3] Joe Alsop, having thought up the line, liked it so much that he constantly repeated it in his private correspondence, applying it to others in addition to Thomas.

McCarthy, following in Thomas's footsteps, had made his debut as a scourge of Communism in government in a February Lincoln's Birthday speech in Wheeling, West Virginia. One night a month or so earlier, when McCarthy was casting about for a theme, one of the senator's friends, a Jesuit priest and professor at Georgetown University who was an academic authority on Communism, had recommended the internal Communist threat as a topic. "That's it!," McCarthy exclaimed, according to McCarthy companions who recalled the incident. "The government is full of Communists. We can hammer away at them!" At Wheeling in February he hammered away and the response was volcanic. McCarthy seemed to have facts and figures. He had even specified a number of Communists still allegedly employed at the State Department: 205. Later analysis showed that McCarthy had loosely estimated the figure from a letter written four years earlier by Secretary of State James F. Byrnes and that the already outdated letter supported neither the arithmetic nor the charges.[4]

McCarthy emerged as the paladin of domestic anti-Communism while Joe Alsop was on one of his lengthy reporting trips abroad. It fell to Stewart to apply the ready-made Alsop yardstick to McCarthy's enterprise. In a coolly sarcastic March 5 column, Stewart speculated that McCarthy, "the big, raw-boned pride and joy of the real estate lobby [McCarthy had been linked to the current Reconstruction Finance Corporation scandals]," might actually have done the nation a service. His much-juggled and -revised figures on Communists in the State Department were so far wrong that "in the forthcoming Senate investigation [by the Judiciary Committee] . . . McCarthy will get his head so thoroughly washed that neither he nor any of his like-minded colleagues will soon again use this particular vote-catching technique."[5]

The prediction proved to be wildly overoptimistic. What Stewart Alsop quickly identified as a routine brand of political opportunism turned out to be more sinister than that. His assumption that facts would provide a firebreak against the growing hysteria was also wrong. His prediction that the investigation headed by Millard Tydings, a conservative Maryland Democrat, would administer a "head-washing" was accurate enough: After investigating McCarthy's charges, the panel dismissed them as "a fraud and a hoax." Tydings, however, would pay a high price for tangling with McCarthy—the loss of his Senate seat two years later. The defeat created the myth that McCarthy was a giant-killer, a man to be appeased, a dangerous man to cross. It also proved that McCarthy would stoop to any measure—including the forgery of photographs—to punish his critics.[6]

Sensing the sudden shift in the wind, Congress could hardly wait to capitalize on it. In September 1950, over Harry Truman's veto, it passed the McCarran Internal Security Act, which created a Senate version of the House Committee on Un-American Activities, required the registration of Communist Party members, set up a "subversive activities control board" that would linger for decades, and even authorized detention camps for political "subversives" in the event of a national emergency. It was a crowning measure of the mood of the time. McCarthy might be, as the Alsops observed a couple of years after his rise, "the only major politician in the country who can be labeled 'liar' without fear of libel."[7]

But unfortunately, the bolder the lie, the harder it was to refute. No one had imagined mendacity on such a large and daring scale.

THE *Saturday Evening Post* of July 29, 1950, carried the first of the Alsops' longer looks at Joe McCarthy. "Why Has Washington Gone Crazy?," the writers asked. "A miasma of neurotic fear and internal suspicion" had spread through the capital after McCarthy's Wheeling speech, "like some noxious effluvium from the marshy Potomac." The secretary of state had begun to worry that his phone might be tapped, and from top to bottom the government was "like a distracted dog endlessly scratching imaginary fleas." McCarthy and his supporters and imitators were exploiting "two shadows"—the shadow of "betrayal from within" and "devastating attack from without," now freshly intensified by the North Korean invasion. Of the two, as the Korean War showed, the external threat was much the more serious. Washington's neurosis was compounded by the cult of government secrecy, which encouraged "the lunatic notion that American government is honeycombed with perversion and treachery." Moreover, "the cheap pleasures of the smear and the spy chase" had become a substitute for "the long, hard effort which this country must make if the free world is to survive."[8]

In diagnosing the temptations of McCarthyism as a distraction from the unpopular and unwelcome burdens of rearmament and international responsibility, the *Post* article sounded a central theme of the Alsops' anti-McCarthy journalism. The question was whether anyone was paying attention.

Certainly McCarthy himself was, for the *Post* article brought an unanticipated dividend. The Wisconsin senator was sufficiently stung by it to write a letter of protest directly to the editor. It was "irresponsibility," McCarthy charged to *Post* editor Ben Hibbs in a letter of August 24, to give the Alsops space in his magazine to question his charges "without yourself delving into the facts."[9] McCarthy was bluffing. The Tydings inquiry had demonstrated that—not only as to the alleged numbers of Communists on the State Department payroll but as to McCarthy's individualized charges against prominent figures like Philip Jessup, ambassador at large at the State Department, and Owen Lattimore, a scholar of Far Eastern affairs at Johns Hopkins University who had served in the State Department during the war.

The Tydings Committee had gone out of its way to ask the FBI

68
Senator Joe McCarthy

whether State Department files on employees whose "loyalty" had been questioned had been picked over and purged in an effort at concealment, as McCarthy charged. The attorney general certified that this charge, too, was false. In short, the Tydings inquiry backed up every criticism the Alsops had offered regarding McCarthy's recklessness with facts. No one had yet grasped, though, how mistaken it was to assume that McCarthy or his followers were interested in facts or could be stopped by the suggestion of their absence.

Meanwhile, the senator's letter to the *Saturday Evening Post* offered an opening for a bit of fun. Resorting to his usual technique in the face of exposure, McCarthy had labeled the Alsops' *Post* article "almost 100 per cent in line with the official instructions issued to all Communist and fellow-traveling members of the press by Gus Hall, national secretary of the Communist Party." They might as well confess, Stewart merrily responded on August 11, "revealing" that under Gus Hall's orders, he and Joe had so carefully camouflaged their undercover labors for the Communist Party that even the *Daily Worker* had been fooled. The *Worker* regularly denounced them as "fascist warmongers," "lackeys of Wall Street," and "presstitutes." Apparently the word hadn't reached everyone in the party apparatus that they were undercover agents.[10]

ON SENATOR MCCARTHY and his motives, methods, and effects, a vast literature has accumulated during the four decades since he died (of acute alcoholism) in 1957 at the age of forty-eight.[11] McCarthy was unusually gifted in the arts of demagoguery. But in other respects he was a particularly spectacular symptom of the neuroses of the age — "a by-product of the Cold War," as the Alsops often said. Had McCarthy not commissioned himself to search the nooks and crannies of government (and subsequently the clergy, the universities, and finally even the U.S. Army) for subversive influences, another such inquisitor might still have been invented. He provided simple and drastic answers to hard, complex, and largely unprecedented questions.

When McCarthy suddenly soared onto the scene, the United States was, by the Alsops' reckoning, four years into the Cold War. They dated its beginnings to the Iranian crisis of 1945, when President Truman compelled the Russians to comply with their wartime pledge to evacuate their forces from Persia's northern territory. Since that episode, public anxieties had been kindled by other events of the same sort — the "loss" of

China; the North Korean invasion of South Korea; and the revelations, true and false, about conspiratorial activities in the thirties and during World War II, whose actual significance and danger were debatable.

There was also the unexpectedly early acquisition by the Russians of the atomic bomb in late 1949 and, most disturbing, the realization that for the first time in its history the continental United States had become vulnerable to long-range attack by air and sea. McCarthy and others harped upon these quite genuine anxieties. How, they demanded, had the United States, leader of a triumphant and all-conquering alliance, come in less than five years to mortal vulnerability? A theory that assumed conspiracy in high places was one way to account for events and forces that were apparently disconnected but that imagination could easily link. This was a variation on the political complex which the historian Richard Hofstadter would later call "the paranoid style in American politics." The idea of an encompassing Communist conspiracy in government was not less appealing to excitable people now that the Hiss and Rosenberg cases had been broken. Had McCarthy anticipated the thunderous public response to his recent foray against "subversion" at the State Department? Perhaps not. But among the inquisitors of the time, none was more unscrupulous and none so loose with facts, although in cruelty and mean-spiritedness some of his less notorious colleagues exceeded him.

"No bolder seditionist," Richard Rovere of the *New Yorker* wrote in his posthumous biography of McCarthy, "ever moved among us — nor any politician with a surer, swifter access to the dark places of the American mind."[12] Yet the Alsops, like Rovere and other students of McCarthyism, soon came to see that much of the McCarthy spell lay in a strange unseriousness. The senator from Wisconsin had a frivolous streak, which emerged in his cavalier treatment of numbers and his clumsily playful demeanor. He seemed at times like an overgrown playground bully, who like many bullies was essentially soft at the core. He could accuse someone of spying one day and the next day slap him on the back in a display of bonhomie. His admirers among young right-wing intellectuals, such as William F. Buckley, Jr., and Brent Bozell, were more "scholarly" and factual about the supposed Red conspiracy than their brummagem hero.

THAT THERE WAS a Communist threat the Alsops did not dispute and never failed to say. But it lay in the danger that the United States

would allow the balance of power to deteriorate and would leave freedom to be chipped away by Communist military power and political subversion. To their minds the vigilantes in Washington constituted a menace exceeding the internal threat they warned against. Joe Alsop was soon writing to friends of his fear that a "native fascism" would flourish. This was typical Alsopian exaggeration; and in any case, Joe thought, this "fascism" might be averted if the Republicans recaptured the White House in 1952 behind the right kind of political leadership. Joe Alsop frequently suggested that if, like the Red-hunters, you tried to gauge secret Communist motives by inferring them from suspect acts, you could make a case that the stalwarts of Republicanism—even Robert Taft himself—were Communists. Hadn't they voted against most of the landmark national security measures—aid to Greece and Turkey and the Marshall Plan in 1947, then the North Atlantic Treaty in 1949? It was a debating point, but it was also a telling spoof on the way McCarthy twisted the rules of evidence.[13]

In this black art, McCarthy was not alone. His chief Senate rival, Senator Patrick McCarran, a Democrat and a former Reno divorce lawyer and Nevada chief justice, also excelled at it. McCarran had made a special project of the alleged wartime conspiracy against Chiang Kai-shek, which had been centered, he claimed, in the Institute of Pacific Relations and the State Department. Joe Alsop's one-man battle to correct the McCarran Committee's attempt to pervert the history of the American effort in wartime China would preoccupy him in 1950–51, though not to the exclusion of McCarthy. McCarran and McCarthy drew on many of the same dubious sources of information.

71
Senator Joe McCarthy

Chapter Six Witnesses

The congressional committees that in 1950–51 were feasting on public suspicions depended heavily on sometimes patently self-interested witnesses—usually penitent former members of the Communist Party who now promoted themselves, sometimes for substantial fees, as experts and authorities on the conspiratorial past. Whittaker Chambers, the anguished *Time* editor who had exposed Alger Hiss and who wrote the best-selling book *Witness*, was the most eminent prototype. His memoir, serialized in the *Saturday Evening Post*, found millions of worried readers and remains a classic of America's second Red Scare era. Years later, a notable occupant of the White House, Ronald W. Reagan, said that Chambers's book had been a major influence in his evolution from New Deal Democrat to conservative Republican. So busy did the Congress of the United States become with special investigations —no fewer than 225 were proceeding in the early 1950s—that in March 1952, the *New York Times* reported that these inquiries had overrun the available office space and had now overflowed into rented hotel rooms.

Of the many professional witnesses who came under the scrutiny and direct rebuttal of Joe Alsop, the most eminent was Louis Budenz, a former Communist functionary whose party affiliation had survived the Hitler-Stalin Pact of 1939. After founding and editing a party newspaper in Chicago, Budenz had ended up as managing editor of the *Daily Worker* in New York. With considerable self-dramatization, he abruptly announced in the spring of 1945 that he had repented, left the party, and returned to the Roman Catholic Church. When he began to sing more or less full-time to the FBI, he was a professor of labor-management relations at Fordham University. Since defecting from the party, he had undergone countless FBI debriefings about the party apparatus and had testified before several congressional committees, always with expansive claims of authority and inside knowledge. It was Louis Budenz who would, with sensational testimony about Vice President Henry Wallace's 1944 mission to China, bring Joe Alsop back into the noisy China debate.

One day in the course of routine testimony to Senator Pat McCarran's Internal Security Committee, which had launched a major investigation of the Institute for Pacific Relations (IPR), Budenz charged that two eminent China experts—Owen Lattimore, a professor at Johns Hopkins University, and John Carter Vincent, onetime chief of the Far Eastern desk at the State Department—had been Communist errand runners. Specifically, he said, the Politburo had viewed with interest and approval their services to Vice President Henry A. Wallace during his wartime visit of inquiry to Chiang Kai-shek. It had been their mission, Budenz testified, to hold Wallace to the party line. "From official reports," Budenz claimed, it was Vincent's and Lattimore's task "to guide Mr. Wallace largely along [Communist] paths," since both of them were "in line with the Communist viewpoint." Budenz's exact words were: "The trip by Wallace to China was followed by the Communists with a great deal of interest in discussions in the Politburo. In these discussions it was pointed out that Mr. Wallace was more or less under good influences from the Communist viewpoint, that is to say, that he had on one hand Mr. Lattimore and on the other John Carter Vincent, both of whom were described as being in line with the Communist viewpoint, seeing eye to eye with it, and that they would guide Mr. Wallace largely along these paths."[1]

The language, closely read, is far from unequivocal, but the gist was unmistakable: Wallace (who in the years intervening between the war and the time of Budenz's testimony had run for president in a Progressive anti–Cold War campaign heavily influenced and supported by Communists) had been a dupe of the party at the time of his China mission in 1944. And the agents manipulating him then, holding him to the party line, were Lattimore and Vincent.

Budenz claimed to have acquired this information through party channels during the war. He happened to tell his story to the McCarran Committee on August 23, 1951, the very day Joe testified for John P. Davies before the State Department loyalty board. The charges, implicating a former vice president and two of the already suspect China Hands, generated blaring headlines.[2]

This time, Budenz had overplayed a weak hand. Of the thirty-seven persons connected with IPR who had been named as conspirators before the McCarran Committee, Budenz was the sole accuser of twenty-four. Moreover, readers of his 1946 account of his reconversion from Communism to Catholicism had remarked that a number of those he now depicted as kingpins of furtive party influence, including Lattimore and Vincent, had not even been mentioned five years earlier. Joe Alsop had more than circumstantial reason to believe that Budenz was lying, however, and his confidence on the matter went back to his personal contacts on the scene with the Wallace mission.

The vice president's journey to China in March 1944 had been one of those irregular, out-of-channels embassies by which President Roosevelt often conducted several overlapping foreign policies at once. The president sent Wallace as a fact-finder. He asked Wallace to explore with Chiang the possibility of once again cooperating with Mao and the Communists against the Japanese. Political observers at home noted later that it was convenient to have Wallace out of Washington, since Roosevelt planned to drop him from the presidential ticket that summer.

Joe's connection with these events could hardly have been more personal. When Wallace arrived in Kunming, Claire Chennault designated his young aide, Captain Alsop, to show the vice president about. Joe had been Wallace's companion more or less constantly, except, he later recalled, during "his frequent periods of violent exercise": impromptu baseball and volleyball games with the young airmen and aircraft mechanics around Chennault's Fourteenth Air Force base. For a number of special personal reasons, Joe wrote in the first of three columns, the charge that Wallace had been a stooge of the Politburo under the tutelage of Lattimore and Vincent made no sense at all. It was in fact completely implausible.

Joe had witnessed first-hand all the major developments of Wallace's visit to Kunming. The startling fact was that he had actually helped Wallace draft two important radio messages to FDR, typing them up in Chennault's quarters. (It was, as he later acknowledged, a highly irregular role for a mere captain, though perhaps not for a captain named Alsop.) These "radios," as they were called, were later dispatched to Washington from Delhi; in them Wallace urged General Stilwell's replacement and suggested, without insisting, that the right successor, from all that he had heard on the scene, would be General Albert Wedemeyer. No advice could have been more anti-Communist in thrust, Joe argued, than the recommendation of Wedemeyer. In the first place, Stilwell strongly advocated cooperating with Mao's forces, while Wedemeyer was much warier of that alternative. In the second place, Vincent had sat in on the Kunming conference in which Wallace formulated his recommendations to Roosevelt. Joe recalled that Vincent had supported them enthusiastically. As for Lattimore, the other alleged collaborator in keeping Wallace close to the Politburo line, he had played no substantive role; he had served as Wallace's interpreter. So much, then, for Budenz's testimony that the Wallace mission had been "in line with the Communist viewpoint."

JOE'S BOMBSHELL newspaper columns on the Budenz testimony, which appeared on September 10 and 12, 1951, startled a capital that was already almost numbed by random accusations of conspiracy and treason, whose very volume almost made them seem credible. Now suddenly it seemed that at least one tale of one of the ex-Communist witnesses (Budenz claimed to have spent some three thousand hours briefing the FBI since his defection) could be tested against authentic recollection and documents. The two Wallace "radios" to FDR were still classified, and in his columns Joe had paraphrased their contents. But the paraphrases were confirmed when the White House officially released the cables. Senator Herbert Lehman of New York, an outspoken critic of the inquisitors, took the Senate floor to read the two Alsop columns into the congressional record. McCarran and his allies, apparently scenting mortal danger to the vast fantasy of treachery the Internal Security Committee was crafting, were quickly on their feet with parliamentary objections.

Under the Senate's Rule 19, no senator in debate could "directly or indirectly, by any form of words, impute to another senator or to other senators any conduct or motive unworthy of or unbecoming a senator." The insinuation that McCarran had welcomed perjured testimony was just such an imputation, he protested. Thus, Lehman's initiative was blunted by the rules of the Senate. But a wider public was listening; and for the first time it looked as if a prominent witness had been credibly accused of fabrication.

But the fight to get the truth on the record had to be pressed to a conclusion, and half measures were not enough. Budenz's testimony might be clearly fictitious in the eyes of Joe Alsop and others who studied the matter in detail and read Wallace's cables. But the forensics of the matter were complicated and needed to be dramatized to the committee and the public.

Joe broke the sensational revelations about Budenz nearly a month and a half before he and Wallace would have a chance to document them in testimony to the committee. Meanwhile, there was work to do, assembling documents and witnesses who would reinforce the challenge. Stilwell had been dead for years, but his successor, General Wedemeyer, now retired from the army, could offer material testimony. Joe wrote to Wedemeyer, who was in business in New York, to ask the general's help in combating "an extraordinary attempt . . . to rewrite the whole China story around a dark imaginary plot." This brazen revisionism practiced by Budenz and others had "forced me much against my will to plunge back into controversy." (To anyone who knew Joe Alsop, it must have seemed among the world's unlikeliest stories that his plunge into any controversy had been unwilling.)[3]

For a month Wedemeyer was mysteriously unresponsive to Joe's plea; he answered only after Joe prodded him again and reminded the general that in the early days of World War II he himself had been the victim of malicious misrepresentation. During this incident Wedemeyer's critics had slyly asked whether, as a 1936–38 alumnus of the Kriegsakademie (the Wehrmacht staff officers' college in Berlin), Wedemeyer might be a German sympathizer. The rumors had intensified when, three days before Pearl Harbor, someone had leaked to the isolationist press documents on the top-secret "Victory Plan," of which Wedemeyer, in his role as chief of war plans, had intimate knowledge. His mentor George Marshall (much abused by McCarthy, McCarran, and others in the China inquisition) had believed Wedemeyer to be innocent and had protected him.[4]

That was the sensitive memory Joe invoked to jog Wedemeyer to his current responsibilities as a witness in favor of others unjustly accused of disloyalty. In his response, Wedemeyer wrote to Joe that he had never thought the China Hands disloyal but had himself told the McCarran Committee that "if I had followed their advice . . . it would have accelerated the conquest of China by the communists for obvious reasons."[5]

The response was at best ambiguous. Wedemeyer did not explain what "obvious reasons" impelled him to think their advice defective. In his 1958 memoir *Wedemeyer Reports!*, the general still seemed ambivalent about the actual effect of the State Department advisers in China. "At the time," he writes, as if to intimate that he had since had occasion to change his mind, "I had no reason to doubt [their] loyalty . . . even though I did not agree with their estimate of the situation in China and their proposals that we should eventually ditch Chiang Kai-shek."[6] Since the record offers no evidence that any key adviser recommended that Chiang be "ditched," it is unclear what Wedemeyer meant. For much the same reason, his ambiguous response to Joe's appeal for help in the Budenz matter was less than useful. The more forthright Chennault was direct and explicit. His response of September 22—Joe had reached him by telegraph in Taipei, Formosa, where he and his old adjutant, Whiting Willauer, were now in the export business—confirmed Alsop's version of the story point by point.

Far the most important witness, of course, was Henry A. Wallace himself, the former vice president whom Budenz had portrayed as a dupe manipulated by sly keepers. The White House had now released Wallace's 1944 cables, and Wallace could supply the most authoritative account of their meaning and context. Wallace also happened to be an old Alsop friend of the sort the Alsops called "tribal." His father, a U.S. secretary of agriculture, had been a progressive Republican and a follower of Theodore Roosevelt in the Bull Moose Revolt of 1912. Like several other eminent New Dealers—the outspoken Secretary of the Interior Harold L. Ickes was another—Wallace had emerged from the same political tradition as the Connecticut Alsops.

The foreseeable hazard lay in Wallace's personality and judgment: He was capable of appearing to be both gullible and misguided. Joe and others thought he had looked naive only three years earlier, when he had allowed his third-party bid for the presidency to be penetrated, almost controlled, by the Communists. With his interest in Rosicrucianism and other mystical cults, he qualified, Joe once said, as "not only a goose but a mystical goose."[7] Now, as the time approached for his appearance before the McCarran Committee, Wallace seemed to be courting disaster once again. He had announced that he planned to appear before the committee without a lawyer. Joe warned him that if he did so McCarran and Jay Sourwine—the artful chief counsel of the Judiciary Committee, who frequently sat in on the IPR investigation—would cut him to shreds. With Wallace's reluctant consent, Joe undertook to recruit a lawyer.

In the poisonous Washington climate, a lawyer willing to stick his neck out even for a former vice president (especially Henry Wallace, still trailing the aftermath of his 1948 campaign) proved very hard to find. After thirty refusals—at least Joe, possibly with exaggeration, remembered it as thirty—Joe finally enlisted George Ball, the future undersecretary of state, a courageous advocate who then and later had a streak of stubborn independence about him. Ball agreed to help, but only on condition that the notoriously headstrong Wallace follow his legal advice to the letter.

Ball's proviso became the hinge of a comic subplot. On the eve of Wallace's appearance before the McCarran Committee, it emerged that he planned to have his say beforehand on a popular Sunday television program, *Meet the Press*. Ball emphatically vetoed the idea. Wallace could foul up his case on the air, Ball said. If Wallace insisted on this advance public appearance, he would quit.

Joe's Dumbarton Avenue house now became the scene of desperate maneuvers. *Meet the Press* had turned up the pressure. If Wallace dropped out, the producers were complaining, the program might lose its most important sponsor, the Curtis Publishing Company, who happened to be publishers of the *Saturday Evening Post*. With George Ball hovering at his front door demanding a yes-or-no answer as a taxi idled in the street, Joe frantically placed a call to his *Saturday Evening Post* editor, Ben Hibbs, in Philadelphia and, explaining the emergency, extracted from Hibbs a pledge that Curtis would not quit as sponsors if Wallace stood the program up. Wallace canceled; Ball stayed on as his lawyer.[8]

There was one final development. The McCarran Committee was beginning to circle the wagons around Budenz's testimony and wished to take Wallace's rebuttal in private session. Wallace, however, insisted on reading his prepared statement to the waiting reporters. The committee agreed to open the doors.

JOE'S CHANCE to testify for the first time came the next day, in executive session, with Senator Willis Smith of North Carolina standing in for McCarran. Speaking in assured terms, Joe methodically dissected Budenz's testimony. In outline his story paralleled the *Saturday Evening Post* account of the wartime events in China. Stilwell, he told the committee, had brought to China "the germ of a military prejudice in favor of the Communists, against the Nationalists," which had become "a violent infection when General Stilwell was brought into sharp collision with the Generalissimo." This "military prejudice" could now be documented from Stilwell's recently published diaries, edited by Theodore White, from which Joe selectively quoted. (White and others, writing later, questioned Joe's interpretation of the diaries, but not on the points that were so fatal to Budenz's testimony.) Joe confidently traced a revealing discrepancy between the wartime Communist Party line and the policies counseled in the Wallace cables, especially the recommendation that Stilwell be relieved by Wedemeyer. Joe could not resist flaunting his personal role in this hinge-of-history episode:

> Mr. Wallace's Kunming cable was at last roughed out in this discussion between Mr. Wallace, Mr. Vincent and me. We drafted it together. I had a typewriter in the house, and I did the typing. After Mr. Wallace had signed it, the cable was sent. . . . [Joe appears to have been wrong on this minor point: Wallace's wires were sent later from Delhi.] This is the way that the accused man, Mr. Vincent, "guided" Mr. Wallace "along the paths of the party line." . . . Again I say, it is not I who convict Mr. Budenz of untruth. It is the facts that convict him.[9]

Joe accused Budenz of lying at three critical points, and to clinch his case he offered for the record the telegrams he had recently obtained from Chennault and Chennault's deputy, Whiting Willauer. McCarran managed to dodge this embarrassing blow to the conspiracy myth he and his chief counsel Robert Morris were assiduously concocting, but the transcript shows that Sourwine, Morris, and several of the very conservative senators on the committee tried their best, then and later, to trip Joe up. Smith, a former American Bar Association president, struck Joe as eminently fair; Joe commended Smith afterward and suggested that his procedures ought to be widely imitated by congressional investigators.[10]

Months after their appearances before the committee, Joe was surprised to learn that Henry Wallace was still quibbling over George Ball's legal fee. In answer to Joe's query, Wallace fumed in a letter of August 18, 1952, "I never thought when I read the Kunming cable to you over the phone that I was letting myself in for an expense of $2,679." It turned out that while Wallace had reimbursed Ball's out-of-pocket expenses, he had failed to add a fee, whose amount Ball had left up to Wallace. Ball had then sent a bill. "You have behaved almost unbelievably badly to George Ball," Joe scolded, adding a brief lecture on the facts of life in the Washington witch-hunting season: "George protected you from being torn to pieces on the radio by . . . Sam Spivak and his female partner, whose malevolent intentions I can now document. I think I am a better in-fighter than you are. I was not on trial before the McCarran committee as, in effect, you were. Yet I considered it necessary to employ counsel for myself; and, although he did far less for me than George did for you, I gladly paid Ganson Percell's bill of $1,000." Joe closed with an apology for writing "roughly," but pointedly asked Wallace to show his letter to Mrs. Wallace, "whose judgment I greatly respect."[11]

Joe Alsop's epic battle to establish the complex truth about the Wallace mission continued behind the scenes. When the *New Leader*, an anti-Communist magazine of liberal origins, printed columns by David Dallin and William Henry Chamberlin that seemed to reinforce Budenz's tall tale, Joe complained to the editor of their "pernicious and foolish untruth." Sympathize as he might with their views on China, Joe wrote to S. M. Levitas in early December, he could not sympathize with "the almost psychotic vengefulness which seeks to convict all those who did not listen to Dallin, Chamberlin and me of Communist tendencies or actual Communists links." Such writings "lend . . . aid and comfort to those who would meet the grim challenge of Soviet imperialism as the Australian bushmen met the white invaders, by mystical exorcisms and the driving out of helpless scapegoats." With this rhetorical flourish, Joe canceled his *New Leader* subscription and rebuffed Levitas's protest that the two columnists had been speaking for themselves and did not represent the magazine's own views. To no avail; the subscription cancellation stuck.[12]

In an April 1952 *Atlantic Monthly* article called "The Strange Case of Louis Budenz," Joe elaborated his campaign for fairness in the China postmortem. Was anyone listening? It often seemed that no one was. The Budenz article had bounced from magazine to magazine before finding an outlet. Rejected by both the *Saturday Evening Post* and *Collier's*, it had come to the notice of Edward Weeks, the *Atlantic*'s veteran editor, who heard of it in a conversation with the Oxford historian and philosopher Isaiah Berlin. In the *Atlantic* piece, Joe expressed the view that in his conversion from a secular to a religious absolute (that is, from Communism to Catholicism) Budenz was typical of former Communists. In those pre–Vatican II days this was a usual Protestant liberal view, but it was one that Catholics often resented. After the *Atlantic* piece appeared, Joe was peppered with letters protesting the parallel and suggesting that his evaluation of Budenz was anti-Catholic. Joe, stung by the suggestion, reminded several correspondents that his brother Stewart had married a Catholic and that his own collateral descendants would therefore be of that faith. The battle over Budenz left other scars as well and briefly imperiled the Alsops' working relationship with the *Herald Tribune* syndicate when the publisher, Helen Reid, ordered one of Joe's columns on the case spiked.

Joe continued to view himself as a far-seeing hard-liner on the China question. He went on strewing personal letters, and sometimes columns, with biting asides. In a Matter of Fact column just before Christmas in 1952, he went so far as to call Lattimore and Vincent, the hapless victims of Budenz, "two of the silliest fellows that this reporter has ever had the misfortune to know"—a condescending slur that took the glitter off his defense of their honor and drew a protest from George Kennan.[13] As in many of his scraps, the stout defense of reputations and personal liberties was flawed by gratuitous sneers. Joe reserved unalloyed approval for John Paton Davies; but even Davies was sometimes depicted as an unduly young and impressionable victim of Stilwell's seductive personal charm. That view began to give way only as it occurred to Joe, perhaps for tactical reasons, that the missed possibility of a "Titoist" China, as advocated by Davies, made a useful debating point. As he battled with the hard right, Joe soon talked himself into the view that "the policy of having no policy" in China, following the ouster of Chiang, had the worst of alternative outcomes, even worse than a policy of outright collaboration with Mao Tse-tung. But this view was too sophisticated, too much shaded by personal experience and observation in China, and perhaps too generous, to impress Kohlberg, McCarran, McCarthy, or their admirers and allies.

In the China fight, Joe at times exchanged the commentator's hat for the citizen-activist's hat. Sometimes the two hats seemed interchangeable. His justification was the citizen's duty to come forward with useful information or a special perspective, both of which he certainly could claim. But his militancy in behalf of the beleaguered China Hands, admirable though it was, was more a reaction against the expedient demagoguery of the Senate than a conversion to the State Department view. That he had almost single-handedly administered a stinging publicity defeat to the McCarran Committee, though, was beyond doubt.

In a parting shot, Joe wrote to McCarran in early 1952 to suggest that it should be Budenz, not the targets of the committee's recent investigation, who should be investigated by the Justice Department as a candidate for possible perjury indictment. "If your committee has the faintest pretensions to fairness or . . . for the honorable traditions of democracy," Joe said, "you must desire a most careful, detailed and serious investigation" of who had been lying.[14] But as Joe must have known, the appeal to fairness and honor was idle. His expectations of McCarran—"this disgraceful old man," as he had called him in a letter to his *Saturday Evening Post* editors two years earlier—were never exalted, and McCarran did not reply.

Chapter Seven Dealing with the "Native Fascists"

To Joe and Stewart Alsop, the uproar over subversion and betrayal seemed a compelling argument for change in the 1952 presidential election. The Republicans, out of power for twenty years, needed fresh leadership and a taste of the disciplines and responsibilities of governing. They had been in the wilderness since March 1933, the longest interval since the party's emergence in the pre–Civil War years. In letters to friends, Joe wrote, with his usual exaggeration, that "something like a native fascist party" would almost certainly take over the country if the Republicans were frustrated again. That clearly strained his resolve that (as he had written to John Lardner when they were quarreling over Wallace's third-party campaign in 1948) he now regarded himself as "a man of the left" and would never again vote Republican, unless for his brother John, a Connecticut legislator with gubernatorial ambitions, or of course "Pa," the perennial first selectman of Avon.

Yet the political picture was blurry. The most appealing candidate for either party, the popular General of the Armies Dwight D. Eisenhower, had been courted by Democrats and Republicans alike, and by President Truman as well. He was playing hard to get. So was Adlai E. Stevenson, the fifty-two-year-old reform Democratic governor of Illinois, about whom the Alsops were soon to write in glowing terms—and to whose followers their brother John soon gave a memorable label: "eggheads."[1] As the warmup for 1952 began, Eisenhower was serving as first supreme commander of NATO forces in Paris, while Stevenson was making witty, tantalizing speeches and refusing to be drawn into active candidacy.

Meanwhile, there was one candidate who made no secret of his ambition. He was Senator Robert A. Taft of Ohio, the son of an earlier president who had himself originally been the handpicked heir of their Uncle Teddy Roosevelt. The Alsops had a cordial and correct personal relationship with Taft, who was eager to run and considered the Republican nomination no less than his due after the 1948 Dewey fiasco. Taft's proprietary claim to the 1952 nomination was backed by a host of regular Republicans, the ideological descendants of the "stalwarts" who had followed his father, William Howard Taft, four decades earlier. But nothing Taft could do or say would persuade the otherwise friendly Alsops that his foreign-policy views were less than calamitous. In their view, his nomination was to be resisted at all cost.

Taft was a hard case for liberal internationalists of both parties. He had voted against the NATO enabling legislation in 1949, though after much quibbling and qualification he had reluctantly agreed (perhaps under the influence of his presidential ambitions) to support the deployment of four American divisions in Europe—heresy, according to the strictest sect of his fellow "isolationists." But, professing indifference, Taft had declined a seat on the Senate Foreign Relations Committee, almost a mandatory position for those seeking to reach the White House by way of the Senate. In some ways his views seemed to echo those of Henry Wallace. His well-known doubts on the doctrine of collective security rested on his assumption that the Soviet Union did not want war, whatever more excitable people might think. He believed that the Russians would be deterred from aggression by U.S. atomic weapons. He also believed that the ballooning post-Korea defense costs—the very budget increases the Alsops had campaigned for—threatened to unbalance the budget, and nothing could be worse.[2]

No view could have been more antithetical to the Alsops' central article of faith—that in the unlikely event that the nation must choose between bankruptcy and military destruction, bankruptcy was by far the better bargain. (This was Joe's patented answer to any suggestion that the arms buildup inspired by the requirements of NSC-68 threatened the country with insolvency.)

Finally, Taft's views on the Korean War had lurched erratically from approval to disapproval. Though he initially supported Truman's use of American forces, he shrank from deeper U.S. military involvement after the Chinese intervened across the Yalu River in the winter of 1951. Once Taft had even told reporters that if he were elected president, he "probably" would pull American troops out of Korea altogether and establish another defensive line based on Formosa, the Philippines, and Japan. (Ironically, that had been the official U.S. strategic position before the North Korean attack in June 1950.)

As the Alsops saw it, Taft's views justified their teasing suggestion that Taft and other Senate isolationists, heirs to the prewar position of Senator William E. Borah and others, had done more to jeopardize non-Communist interests than any of the alleged "subversives" hounded by their pet watchdog, Joe McCarthy. In any case, Taft's weakness on critical foreign-policy issues made it imperative that they work to stop his nomination. Stopping Taft had become a top-priority item on the columnists' agenda by the midspring of 1952. Eisenhower had finally been prevailed upon to announce his candidacy. But he lingered in Paris; and in many crucial states, especially in the border South, a decisive knock-down struggle loomed between the pro-Taft regulars and insurgent pro-Eisenhower factions, the latter swollen by Democrats, volunteers, and independents. Meanwhile, because the party rules were heavily stacked in favor of the party regulars in most key states, Taft was building an impressive lead in delegate commitments.

Thus, states where delegates would be named by convention were critical, and none more so than Texas. Another of the Alsops' tribal friends, Senator Henry Cabot Lodge, Jr., of Massachusetts, had been monitoring the crucial Texas showdown. It was Lodge who urged Joe Alsop to journey to Texas for a big late-May gathering at the hill country resort town of Mineral Wells, where the Texas party would choose thirty-eight delegates to the national convention. The setting was unusual and the stakes high. In view of the long Democratic reign in the state, "an important Republican gathering in Texas," wrote Joe on May 28 in his first dispatch from Mineral Wells, "used to seem about as likely an event, by the ancient rules of American politics, as a synod of atheists in St. Peter's cathedral."[3]

Joe arrived at the "bleak little resort town" armed with a zeal for "fair play" as the Eisenhower partisans defined it. Their definition did not, then or later, quite fit the byzantine complexities of Texas politics; and certainly the rights and wrongs of the contest for party power were not so stark or clear-cut as the Eisenhower forces proclaimed.

The factional battle for control of the Texas delegation had opened two years earlier, with the death of a powerful national committeeman. The Texas Republicans had fought it out in a preliminary round to fill the vacancy; the victor had been Henry Zweifel, a Fort Worth lawyer and onetime U.S. attorney (and also, as Joe would note, a leader in the anti-Catholic campaign against Al Smith in 1928). Zweifel, a Dewey supporter in 1948, was now solidly for Taft. He was using his considerable influence to stretch the rules, even scheduling furtive precinct meetings in the privacy of his house. The aim was to avoid a takeover of the party by the swelling Eisenhower forces, who happened to be led by Zweifel's vanquished rival for the national committee post.

To complicate matters further, Texans apparently often declined to accept numerical defeat as a finality, even when it came by the rules. Losers had a disconcerting way of simply splitting off into rump factions and going their own way. That was the key tactic by which Zweifel and the Taftites were attempting, in the face of overwhelming defeats in all the big Texas cities, to retain their control of the Texas delegation for Taft.

Joe Alsop's arrival in Mineral Wells was noted by both sides, not only because he was a recognized reporter and commentator but also because his flagship paper, the *New York Herald Tribune*, was considered to be the virtual house organ of the Eisenhower "internationalists" who were trying to "take over" the Republican Party. Joe's most important source of tactical information at Mineral Wells was Herbert Brownell (later Eisenhower's attorney general), who was managing the general's interests on the scene. Brownell was feeding Joe information about the Texas fight, and his briefings were unabashedly slanted in favor of Eisenhower.

But Joe was in Texas as an advocate as well. He did not shrink from using strong language in his dispatches from Mineral Wells: The Texas delegation to the Chicago convention was being "stolen," he charged, by the Republican establishment. A "nasty club" of GOP insiders, led by Zweifel, had ignored overwhelming Eisenhower victories in recent precinct meetings. The Taft forces claimed that many of the pro-Eisenhower voters were not "real" or "true" Republicans as defined by the old party rules. Many of them were indeed Democrats who had not voted Republican in the last election. On this thin pretext, Joe reported, most of the thirty-eight Chicago delegate seats had been awarded to Taft. It was "theft" and "skulduggery," made no more savory by being committed in broad daylight. In his partisan zeal, Joe missed a crucial nuance. He reported that Zweifel had openly invited Democrats and independents to participate in the precinct meetings. In fact, that had been the ploy of Zweifel's rivals, who displeased the party regulars even further by adding that the newcomers should not hesitate to pledge to vote Republican in the fall, whether they meant to or not.

Joe's main argument, developed more fully in a follow-up dispatch from Dallas on June 1, was more persuasive than his account of the tactical byplay at Mineral Wells: The Republicans would need Democratic and independent votes to carry Texas and other Democratic states, especially in the South. Since the Taft Republicans were "justifiably denouncing the corruption that has crept into American government," the issue of honesty mattered in Texas too, for "honest government depends on honest politics." In short, "stealing" delegates from the Eisenhower forces in May made a shaky platform from which later to accuse the Democrats of stealing money from the taxpayers. No doubt Joe would have recalled, though he did not mention, that in 1912 a disputed Texas delegation had made ammunition for Uncle Teddy Roosevelt's charges that Robert Taft's father was using "steamroller" tactics to capture the Republican nomination. Forty years later, the Texans "had at least had the grace not to pretend that these transactions are either savory or honest." Joe singled out a symbolic figure who exemplified the attitudes and tactics of the Taftites: "The case was put rather plainly by the state chairman, an amiable old gentleman named Orville Bullington, whose war cry is, 'To hell with foreign policy.' He told this reporter: 'They'll barrelhouse 'em through. Whoever controls the committee can always barrelhouse 'em through. You'll see, it'll be the same at Chicago.'"[4]

The vivid lines about the "barrelhousing" Bullington soon brought a stiff reply. Bullington wrote to insist that Joe had not heard him correctly and even seemed to be challenging Joe to a duel or some other affair of honor in Chicago. On June 7 Bullington wrote from Wichita Falls,

> Either you cannot hear well or you are a common liar, and if you will come to Chicago I will repeat just what I have said in this letter to you, because I expect to be there. . . . What you said about my putting the case plainly and saying "To hell with foreign policy," is not true. . . . What I did say was "Away with bipartisan foreign policy." There is no such thing. . . . With reference to "barrelhousing them," I said that I personally had been railroaded and barrelhoused in many conventions, but that I had never bolted one. I also said that anyone who controls a political committee can do that if they want to.

Orville Bullington closed with a ringing condemnation of the *Herald Tribune*, which he said was "controlled by people who are more interested in foreign bonds and taking Americans' money to pay the interest on them. . . . They put the dollar first and principle second, in my judgment. They did this in Willkie's campaign, and they have done it ever since. I just want to set you straight about this," Bullington concluded in a challenging tone, "and if you do not like it you can find me in Chicago." Joe, so far as we know, did not take up the challenge. "I hear extremely well," he wrote Bullington on June 17. "I have detailed notes of what you said. And every word that I printed came straight from my notes."[5]

In the critical struggle over delegates in early July, the exposé of the "Texas steal," as the Eisenhower forces called it, was among the issues that tilted the Chicago convention Eisenhower's way. The Eisenhower forces spent some $3 million to publicize the issue. Joe's reporting from Mineral Wells had helped nationalize what was now being portrayed less as a struggle for political power than as a crusade for morality in precinct politics. Robert Taft arrived at his convention headquarters at the Hilton Hotel to find a sound truck circling the building and blasting out the admonition "THOU SHALT NOT STEAL."[6] If it mattered to keep the "isolationist" Taft out of the White House and put the "internationalist" Eisenhower in, and if the dispute in Mineral Wells was a critical point in the battle, it must be said that Joe Alsop had played no small role.

But in the end the Texas issue was perhaps of greater psychological than mathematical importance at Chicago. The disputed Texas votes never were decisive. But everyone agreed that in exposing himself to the "theft" issue, Taft had committed what his biographer James T. Patterson calls "his grossest blunder":

> Surely, it hurt badly. If [Taft] had repudiated Zweifel, he would have deprived Eisenhower of the moral issue and Lodge and Langlie might not have dared to try to change the rules over the lesser controversies in Georgia and Louisiana. But these were might have beens, for every vote taken at the convention revealed the overriding fact that Taft simply lacked enough delegates. . . . To have written off Texas might have preserved Georgia and Louisiana, but nothing suggested that such a move would have given him Michigan, Minnesota, Pennsylvania or California. Without these crucial delegates Taft could not have won, and that was that.[7]

Still, it was the impression of the day that Joe Alsop's exposure of the Texas regulars had vitally contributed to the strategic objective of keeping the nomination out of Taft's hands, thus assuring that the 1952 contest would not be a referendum on American commitment to the defense of freedom in Europe and Asia. Certainly that was as Joe Alsop liked the episode to be remembered, though, as we shall see, Eisenhower's failure to follow Joe's agenda while he was in office left the columnist contemptuous of him.

SINCE EISENHOWER and the Republicans were the ultimate winners, Joe's 1952 romance with Adlai Stevenson (which in later years he tried energetically to paper over) mattered less in the end than it might have. But while it lasted, the affair was ardent.

The witty and captivating Illinois governor, grandson of Grover Cleveland's vice president of the same name, for a time had no more enthusiastic promoter than Joe Alsop. Stevenson's urbane internationalist outlook, his patrician manner, and his winning performance as a reform governor of Illinois won impartial admiration. President Truman begged him to be the next Democratic presidential candidate. Others plotted ways to overcome his reluctance and, if necessary, to draft him for the role. Joe Alsop was not alone.

Stevenson seemed to Joe and Stewart Alsop to occupy a special niche in outlook, equidistant from the insularity of Taft and the rank amateurism of Dwight D. Eisenhower. Joe's enthusiasm showed in several glowing columns and in an admiring *Saturday Evening Post* profile in which

Stevenson was vividly portrayed as a "political Penelope," working his spindle at the statehouse in Illinois, and saying funny and sometimes contradictory things about his reaction to a possible draft, while suitors from every state and party faction courted him.[8] The outcome of the Democrats' courtship of Stevenson would hinge, Joe predicted in that article, on what happened to Bob Taft's candidacy. The nomination of Taft would force the Democrats to turn to Stevenson, and "this complex, reluctant and self-doubting politician" could "become the victim of the first genuine presidential draft in American twentieth-century politics."

Stevenson's appeal lay in "strict adherence to his rule, 'Be yourself.'" But Joe thought the Illinois governor carried self-doubt to "painful limits," and in it there was "a pitch of almost self-questioning that comes near being ludicrous." But the unmistakable egotism of his self-questioning was offset by "the air of being a humorous, intelligent, sensible man who has strayed into politics by mistake." That was the appearance; but according to the preliminary Alsop assessment, Stevenson's record at the governor's office in Springfield showed that beneath the suave, self-deprecating façade there was some toughness, even a bit of ruthlessness.[9]

The waspish strokes in the *Saturday Evening Post* profile may have been afterthoughts, given the piece's generally laudatory tone. What readers didn't know at the time was that Joe's piece had come near being canceled at the last moment, when Stevenson abruptly strengthened his statements of renunciation. He had angered President Truman by playing hard to get; Truman had now turned to Alben Barkley, his seventy-four-year-old vice president from Kentucky, and was using a president's far-from-inconsiderable influence within the party on Barkley's behalf. By the political standards of the day Barkley seemed too old. Yet it was beginning to seem, by midspring, that he might sew up the nomination by default. Joe wrote Martin Sommers at the *Post* on April 21, "Had I had the faintest inkling that Stevenson's statement [of non-candidacy] could possibly go so far I should have warned you long in advance. It made me more angry than I can say, and not only because it threatened me in the pocketbook nerve."[10]

This might be the point at which Joe's enthusiasm for Stevenson first began to cool a bit. Stevenson's acceptance speech following his draft at the convention included biblical imagery, thrilling at the time, which would later imply an unfortunate comparison. "I have prayed the merciful Father of us all to let this cup pass from me," Stevenson intoned, in an unmistakable allusion to Christ's anguish in Gethsemane. This statement would plant the seed of what was later to become a wholesale rearrangement of the essentials of the story in Joe's memory.

By the late 1980s, when Joe began composing his memoirs with the help of Adam Platt, historical revision on the subject of Adlai Stevenson had worked a transformation. He and Stewart had, he admitted, "briefly entertained high hopes" for him and had even gone to Springfield, Illinois, to interview him. But they had been "alarmed," Joe recalled, "by his tendency to bring Abraham Lincoln into the conversation," a sign in their rule book that it was time "to send for a psychiatrist." The alarm had been strengthened, according to this later account, "by Stevenson's famous acceptance speech in which he compared his agony in reaching his decision to run . . . with no less than Christ's agony in the garden. . . . Indeed, when he used Christ's anguished plea to our Lord 'Let this cup pass from me!' as a highlight in his speech, I am afraid I was driven, quite literally, to drink."[11]

This later rearrangement of Joe's reaction at the time shows the chemistry of what George Orwell called "double-think." There is little if any contemporary evidence of distaste for Stevenson or his biblical imagery; quite the contrary. By July 24, with the Stevenson draft now a reality, Joe had persuaded himself that Stevenson's reluctance to run had been craftier than it seemed from the outside. Stevenson had maneuvered with a "curious double vision," genuinely hoping to avoid the nomination but positioning himself to make the most of it if it could not be turned aside. "If you take a good look at all the facts," the Alsops wrote from Chicago, "you must . . . see that behind Stevenson's sometimes disturbing mask of the tortured intellectual, there is the face of a bold and intelligent leader, very clear in his own mind about the terms and limits of his nomination."[12]

This estimate was confirmed, for Joe Alsop, by Stevenson's stirring speech to the potentially hostile American Legion, in an early campaign appearance. The Legion was deeply tainted with superpatriotic McCarthyism. The organization had supported the Mitchell Palmer antiRed campaign following World War I; indeed, it had been founded in 1919 in large measure "to foster and perpetuate a one hundred per cent Americanism" and, by battling for the arrest or deportation of alleged "radicals" and "Bolsheviks," to reassure the country that the doughboys had not returned from France contaminated with revolutionary ideas. Now, true to form, the Legion had joined the crusade to redefine American patriotism in the Wisconsin senator's way. Stevenson boldly took "patriotism" as his subject and admonished the Legionnaires that it was not a spasmodic reaction to current tensions but "the patient, steady dedication of a lifetime." Joe's reaction to the speech was ecstatic. He wrote on August 29 that Stevenson was a Daniel in the lion's den. Stevenson had bearded the lion and made the lion like it by lacing his bold words with winning wit. "He came out unscathed and in glory . . . a virtuoso performance."[13]

Privately, Joe's reaction to the prospect of a Stevenson candidacy had all along been warmer than his public applause for the Legion speech would suggest. When he wrote to Stevenson in the spring to thank him for the interview for the *Saturday Evening Post* article, he said he could not recall "an experience . . . with an American political leader since the end of the war which has so much instructed, enlightened and encouraged me." At the time, Stevenson was still on the fence, and Joe couldn't resist putting in his plea with all the others: "In the most dreadful crisis America has ever entered, you are quite obviously the best qualified man to lead the country." He admonished Stevenson not to allow humility to "muffle the clear call of duty."[14]

Now, six months later, with Stevenson drafted and running, Joe sent "a line of jubilation" to Carl McGowan, Stevenson's aide in Springfield. Joe's view of the governor's Chicago acceptance speech was exalted. It had, he told McGowan, only three rivals as a happy turning point in recent American history—Franklin Roosevelt's first inaugural and post–Pearl Harbor speeches and "the release of the news that we would not take Korea lying down." He had found the moment at Chicago stirring, he told McGowan, because "we were seeing another national leader with the potentiality of greatness . . . stepping boldly onto the national stage."[15]

Again, the ecstasy was not long-lived; it did not even survive the campaign. By October 20, Joe was writing Isaiah Berlin in Oxford that the campaign "has been really horrible—like a trip through the Paris sewers." That unpleasant image of the campaign recurs in personal letters throughout the autumn election season. Stevenson was "admirably qualified," and Eisenhower plainly unfit (a dim view of the hero of the European crusade, and a view from which Joe never receded). Yet Joe felt "blackmailed by the virtual certainty that we shall have a first-class fascist party in the U.S. if the Republicans don't win."[16] He had now returned to the feeling that the alternative to giving the Republicans a turn in the White House was so dire as to qualify as "fascist."

It was an argument he had made before. Now his archrival Walter Lippmann had taken up the same argument, though in less exaggerated form, and that was a good reason for not repeating it. Yet, Joe admitted ruefully to Berlin, "there is truth in [it]." After all his praise of Stevenson, Joe seems to have swallowed his real preference and cast a vote for Eisenhower to avert, as he thought, the "first-class fascist" surge—whatever he meant by that. Conceivably it was the sour memory of having betrayed his instincts that pushed him in later years to revise his distinct enthusiasm for Stevenson. It was a slow change, and perhaps not entirely conscious or calculated; it was only when he wrote his memoirs thirty-five years later that the transformation was complete. His contemporary letter to Carl McGowan shows that he had actually found in Stevenson's acceptance speech "the potentiality of greatness." In this, of course, he had the company of millions.

All three Alsop brothers had participated in making Adlai Stevenson something of a joke. The columnists' brother John had told Stewart that even with "all the eggheads" behind him, Stevenson could not win in 1952. This word of John Alsop's coinage entered the language. He said later that it had come to him when he thought of the bald, shiny domes typical of intellectuals, at least as cartoonists draw them. Much later, during the Kennedy administration, Stewart would collaborate with another Washington journalist, Charles Bartlett, in an instant-history piece for the *Saturday Evening Post* on the 1962 Cuban missile crisis. They quoted someone (possibly the president himself) as believing that "Adlai wanted a Munich." The outrageous quotation ultimately proved to be full of irony: It finally came out that Kennedy had accepted Stevenson's suggestion for the solution of the standoff and secretly promised Nikita Khrushchev to withdraw U.S. missiles from Turkey.[17] In his last years Joe remembered viewing Stevenson as a tortured, neurotic man. The contemporary truth was very different.

IT WAS ODD that the candidate in whom the Alsops had shown the least interest—at least after the Texas battle over delegates—was the eventual victor. Since Eisenhower's aim was to prevent a slide back into isolation and to tame the cruder instincts of the Republican primitives, the columnists' strategic objections for 1952 had been accomplished— for the moment, at least. With the popular Eisenhower installed in the White House as the first Republican president since the Great Depression, the "first-class fascist" movement that Joe thought of as a native tendency was quiescent.

Joe (left) and Stewart Alsop looking slightly foppish in their younger years. This photo by the famous French master was a favorite family conversation piece, and enlarged prints were to be found in a number of family houses. (Henri Cartier-Bresson/Magnum)

*Corinne Robinson Alsop, "Ma" to Joe and Stewart. She was, a friend recalled, "the only one who could tell Joe to shut up and get away with it." She was also an active and accomplished Republican politician. (Dick Spafford/*Hartford Times*)*

The young Joe Alsop in a favorite pose. He ordered books by the score from Blackwell's in Oxford and read them all. (Carl Mydans for Time/Life)

*Joe in his showpiece formal garden on Dumbarton Avenue in Georgetown. His friend and occasional house guest, the historian Arthur Schlesinger, Jr., warned Joe after a visit that his "sinister plants" might someday attack and devour him. (*Washington Post*)*

Grandmother Corinne Roosevelt Robinson, the favorite younger sister of President Theodore Roosevelt and a strong influence in the lives of the Alsop brothers. Through her connections with Mrs. Ogden Reid, she got Joe his first reporting job, on the New York Herald Tribune. *(Alsop Papers/Library of Congress)*

Joe and Susan Mary Alsop leaving St. John's Church, Lafayette Square, after her daughter's wedding. For the reception, Joe had fresh grapefruit hung on some of the magnolia trees in his garden. (Alsop Papers/Library of Congress)

Henderson House, Grandmother Robinson's mock Scottish baronial country house overlooking the Mohawk Valley. It was fondly remembered as the scene of the summertime "rolling house parties" that took place when Joe and Stewart were boys. It is now owned by the former music director of the National Symphony Orchestra, Mstislav Rostropovich. (Alsop Papers / Library of Congress)

George F. Kennan during his brief tenure as U.S. ambassador to the Soviet Union. No friend of the Alsops was a more respected source of information and views on American foreign policy. (Associated Press)

*Joe Alsop and his "tribal" friend Henry A. Wallace at the time of the McCarran Committee hearings on China. Joe considered Wallace a "mystical goose" but sprang combatively to his defense when he was accused of having been a Communist dupe during World War II. (*Washington Post*)*

*Above: Boston lawyer Joseph Welch (left) and Senator Joe McCarthy at the 1954 Army-
McCarthy hearings. As the army's special counsel, Welch proved to be McCarthy's most
effective adversary.* (Washington Post)
*Below: Joe McCarthy (right) and his young chief counsel, Roy Cohn. Cohn's bullying of
the army for favors to his young friend David Schine set the stage for McCarthy's undoing
and subsequent censure by the Senate.* (Washington Post)

J. Robert Oppenheimer at the time of the Gray Board hearing. As America's leading theoretical physicist, Oppenheimer directed the building of the first atomic bombs at Los Alamos and later sought to "internationalize" the control of nuclear energy. He was the most distinguished victim of the McCarthy hysteria. (Washington Post*)*

Paul Nitze in 1988. As director of policy planning at the State Department and chief author of National Security Memorandum 68 in earlier postwar years, Nitze was an architect of the U.S. containment policy. He was also a close friend of the Alsop family. (James K. W. Atherton/ Washington Post*)*

Stewart Alsop poses in Red Square, Moscow, during a 1950s reporting trip to the Soviet Union. (Courtesy of Mrs. Stewart Alsop)

*Joe Alsop in 1977 as the author knew him, looking characteristically bellicose and ready to bark behind his trademark oversized coffee cup. (Harry Naltchayan/*Washington Post*)*

Chapter Eight **Showdown with Joe McCarthy**

J oe Alsop's belief that a Republican victory in 1952 and a renewed taste of the responsibilities of governing would curb the surging inquisitorial spirit in the country proved to be unfounded. The new president, Dwight D. Eisenhower, enjoyed great popularity in both parties and had no taste for demagogues. But to critics like the Alsops, his administrative methods seemed to invite anarchy and left much room for mischief-making. With the simultaneous advent of the Republicans to power in the Senate, Senator Joe McCarthy, the boldest of the new inquisitors, soon began to use an almost derisory committee assignment (the chairmanship of the Government Operations Committee and its investigative subcommittee) as a base for widespread pursuit of alleged Communist subversion.

In the last two years of the Truman era, McCarthy had made speeches, occasionally terrorized public officials fearful of their reputations, and manipulated the headlines. But so long as the Democrats controlled the Senate, he lacked a power base. Now at last he could assemble a staff of sleuths and gumshoes to go abroad in search of scandal and subversion and could use the subpoena power to hail witnesses before him.

There was a view within the new administration that it was a mistake to use presidential prestige against McCarthy. Instead he should be paid out the rope to hang himself with. If the spotlight could somehow be shifted away from him he would wilt, according to this theory, for he was first and last a publicity-seeker. That remained the view of McCarthy's most important enemy within the administration, the president himself. In the first year of his administration, Eisenhower confidently analyzed the Wisconsin senator in his personal diary as a man "anxious for headlines . . . [and] prepared to go to any extreme . . . to secure some mention of his name in the public press." Eisenhower believed that the one thing McCarthy couldn't stand was to be ignored and intended to use a strategy of studied neglect to defeat him.[1]

In fact, it hardly mattered whether or not the president and his aides noticed McCarthy. The public worry over the supposed Communist influence in government had now so intensified that McCarthy could command the spotlight with or without White House approval. He soon established himself as a rival to the White House as a source of news and of Republican doctrine in his fields of specialization. McCarthyism (as the *Washington Post* cartoonist Herblock was the first to call it) was a fever that now seemed fated to run its disturbing course, whatever his foes and critics did. Joe's friend Lydia Lewis of Farmington, Connecticut, sensed it when she visited Washington briefly in May after McCarthy's emergence the previous winter. She was "shocked by the poisonous atmosphere," she wrote Joe, "a form of gangsterism devoid of any taint of justice."

AS A HARVARD ALUMNUS and member of the university's Board of Overseers, Joe Alsop was soon drawn quietly into a representative episode of the Red-hunting period. McCarthy and other inquisitors entertained a theory that the most fertile breeding ground for subversion was, paradoxically, not the slums or even the places where working people lived their dim lives but the most privileged sectors of American society—the State Department, to be sure, but prestigious colleges and universities as well.

After becoming a committee chairman, McCarthy had lost no time focusing attention on Wendell Furry, an experimental physicist at Harvard. Furry was already in trouble with the authorities at his own university, because he had failed to disclose his Communist Party membership while working at the Radiation Lab at MIT, which had been a center of weapons and radar research during World War II. Furry had undoubtedly been on the left in the thirties, when joining the Communist Party was not unlawful; this still was the case, although by prosecuting Junius Scales and others under the 1940 Smith Act, the Eisenhower Justice Department was now attempting to turn "knowing membership" in the party into a criminal act. No act of disloyalty or espionage had been charged against Furry, and he had quit the party. But two decades later, even nominal party membership, and even in the distant past, spelled trouble.

From 1943 on, Furry had performed low-security radar research at the Radiation Lab. In view of his political predilections, Furry's colleagues had recommended him only for low-security work and only when the shortage of scientists began to pinch. By all reports, Furry performed diligently. But in answering an FBI security questionnaire in 1944 he made a mistake that would continue to haunt him and threaten his good standing at Harvard a decade later: He concealed his former Communist Party link.

By the time McCarthy's committee summoned Furry, the furor over so-called Fifth Amendment Communists was reaching its height. The Fifth Amendment provides that in a criminal case no one may be "compelled to be a witness against himself"—a form of forced interrogation commonly known as self-incrimination. Strictly speaking, the protection applied only in a court of law, not in a congressional hearing. But the many special investigations, especially those conducted by McCarthy, had taken on the air of trials, and many witnesses called to testify about their political pasts had, for various reasons, invoked the privilege. What their silence might conceal—past or present party membership, fellow traveling, "parlor pink" leftist sympathies, a desire to protect unidentified friends or colleagues or nothing more than their rights of privacy—could only be guessed at. But witnesses who "took the Fifth" often found themselves objects of persecution or even fired.

The nation's schools and colleges, weakened by the general hysteria, often lacked the financial strength or political standing to resist the political crosswinds. Many had adopted the policy of routinely firing teachers who declined to testify fully about their political associations. In the eyes of McCarthy and his colleagues, those who took the Fifth convicted themselves by inference of whatever the charge against them happened to be—disloyalty or worse—and had no business in university or government work. A shaken, fearful academic community was divided over how to respond. And while bullying investigations were widely deplored, some academics earnestly asked whether concealment was consistent with the scholar's obligation to be open and candid. Openness and candor were central values in science, Wendell Furry's field. And what about his falsification of the wartime questionnaire?

The Furry case had been further complicated by a legal technicality. In several cases arising from the congressional hearings, the courts had invoked a longstanding doctrine that witnesses could not invoke the Fifth Amendment selectively. In response to a line of related questions, they must answer all or none.[2] Furry, however, had courted contempt of Congress by announcing that while he was willing to speak candidly about his own past, he would refuse to name friends and colleagues who had abandoned their old party ties but had not been harrowed up by the ongoing inquisition.

The Furry case had become a cause célèbre at Joe Alsop's alma mater, and the Board of Overseers, the Harvard Corporation, and the alumni all were sharply divided. There was a case for firing Furry, tenure or no, since he had violated the university's own regulations. Joe, who as an Overseer had served on the visiting committee to the physics department, proclaimed that he very much disliked Furry and was defending him only for principle's sake. He made a point of saying repeatedly that Furry, like some of the China Hands, had behaved foolishly, a disclaimer that usually turned up in letters of solicitation to friends and other Harvard alumni for contributions to Furry's defense fund. But Joe's fundamental argument was that the university must put likes and dislikes aside to resist McCarthy and his House of Representatives counterpart, Harold Velde, who was also in pursuit of Furry.

The Furry case struck Joe as a mere warmup for a bolder and broader assault on higher education. If Harvard appeased McCarthy by firing Furry, he argued, the Wisconsin senator's attack would shift to weaker institutions. Harvard would then appear as the "judas goat" for a general onslaught. At the very least, the embattled physicist—whose colleagues regarded him as a man of spectacular absent-mindedness—should have a competent lawyer and a sound legal strategy. Furry had already courted a contempt of Congress citation by vacillating on the Fifth Amendment. In his appearance before the Velde Committee, he had used the Fifth as the courts had directed. But when summoned by McCarthy he had invoked the protection against self-incrimination selectively—only when asked about the political associations of others.

This issue touched off a merry argument in letters between Joe, in Washington, and Paul Cabot and Charles Coolidge, the treasurer and general counsel of the Harvard Corporation. Joe observed that Furry "was not afraid to admit his own past membership in the Communist Party, but was not willing to turn informer and so expose others to the loss of their jobs and the other penalties that are now imposed on this brand of political folly." The threat of a contempt citation proved "the unwisdom of the Pontius Pilate policy which Harvard adopted at the start," and the university was in part to blame for Furry's "present plight." Besides, "technical contempt" of McCarthy's showboating committee should not be regarded as misbehavior; it would be "squalid and cowardly" to punish Furry after he had "made a clean breast of his own past."

Coolidge was less sympathetic. On January 26 he asked,

> Would you be willing to admit that arrogating to himself the right to decide whether five commies working in the Radiation Lab were or were not a spy ring, is somewhat different from refusing to name friends for the usual reason of saving them from the "persecution" and possible loss of jobs? . . . I am pretty clear that there is a point where the activities of one's friends make it highly immoral to refuse to testify about them. . . . If I had known that Furry's use of the Fifth Amendment hid five commies in the Radiation Laboratory, I would have been more concerned about it than I was. Bear in mind that we have already found Furry guilty of grave misconduct in lying to the FBI back in 1944, so that he can be removed for misconduct amounting to less than grave misconduct.

Joe stuck to his guns. The Rad Lab sounded "secret and important," he responded on January 29, but well-informed friends, scientists themselves, had told him that it was "never a project of the highest importance."[3] That assumption was certainly false, and Joe's argument failed to meet Coolidge's point squarely, since to second-guess a lawful security system in wartime could indeed be classified as grossly irresponsible behavior, just as Coolidge argued; this idea would soon be an issue in the Oppenheimer case. Joe's contention that Furry's discharge would "look to the world like an act of appeasement" of McCarthy and damage the Fifth Amendment was stronger. "The founding fathers," Joe admonished the university's counsel, "foresaw such a period as we are now, unhappily, living through." It was precisely because Furry was "bad public relations" for Harvard that "we must be all the more determined not to be browbeaten by the new Fascism into staining Harvard's record." Coolidge replied several days later, thanking Joe for his "eloquent letter" and pronouncing it "really . . . very good." Joe went on lobbying for Furry and raising money for his defense fund, to which he personally contributed $100.[4]

The Furry case yielded a useful journalistic by-product. In a letter addressed to William Marbury, a member of the governing body of Harvard, Joe had deployed his best eloquence in defense of Furry. In fact, Joe liked what he had told Marbury so much that he sent it to the *Atlantic Monthly*, which published it as an open letter without Marbury's name. "Freedom of personal choice within the limits of the law," Joe wrote, "is the first great principle of academic freedom [and] the second principle is unrestricted freedom of thought. . . . [including] the freedom to hold unpopular and pernicious political views and to belong to unpopular or pernicious political parties, so long as they are legal." After forty years, the letter to Marbury seems boiler-plate free speech and free association doctrine. But in the early fifties that was far from so. To reiterate these fundamentals in those troubled days was to remind frightened Americans of a legacy of free thought and free speech that many did not wish to think about.[5]

BY MID-1953 distaste for McCarthy was growing within the divided Eisenhower administration. Vice President Nixon, pragmatic as ever, was among those who argued for artful containment, lest a violent collision with the senator split the Republicans in Congress and imperil the administration's legislative program. Some of the president's aides at the White House—his adviser and speechwriter C. D. Jackson, for instance—were pushing for open and explicit resistance. Then, just as McCarthy seemed to be creating a myth of invulnerability, he blundered into a fight with the United States Army that was ultimately to prove his undoing.[6]

This colorful episode opened with a McCarthy investigation of alleged Communist influence at the Army Signal Corps laboratories in Fort Monmouth, New Jersey. But why so solid an institution as the U.S. Army? The Alsops had been among the first to report that Communists had gained some marginal influence within the U.S. command in occupied Germany. This infiltration had taken place during Dwight D. Eisenhower's time as chief of staff of the army; and, as we will see, Joe Alsop had a theory that McCarthy planned to attack Eisenhower over this issue in due course.

He believed that McCarthy, having taken the measure of the lower brass, also planned to revive the controversy over Eisenhower's wartime strategic decisions—those in which he had supposedly passed up British and American opportunities to seize Berlin and Prague before the Russians got there.[7] This theory was plausible, for two years earlier McCarthy had delivered a tedious and pseudoscholarly 72,000-word indictment of General George C. Marshall, beginning with Marshall's influence on high strategy during the war and going on to his allegedly treacherous handling of China policy during his tenure as secretary of defense. The lengthy screed—ghostwritten by one of McCarthy's scholarly allies—had been published as *America's Retreat from Victory*. Eisenhower's decisions could similarly be represented not as military judgments (which in fact they were) but political policies calculated to promote, almost to invite, a Soviet military incursion into the heart of Europe. The columnists were not alone in expecting that McCarthy planned to spring that and other surprises on the president. In a telephone conversation recorded by Pentagon stenographers during the controversy, General Lucius Clay told Eisenhower, "I'm willing to bet [McCarthy] has information on honorable discharges while you were chief of staff." Eisenhower angrily replied to his old friend that he had never knowingly given an honorable discharge to a Communist.[8]

In the rancid and fearful climate of the McCarthy period, no wartime strategy decision, whether in Europe or at Yalta, Cairo, Potsdam, or elsewhere, was immune to the imputation of sinister or conspiratorial motives. The whole line of accusation was of a breathtaking shallowness, worthless as history or even polemic. But most Americans aren't trained in historical analysis.

Meanwhile, the Army-McCarthy confrontation began with a draft notice to a junior McCarthy staff aide and "consultant"—G. David Schine, a handsome blonde youth in his twenties. Schine's credentials as a "consultant" on the Communist conspiracy consisted of a single puerile pamphlet, "Definition of Communism," which he had written as a Harvard term paper. Schine's father, a wealthy hotelier, had had this amateurish tissue of bromides printed and placed in rooms throughout his hotel chain as a "public service." Schine had been hired by his friend Roy Cohn, the McCarthy subcommittee's chief counsel. As a precocious Columbia Law School graduate of twenty, Cohn had assisted in the prosecution of the accused atom-bomb spies Julius and Ethel Rosenberg and was now a rising star on the anti-Communist scene. The names of Cohn and Schine were soon as closely linked as those of famous comedy teams (or, as Lillian Hellman later cracked, Bonnie and Clyde); and their antics produced an abundance of low comedy. In the summer of 1953, they toured U.S. libraries in Europe, attacking books like Dashiell Hammett's *Maltese Falcon*. In mischief or fright, one librarian actually burned some of the books Cohn and Schine labeled subversive—an episode that drove an infuriated President Eisenhower to plead in a commencement speech at Dartmouth College, "Don't join the bookburners."

Even in the face of these provocations, to Joe's dismay the administration still shied from an open battle with McCarthy. When it came, the fight was unsought and occurred almost inadvertently. The Wisconsin senator and his aides began to bully the army over the draft status of G. David Schine. When Schine's draft notice came, his friends on the subcommittee staff—Roy Cohn and Francis Carr, a roly-poly former FBI man—sought unsuccessfully to get Schine exempted. When that attempt failed, Schine cheekily proposed himself, with the committee's backing, as a commissioned officer and special aide to the secretary of the army, Robert T. Stevens, a mild and obliging textile executive. Stevens went through the motions of exploring the idea but found that regulations barred it. Schine was then represented as so vital to the work of the subcommittee that he needed special leaves and passes, which the army lavishly provided during his weeks in boot camp and after. Yet the bullying of the army continued, and the stage was thus set for one of the most spectacular of all the great stories of the 1950s. It was not only a story that Joe and Stewart Alsop reported with relish; it was also a story in which Joe, behind the scenes, would play a decisive role.

THE MANAGEMENT OF the David Schine–Roy Cohn problem had fallen, as it happened, to two earnest and undesigning men, Secretary of the Army Stevens and the army's legal counsel, John G. Adams. These two upright and accommodating civilians suddenly found themselves facing an underground struggle that was byzantine beyond their innocent imagining. Yet their inept handling of the pressure of McCarthy's henchmen on the army sped the chain of events that would bring McCarthy down.

Still, the showdown might have been delayed if Stevens and Adams had simply rebuffed Roy Cohn's insolent pressure for the special treatment of Private First Class David Schine, the young Harvard graduate who had now become Cohn's protégé. But it was beyond the two army officials' personal style to be abrupt about these unseemly and irregular matters.

For one thing, it was known throughout the administration that President Eisenhower believed that Harry Truman's great failing as a president had been his disrespect for congressional prerogatives. Eisenhower had accordingly brought with him to the White House a prejudice that twenty uninterrupted years of Democratic control of the executive branch had made presidents habitually highhanded. This doctrine had been assiduously preached to the president's subordinates. Administration officials were admonished to go the last mile in soothing congressional vanity, even when such cajolery meant overaccommodating the likes of Joe McCarthy and his bully-boy staff.

This Whiggish doctrine pervaded the administration. It was perhaps too much to expect that mild-mannered men like Stevens and Adams would steel themselves to resist Cohn's insolence. If the Alsops had not already sensed this deference as the root problem in the Eisenhower administration's kid-glove handling of McCarthy, they soon were alerted to it by William Chanler, a friend of theirs who had recently served as corporation counsel for the City of New York. On March 19 Chanler wrote to Joe that while "all of us recognize . . . the congressional right to inquire and investigate into every phase of [the executive's] public operations," the probing had gone far beyond sane or useful limits and put the separation of powers principle under critical strain.[9] Secretary of Defense Charles E. Wilson, Steven's boss, had even gone so far as to call the members of Congress "bosses," an attitude that seemed to Chanler ignorant of American constitutional practice.

Meanwhile, the McCarthy Committee had begun investigating charges of subversive influence at Fort Monmouth, New Jersey, the site of the

Army Signal Corps radar laboratories, which were then working on warning systems against ballistic missile attack. The investigation had trivialized itself by focusing on the ludicrous issue of who had "promoted" Irving Peress, an army dentist at Fort Monmouth, from captain to major. (In fact, no one had done so except in the most routine sense; the promotion had been automatic under the Doctor Draft Law.)

Peress was believed to have left-wing opinions or connections of a sort never clearly defined and almost certainly irrelevant to his ability to drill GI teeth properly. When Peress found himself, to his dismay, a target of a congressional investigation, he began scrambling to get out of uniform and was quietly allowed to do so. McCarthy then summoned Peress's nominal superior, General Ralph Zwicker, a highly regarded and much decorated combat officer. In executive session, McCarthy and his bloodhounds berated Zwicker; for example, McCarthy said that he had the mind of a nine-year-old child and was "unfit to wear the uniform." Zwicker was not allowed to have a lawyer present during this humiliating ordeal. When the transcript of McCarthy's hazing was leaked to the newspapers, it enraged the officer corps and made a vigorous response from the army and the administration imperative.

In the Senate, an anti-McCarthy Republican, Ralph Flanders of Vermont, ridiculed the Fort Monmouth follies: "[Senator McCarthy] dons his warpaint . . . goes into his war dance . . . emits his warwhoops. He goes forth to battle and proudly returns with the scalp of a pink army dentist. We may assume that this represents the depth and seriousness of the Communist penetration in this country at this time." Eisenhower sent Flanders an approving note but otherwise kept his silence.[10]

Meanwhile, Secretary Stevens, bombarded by protests from within the army, sternly announced that Zwicker and other officers would make no further appearances until McCarthy and his committee promised to treat them courteously and fairly. McCarthy was unimpressed. He telephoned Stevens to issue the usual menacing threats: "Just go ahead and try it, Robert," he was heard to growl. "I am going to kick the brains out of anyone who protects Communists. . . . You just go ahead. I guarantee you that you will live to regret it."[11] (McCarthy did not know that Pentagon secretaries were taking down his words in shorthand.) Soon the guileless Stevens allowed himself to be trapped into a Capitol Hill luncheon with Republican senators and wholly reversed himself: He made a gentleman's agreement with McCarthy and his friends that seemed to promise a continuing ordeal for the army. It now became clearer than ever to Stevens's more seasoned superiors in the administration that reinforcements and a new strategy were needed.

Summoned to a January 21 meeting at the Justice Department, Adams, the army counsel, regaled several of the Eisenhower administration's most powerful figures, including Attorney General Herbert Brownell and White House Chief of Staff Sherman Adams, with accounts of the threats the Schine problem had brought the army's way—including Roy Cohn's threat to "wreck the army" if Private Schine were assigned to duty overseas. The additional threat of more inquisitions like the Fort Monmouth hearings was also being held over the army's head. The clear purpose was to assure special treatment for McCarthy's young "consultant." From mid-July 1953, when Schine's draft notice arrived, to March 1, 1954, some sixty-five telephone calls and nineteen meetings between Schine's protectors on the McCarthy Committee and Stevens, Adams, or their aides had been carefully recorded. Most of the threats, cajolery, and abuse—at times featuring obscene language—had been noted by Adams or recorded by stenographic secretaries at the Pentagon. Someone now made a fateful suggestion. John Adams, the army's general counsel, who had been the butt of this assault, ought to compile the record. This document—the record that became known as "the chronology"—was, in a way, Joe McCarthy's political death warrant.[12]

Enter, now, Joe Alsop; for it was this chronology compiled by Adams that would bring him in for an important role in the showdown.

BY FEBRUARY, word was leaking out at the Pentagon about the Adams chronology, and Joe invited himself to Adams's Pentagon office and persuaded the army's counsel to let him examine the document. The date of this examination is uncertain, but it followed the committee's hazing of General Zwicker and Stevens's limp response, which had laid the story at the White House doorstep. Before the age of electronic copiers, documents could still be closely held, and this one hadn't leaked. Nor did Adams leak it to Joe Alsop. He did let Joe read it in his office—"a long series of memoranda . . . at various dates," Joe later recalled, "between 14,000 and 16,000 words." Joe, with his nose for a good story, could see that the material was explosive. He begged Adams, without success, to let him publish it.

Meanwhile, Eisenhower, under intensifying pressure to intervene openly in behalf of his old service, was sticking firmly to his refusal to "get down into the gutter" with McCarthy. In a March 3 press conference in the White House East Room, at which everyone expected him to speak firmly for the army, he mildly said that the army had made mistakes in the Peress matter and that the administration would continue to cooperate with the investigation at Fort Monmouth.

Joe Alsop was flabbergasted. For one thing, the president of the United States was, not for the first time, refusing to take his advice. The Alsops had warned in their column that very morning that "if the President permits just one more appeasement of Senator McCarthy he can say goodbye to his own authority in his administration, in his party and in the Congress."[13] Taking the same line, Walter Lippmann wrote that McCarthy was now "a candidate for . . . the dictatorship of the Republican Party." Eisenhower was not yet ready, however, to abandon his strategy of indirection. "Why the yellow son of a bitch!," Joe exclaimed to a reporter seated beside him.[14]

A week later, exasperated by McCarthy's continued surliness and perhaps prodded by Joe Alsop, the administration finally struck back. Ostensibly in response to inquiries about the Schine affair from Richard Russell of Georgia and John McClellan of Arkansas, two powerful southern senators with jurisdiction over armed service matters, the army forwarded a scrubbed-up version of the Adams chronology to Capitol Hill on March 8. Joe Alsop suddenly found himself in the catbird seat, having seen the juicier unexpurgated original. He must have relished every word he wrote in his jolting column of March 15, "The Tale Half Told."

Joe drew on his remarkably accurate memory to point out that the story of McCarthy's and Cohn's badgering of the army was far more sordid and shocking than the cleaned-up chronology suggested. If the nation could examine the original it would be astonished, for "the whole document was studded with the disgusting obscenities in which Cohn persistently indulged, whenever he was bullyragging Army Department officials to give Schine special favors." There was, Joe continued, a sense of "the unbounded arrogance, the inflated egotism, the Nazi-like sense of power" of McCarthy's chief counsel. In addition, the army had removed from the cleaned-up version certain insinuations concerning the relationship between Cohn and McCarthy, as well as McCarthy's curious pleas—behind Cohn's back—that the army "give Schine the works." In its earthier form, the document had been circulating in the administration's upper echelons "for a good many weeks" and had been known to the Justice Department and the White House more than a month earlier. Surely, Joe concluded (continuing his campaign to prod Eisenhower into the fight), the exposure of this story would not have come without the president's approval. Now the "full facts"—the colorful and unsavory original—ought to be published "as the answer to McCarthy's and Cohn's howls of indignation." And they were indeed howling.[15]

The Alsop column was a journalistic sensation in Washington on the morning of March 15. At 12:31 P.M. the Defense Department's top lawyer, Struve Hensel, telephoned Stevens. "Did you read Alsop?" he asked. "Either Joe's memory is awful damned good, or Joe has a copy—no matter what John Adams says." Hensel's speculation was plausible, but no copy of the original bill of particulars seems to exist in the Alsop Papers today, and it is probable that Joe was not allowed to take it out of Adams's office.[16]

In fact, there was no need for further detail. If the release of Adams's chronology had been intended to force a showdown with McCarthy, it achieved that purpose. The uproar made some sort of formal investigation inevitable. Ordinarily, the logical investigating body would have been the Senate Armed Services Committee. But that committee's chairman, Leverett Saltonstal of Massachusetts, was up for reelection and feared irritating McCarthy's Boston Irish following. No senator had forgotten the fate of Millard Tydings, who had led the damaging probe of McCarthy's initial charges against the State Department four years earlier. Thus the investigation fell, improbably, to the McCarthy subcommittee itself: McCarthy temporarily stepped aside for a placid former South Dakota schoolteacher, Karl Mundt, who filled in as chairman. Mundt had predicted—it was perhaps the measure of his perspicacity—that the investigation would last a week. In fact, along with Senator Estes Kefauver's crime investigation of some years before, it became one of the first of the great television spectacles from the Senate Caucus Room, and it riveted the attention of the American public for thirty-six vivid days. It would have no rival as a clash of personalities and issues until the gaudy parade of characters at the Watergate hearings nearly twenty years later.

NOT EVEN THOSE who were spellbound by them could say what the aim of the hearings was nor specify their ultimate findings. It was obvious that McCarthy and the army had clashed over special privileges for

Private Schine and that General Zwicker had been crudely browbeaten. But what else? In the end, the findings mattered a good deal less than the visual impressions that had been left—above all, the unsettling spectacle of McCarthy bellowing "Point of order, Mr. Chairman," and the army's shrewd outside counsel, Joseph Welch, a tweedy Boston lawyer, needling McCarthy and his aides with silken wit and polished sarcasm.

An agreement between the parties tended to limit, in advance, the material conclusions. The army agreed not to sum up its case; the McCarthy forces agreed not to call General Lawson, the Fort Monmouth commandant, who was prepared to testify that the army had indeed been lax about Communist infiltration. The evidence of favor-seeking for Schine, the bullying of the army and its officers, and even the appearance that the committee had doctored photographs and forged memoranda—these facts spoke for themselves, and not favorably of McCarthy.

The Wisconsin senator, having rashly attacked an American institution, seemed fated to overreach and finally did so. One day as Welch was teasing Roy Cohn about the Communist danger ("May I add my small voice, sir, and say whenever you know about a subversive or a Communist or a spy, please hurry"), McCarthy suddenly broke in.

"In view of Mr. Welch's request," he said, "I think we should tell him that he has in his law firm a young man named Fisher . . . who has been for a number of years a member of an organization that was named, oh, years and years ago, as the legal bulwark of the Communist Party." The reference was to a young Welch associate, Fred Fisher, and his membership in the Lawyer's Guild. Welch had been sufficiently concerned about this very danger that he had sent Fisher back to Boston before the hearings started.

Now Welch dramatically turned on McCarthy with words that rang for days: "Until this moment, I think I never really gauged . . . your cruelty or your recklessness. . . . Little did I dream you could be so reckless and so cruel as to do an injury to that lad. . . . Have you no sense of decency, sir, at long last? *Have you left no sense of decency?*" With that, Welch stalked from the hearing room to loud applause. McCarthy, stunned and surprised, sat with his palms turned up as if to ask: "What did I do to deserve this?" The scene was long remembered as the beginning of McCarthy's fall, leading to his formal censure by the Senate the following December and his lapse into obscurity and an early death of alcoholism.[17]

Even before the Welch-McCarthy finale, however, Joe Alsop's March 15 column on the Adams chronology continued to reverberate. Testifying on May 6, the secretary of the army, the hapless Stevens, was asked whether the army had been "helped" to prepare Adams's chronology by someone in the press corps. Stevens seemed not to understand the question.

"Did [Adams] tell you that one member of the press helped prepare" the charges, McCarthy asked.

"He did not," Stevens answered. McCarthy suggested that Stevens check his records "before the record [of the hearing] goes to the Justice Department"—a clumsy threat that perjury charges might be brought. Stevens stood his ground; so far as he knew, Adams had talked to no journalist.

"Turn around to Adams and ask him," McCarthy demanded. Stevens, Adams, and Welch huddled. "Mr. Adams says the name of the newspaperman is Joseph Alsop," Stevens said, revising his previous denial.[18]

The next day Mundt and the subcommittee's assistant counsel, Thomas Prewitt, called Joe Alsop to a closed hearing, also attended by Roy Cohn, who was in a hostile and combative mood. It was soon clear what the plan was: The questioners groped for an admission that Joe had served as a ghostwriter for Adams in preparing the chronology. Had he not "conferred" with Adams, Alsop was asked. There was no question of "conferring," Joe said. He had gone to see Adams as a reporter in pursuit of a story. Adams had the story and gave it to him. He had naturally urged Adams to release the tale of the committee's meddling on Schine's behalf because it was "affected with the public interest . . . [and showed] the most shocking malfeasance." Well then, Prewitt pursued, hadn't Adams tried to use Alsop as an intermediary to threaten "that if Senator McCarthy did not forego this investigation of the army the report would be issued?" That also was false, Joe replied.

Cohn, taking up the questioning, then asked about Joe's assertion in the March 15 column that in its original form the Adams chronology "is also understood to contain an indication that Cohn was receiving substantial financial assistance from Schine while he was threatening to wreck the army." Where had Joe gotten that? From the documents? From other sources, Joe replied. Cohn clearly hoped that the damning tale told by the army's chronology could be discredited by portraying it as journalistic invention, concocted by the Alsop brothers rather than recorded item by item by Adams, Stevens, and the sharp-eared Pentagon stenographers.[19] There were also hints, Joe later learned from the *Herald Tribune*'s lawyers, that Cohn was threatening to file a libel suit against him and the newspaper when the hearings ended. No such suit was ever filed.[20]

With Joe's brief testimony, his active role in the McCarthy matter ended. The rest is history. Within months, McCarthy had been officially censured by the Senate, and within a few years he was dead and his investigative methods so discredited that "McCarthyism" soon became a word universally—sometimes loosely—used of undiscriminating attack or accusation. In his exposure and discrediting, the Alsops had played a key role through their reporting and, in Joe's case, through personal action.

Years later, Joe recorded in his memoir *"I've Seen the Best of It"* that one day he had paid a confidential call on Sherman Adams, the White House chief of staff. The White House was still pursuing its appeasement policy, and Joe, by his account, came to Adams with what can only be called polite blackmail in mind. Joe put it to Adams (as he had written elsewhere to friends) that, unless fought and beaten, McCarthy soon would seek to use the issue of Communist influence in Eisenhower's wartime and postwar commands in Germany: "On a foolscap pad, I had made my notes of the names and offices of Communists who had been important under Eisenhower's German command. . . . I droned on undiscouraged for fifteen minutes. I explained the situation, as Nicholas Nabokov had laid it out for me years before, at Camp Ritchie, Maryland, listed each of the suspect newspapers, and ran through all the names of the Communist party members on the various governing boards and military staffs which ran occupied Germany."

He and Stewart had reported the same issue some years earlier. Now, to anticipate and deflate the threat posed by McCarthy, he and Stewart proposed to revive the story in their column—unless, of course, the Eisenhower administration planned to go hard after McCarthy. "We had considered . . . publishing the material in our column because if it were to appear so publicly and in such a straightforward way, it would not cause the kind of sensation that McCarthy was reaching for." Adams got the point; he said, "Alsop, we'll fight."[21] The story finds no echo elsewhere in the record or the Alsop Papers, though that hardly means Joe Alsop's account is faulty. Perhaps Joe's memory had reworked the gist of a conversation with Sherman Adams, as it had done regarding other matters—notably, the early Alsop enthusiasm for Adlai Stevenson. Whatever its historicity, it forms an intriguing footnote in the chronicles of the age.

McCARTHY HAD taken advantage of the press's thrall to the rule of reportorial "objectivity," wherein newspapers in the hands of shrewd liars often became passive conveyors of their untruths. As Douglass Cater wrote in his influential book *The Fourth Branch of Government,*

> Few of the reporters who regularly covered McCarthy believed him. Most came to hate and fear him as a cynical liar who was willing to wreak untold havoc to satisfy his own power drive. But though they feared him, it was not intimidation that caused the press to serve as the instrument for McCarthy's rise. Rather it was the inherent vulnerabilities—the frozen patterns of the press—which McCarthy discovered and played upon with unerring skill. "Straight" news, the absolute commandment of most mass media journalism, had become a strait jacket to crush the initiative and the independence of the reporter.[22]

The Alsops, who combined fact-gathering with the columnist's license to frame events and issues in a deeper context, were critical to McCarthy's undoing. So were other important journalists of the time— Walter Lippmann; James Reston of the *New York Times*; Richard Rovere of the *New Yorker*; Alan Barth, a superb editorialist on legal and constitutional issues, and Murray Marder, both of the *Washington Post*; and Henry Luce and the editors of *Time* (once they saw that McCarthy's shabby crusade could not safely be treated as an amusing political windfall for Republicans). Edward R. Murrow played a part too. Murrow's "See It Now" television exposé of McCarthy on March 9 (the day the army forwarded the fateful chronology to Senators Russell and McClellan) had substantial if belated mass impact. The Alsops, however, had made McCarthy a special project from the outset. Their counterattack was not free of snobbery, but it transcended that defect and illuminated the issues McCarthy's investigative techniques raised. Long before the television cameras spotlighted his brutal incivility, the Alsops had made a principled case in print against one of the century's truly gifted American demagogues.

Chapter Nine The Dien Bien Phu Plot

At the beginning, few people foresaw that 1954 would become the pivotal year of the inquisitorial hysteria. The year opened with mixed gains and losses for those who were resisting it, but then the fear and hysteria that had broken out six years earlier gradually receded. Senator Joe McCarthy's spell would finally be broken in his head-on collision with the army, though it would take a while for the totality of the defeat to sink in. At the same time J. Robert Oppenheimer, the nation's most distinguished atomic scientist, would be humiliated in a messy affair that ended with the official withdrawal of his security clearance and his access to national defense secrets which, in any event, he carried in his own memory. No case of the "security" era, before or after, so completely illustrated the self-defeating lunacy of a system that alienated many of the nation's scientists.

It was also the year in which the continuing collapse of the European colonial empires set much of the agenda for debate about international security. A troubled peace had been signed in Korea the year before on the basis of a standoff at the 38th Parallel dividing north and south—the de facto boundary that the North Korean armies had violated three years earlier. Meanwhile, hundreds of miles to the south, the French were clinging to their last colonial foothold in Indochina. Joe Alsop was, as usual, deeply involved in both advocacy and agitation behind the scenes.

One evening in the mid-1960s, a young correspondent of the London *Times* named Peter Jay (later the British ambassador to Washington during the Carter administration) and his wife Margaret encountered Joe Alsop for the first time at a Washington party. The three later became close friends, so close that Joe Alsop and Margaret Jay would share a birthday party—his seventieth, her fortieth. But on this first meeting, the Jays had never before encountered Joe and did not know who he was. Their talk turned to Vietnam. Joe, as usual, pressed his unabashed views on the visitors, soliciting agreement at intervals with the loud "Huh?" that tended to punctuate his more assertive talk, and also seeking the Jays' continued company as the party began to break up. Could the Jays return with him to his house for a drink? Stay for dinner? If not, what about lunch the next day? The Jays were astonished by both the intensity of Joe's absorption in the foreign scene and the strength of his views. Peter Jay said, "You sound as if you believe in the 'domino effect.'" "Dear boy," Joe said, "I invented it."[1]

Long after his retirement from these far-off battles, Joe Alsop would be remembered as Washington's stoutest—some thought bitterest—advocate of the U.S. war in Vietnam. The American effort was in fact a continuation of the last stand of the French expeditionary force in 1954 at a place called Dien Bien Phu—"hell in a very small place," as Bernard Fall, one of the best reporters of that earlier Indochina war, called it.[2] Joe had zealously backed the French stand then, a decade or more before the United States crept slow-motion into the same tragic enterprise. The later defeat of the American-backed government of South Vietnam was, for him, the crowning testimony to the perils of what came to be called the "domino effect," his trademark thesis. He believed that if the United States accepted the collapse of Western interests in Vietnam in the same way that it had accepted a "concealed surrender" in Korea, it risked the collapse of freedom all across Asia. This was the theme of much of what Joe Alsop wrote about Indochina in 1954.

IN THE SPRING OF 1954, the French had concentrated their beleaguered force at Dien Bien Phu, a remote administrative post occupying a
valley in the highlands of northeastern Vietnam. The place was ringed by
hills controlled by the insurgent Viet Minh forces, commanded by the
same General Giap who would direct the struggle against U.S. intervention a decade later. But it was assumed that the foe would never manage
to get its artillery to the high ground—an assumption that, in early January, would prove to be a costly and decisive tactical miscalculation. The
Alsops anticipated the problems at Dien Bien Phu: Not long after the
French deployment there, an Alsop column titled "French Want More
Help in Indochina" astonished and upset the French government.[3]

The burden of the column was that unless France's allies (which could
only mean the United States and Britain) sent reinforcements in the next
three to six months, the French might recall their force from Indochina
and abandon the struggle against the Communists and their nationalist
allies. Joe Alsop said that he had been told in Paris that this capitulation
would come in "a matter of weeks" unless American troops were sent to
back up the faltering French effort.

Whether Joe's information was accurate or was simply the product of
his passionate conviction about the virtues of the French effort is hard
to say. It is certain, however, that the report jolted the French government. On January 5 Joe's friend Robert Joyce, U.S. chargé d'affaires in
Paris, cabled the State Department that the Quai D'Orsay was "in-
censed" at what it termed Joe's "deformation of [Jacquet's] comments
on Indochina." Marc Jacquet, secretary of state for the Associated States
(France's official name for Indochina) had told Joyce that Joe candidly
admitted to him that he meant to write a piece sufficiently provocative
to get Washington's attention. He "intend[ed] to force the hand of the
American government in this matter as the only means of saving the
situation."[4]

As we have seen, this was hardly the first occasion on which Joe Alsop
seemed to mix reporting—or, in any case, the supercharged opinionizing
that he represented as reporting—with backstage intrigue. The French
had been startled by the "unexpected suggestion" that American troops
might be called into Indochina. Jacquet told the U.S. chargé d'affaires
that in his conversation with Joe he had merely outlined several options,
mainly diplomatic. What French public opinion was demanding was a
decisive plan of action. (Years later, precisely the same public psycholo-

gy would operate as a constraint on American policy in Vietnam, when it seemed to many Americans that that policy's most striking characteristic was flabbiness and hesitation.) The real point Jacquet had tried to make, Joyce had learned and now cabled to his superiors in Washington, was that "within three to six months French public opinion will oblige the National Assembly to support only that government which can promise a solution to the Indochina problem, even if the solution is withdrawal." Moreover, "the policy of the French government for years has been to seek all forms of American aid other than direct troop intervention." Then Joyce came to the key point: "Jacquet attributed Alsop's distortions of what was said to the latter's emotional fervor and personal belief in the need for sending U.S. troops. He quoted Alsop as saying that if U.S. troops were sent to Indochina he 'wanted to take part in the campaign.' Jacquet said that rather than seek his opinion, Alsop inflicted his own. He also described Alsop's French as being poor and admitted the possibility that this may have been a contributing cause to his misrepresentation."

"Rather than seek his opinion, Alsop inflicted his own": a classic summary of numberless conversations Joe Alsop had, over the years, with high officials who were sought out for their views and information because they knew policy from the inside. This was not the end of the intrigue, however. In a classified cable from the State Department's Southeast Asian Affairs office to the U.S. embassy in Saigon, Philip Bonsal informed the U.S. ambassador that "a good deal has been going on in the Indochina field lately." A new National Security Council policy paper was being prepared. Additional American B-26 bombers would be sent to the French in Indochina, but so far there was "no practical answer" as to whether American pilots would also be provided to fly them. Air force ground crews in civilian clothes might be sent temporarily to keep the French airlift to its Dien Bien Phu garrison in operation. But U.S. officials would have to guard against the risk of the crews' involvement in combat or exposure to sabotage.

At the end of this long fill-in for the U.S. ambassador in Vietnam, Bonsal noted that he was scheduled to lunch shortly with Joe Alsop, who had "become extraordinarily pessimistic about the military situation" and "thinks that Dien Bien Phu will turn out to be a hopeless trap because the enemy will be able to cut off the French airlift." Bonsal believed, however, that Joe was wrong. The date was January 22, two weeks after the French government reacted so heatedly to what it viewed as Joe's "deformation" of its policy.

FIVE DAYS LATER, a cable from an embassy officer in Paris, Theodore Achilles, reported that the Paris *Herald Tribune* of January 27 had featured an Alsop column ("Where is Dien Bien Phu?") "which reveals details [of a] top secret French request [for] additional U.S. aid [in] Indochina." The Paris embassy now deplored the leak of "important military news" and, it continued, the Alsops' willingness to report "items of considerable interest to enemy and potentially great harm to allies for sake of scoop." The French government, Achilles informed Washington, was deeply worried that word of American involvement with the French forces might easily give the Chinese an excuse to step up their own low-level intervention. How, Achilles asked, could the Alsops have learned of this "top secret project" (using American civilian pilots to fly airlift transports) even before the United States had officially transmitted its response to the French request? Putting two and two together, it would seem clear from the sequence of these exchanges that in the luncheon meeting of which he had spoken in the January 22 cable, Bonsal had attempted to talk Joe Alsop out of his gloom over Dien Bien Phu by telling him of the proposed American reinforcements and that Joe had indiscreetly used the leak in his column. The leak was so disturbing to the French government, Achilles reported, that the cabinet had held two special meetings on the matter.[5]

The little journalistic drama continued. Responding on February 9 to Bonsal's long cable, Ambassador Donald Heath in Saigon took a hawkish view. If the Allies had the nerve to "throw American or Korean battalions into the breach," said Heath, the war could be brought to a quick and favorable conclusion. Heath did not believe the Chinese would intervene. But if they did, "so much the better. We would then take up the war where we left off with the unfortunate armistice in Korea and we would win it. . . . We would put Chiang Kai-shek back on the mainland in southern China and shake, maybe even destroy, the power of the Chinese Communist government." This was the maximalist program and a giddily optimistic one in the light of both the French experience and later American efforts to do far less. In its optimism Heath's outlook of course contrasted with Joe Alsop's gloomy prognosis. "I was amused at Joe Alsop's pessimism," Heath wrote. "He is an emotional young man."[6]

By spring, the situation in Indochina had gone from worrisome to desperate. The French army's area of control at Dien Bien Phu had narrowed to less than a square mile. The Viet Minh forces, directed by the same General Giap who would later direct the effort that drove the Americans from Vietnam, had managed (in the face of expert predictions against such a move) to drag artillery up into the surrounding hills, affording them a deadly plunging fire into the French stronghold. The Alsops reported—accurately, as we know now—that the Eisenhower administration had decided in principle to help the French out of their jam. But there was a big *if* attached—*if* the European Allies, meaning mainly the British, would join the effort and lend at least token approval and support. President Eisenhower, for reasons later to be disputed, had made that the sine qua non of U.S. intervention, and ultimately it was the refusal of the British to cooperate that blocked the aggressive course of action advocated by Vice President Nixon, Admiral Arthur Radford, and others.

The Alsops' columns tracked the internal administration debate in detail and warned that failure to act risked the "loss" of all Asia to what the columnists still called "the Soviet empire." The closest parallel, the Alsops suggested, resorting once more to cautionary historical precedents of pre–World War II vintage, had been the failure of the Versailles Treaty guarantor powers to respond forcefully to Hitler's remilitarization of the Rhineland in 1936. The view, if not the historical parallel, was vigorously embraced by the interventionists in Eisenhower's inner circle. Yet it remained unclear just what sort of game the French were playing. A Geneva conference on Indochina had now convened, and as the debate continued, the American secretary of state, John Foster Dulles, adamantly opposed even a de facto partition and later refused to initial the Geneva accords which embraced that short-lived solution. It was unclear, however, whether the French themselves opposed such a compromise settlement. Did they really want American help—an "internationalization" of the battle to shore up their position in Vietnam? Or did they want only the credible threat of such an intervention to strengthen their bargaining position at the table in Geneva?

Was this, in fact, the "End at Dienbienphu?," an Alsop column asked on April 30; and again their commentary was seeded with historical parallels: "The battle at Dienbienphu now resembles the battle of Yorktown. One hundred and seventy-five years ago, when Cornwallis surrendered to Washington, the British were still able to carry on the war in America. They had the men and the resources to do so. But they did not want to do so. Official reports have warned the American policymakers that a defeat at Dienbienphu will be the same kind of psychological blow to the French, causing them to want to end the Indochinese war at all costs."[7]

The shift in historical examples from the Munich period to the American Revolution seems almost refreshing. But as usual, the prospect was described as ominous. No less than the world's strategic balance was at issue, according to this column, since the president and the National Security Council had agreed "long ago" that the loss of Indochina meant the eventual loss of "all the rest of Asia." And that gloomy prospect reinforced Senator William F. Knowland's still gloomier forecast, the Alsops wrote, that "once Asia is absorbed, Communism can turn upon the West with invincible power."

As late as the middle of May, the French still appeared to be testing U.S. interest in an "internationalization" of the war; and the Alsops were reporting that within six weeks the White House would seek congressional authority for American intervention. Their information clearly came from the administration hawks. They ignored or discounted the far more hesitant congressional attitudes, which as we know now were the decisive sentiments. In a famous remark long remembered by the voters of North Carolina, their junior senator, Kerr Scott—a dairyman whose large farms lay near the small mill town of Haw River—remarked that "Indochina is a long way from Haw River"; he probably spoke, at the time, for more Americans than did Joe Alsop or, behind the scenes, Richard Nixon. Nor did the interventionists understand Dwight D. Eisenhower's "hidden-hand" management of the opposition to intervention, as his biographer, Fred Greenstein, would later characterize it. In any event, the administration again declined to ask for congressional approval for the use of American forces unless the British would join; and at Geneva the British were clearly seeking a negotiated settlement— a "Munich," as Joe Alsop naturally called it.

In fact, there was another and deeper level of intrigue. By early June, it became more and more evident that the French had been playing a more subtle diplomatic game than the Alsops had imagined in their heroic cheerleading for an American rescue party. The French, they now reported on June 11, had "seemed to want American aid" in the war and had twice sought "one-shot" bombing. But "appearances have been misleading" (an understatement). A majority of the National Assembly and the Laniel cabinet wanted a negotiated settlement in Indochina. Thus the overtures for American aid had been "intended to impress the communist negotiators at Geneva." The proof was that "we have only been asked to talk about entering the war," but "have most conspicuously not been asked to join the fighting."[8]

This discovery of French duplicity plunged Joe Alsop into his gloomiest musings yet about the future of freedom in Asia and elsewhere. With French capitulation at hand, General Douglas MacArthur's judgment about Korea had been "vindicated." China's military power should have been smashed while it could be, while the U.S. atomic monopoly, a wasting asset, was still intact. Failure in Indochina was "the direct result of the failure in Korea."[9] Thus the dominos continued to fall, at least as the world looked from 2720 Dumbarton Avenue in Washington.

Chapter Ten Oppenheimer, The Bomb, and Survival

The showdown with Senator Joe McCarthy unfolded, in this busy spring of 1954, against a background of crisis in Southeast Asia—the final collapse, at Dien Bien Phu, of the nearly decade-long French effort to recapture a foothold for the *mission civilisatrice* in Indochina.

Again, the prospect of that collapse had kindled serious thoughts of U.S. armed intervention, and Joe Alsop had been actively promoting such an intervention. The Eisenhower administration's decision to refrain stimulated the usual apocalyptic musings: The negotiated partition of the country at Geneva was, like the Korean armistice before it, a "concealed surrender" that would invite further aggression. Sooner or later there would have to be a showdown; and for a time in the mid-1950s Joe began to toy (not, in the end, very seriously) with the idea of a so-called preventive war—or, in the less drastic version, preventive showdown—with the Soviet Union.

By mid-1954 these doomsday musings had become even more theoretical than they had been a few years earlier, when the United States had held an unchallenged nuclear monopoly. As Sir Winston Churchill and others immediately understood, the nearly simultaneous development of American and Russian hydrogen weapons had placed a nuclear exchange of any character beyond the pale of rational strategic purpose, where it was to remain at least for the rest of the Cold War. In Churchill's words, addressed to the House of Commons just after the news of the Soviet detonation of a thermonuclear device, the world's safety had become "the sturdy child of terror, and survival the twin brother of annihilation." In time this poetic Churchillism would be reduced to the prosaic acronym MAD, or "mutual assured destruction." Others, including for a time Joe and Stewart Alsop, came more slowly to the acceptance of this stalemate. The enduring dream of a nuclear strategy that might confer superiority, by some ingenious combination of offensive and defensive capabilities, continued to intrigue scholastic theorists of nuclear deterrence. The theory of "preventive" or "preemptive" war was one passing manifestation of the dream; continuing recriminations and interservice rivalries flowing from the strategic nuclear policy choices of the Truman years were another. The year 1954 witnessed Joe Alsop's apparently contradictory preoccupation with both. The Alsops' passionate sally into the battle over the Oppenheimer security case was, as we shall see, much the more heartfelt. But there was a link. Seeking to document J. Robert Oppenheimer's hard-headedness about the Soviet threat (in the face of suspicion that he was a poor security risk), Joe Alsop wrote this approving passage in his tract *We Accuse*: "As time passed, indeed, Oppenheimer became the only truly eminent American outside the armed services . . . who was willing to discuss dispassionately the idea of preventive war to save the world from Communist tyranny." Oppenheimer's views on this point were shocking to his fellow atomic scientists. But given Joe's regard for Oppenheimer, his was imprimatur enough—at least for purposes of theoretical speculation. In a way perhaps more teasing than serious, Joe pretended to find the idea of a preventive strike at least faintly credible.

With the exception of Oppenheimer, whose views Joe might have exaggerated to make a debating point with the great physicist's accusers, the idea had never enjoyed serious support—not, at least, among civilian strategic thinkers. It had been openly discussed in speculative terms at military seminars and the like. For instance, in a lecture at the Air

121
*Oppenheimer,
The Bomb, and
Survival*

War College on April 10, 1947, the always sober and serious strategist George F. Kennan, who enjoyed the highest prestige with the Alsops, reflected briefly on the subject. But as his biographer John Lewis Gaddis writes, Kennan thought of it "only as a last resort, to be considered if Soviet war-making potential was exceeding that of the United States and if opportunities for peaceful solutions had been exhausted."[1] In those 1947 remarks, Kennan was probably responding in reflective and rational terms to a hypothetical question raised by someone in his audience.

Yet the idea itself enjoyed an underground life, never close to becoming policy but provoking discussion and popping up now and then for speculation, even at high levels, through the early years of the Cold War. Until late in the fifties, even sophisticated opinion held that the Soviet Union was in league with China and was steadily gaining ground toward strategic weapons parity, or even superiority. In September 1953, discussing the problems of nuclear deterrence in a memorandum to Secretary of State Dulles, President Eisenhower mused on the hypothetical situation in which "we would be forced to consider whether or not our duty to future generations did not require us to initiate war at the most propitious moment that we could designate." A year later, however, Eisenhower publicly dismissed the idea as "an impossibility" to which he would not listen if anyone seriously proposed it.[2] The later reaction was surely closer to his considered view.

Thus, when Joe Alsop began airing the idea in occasional columns of the time, it was not exactly an original thought; it had been around. Few of Joe's friends and regular correspondents shared his gloomy view that the Geneva settlement on Indochina had sprung directly from a "failure" in Korea or would in itself lead inevitably to other strategic defeats and setbacks. These colleagues—particularly the historian Arthur Schlesinger, Jr., and Paul Nitze, with whom Joe privately shared his ruminations—were even less prone to share Alsop's entrancement with the idea that the time might be approaching for a preventive showdown.

THE CHRONOLOGY of their exchanges of correspondence on this alarming subject leaves little doubt that it was a by-product of the approaching "capitulation" in Indochina. It was argued that by mid-June 1954 a window was closing—the mirror image of that "window of [strategic] vulnerability" which would figure in the nuclear debates of the 1970s and 1980s. With its strategic superiority intact, ran the argument, the United States could wreak such heavy damage on the Soviet Union that with luck, a political revolt and a salutary change of leadership and ideology would follow.

Josef Stalin had died a year earlier, in March 1953, and the new Soviet leadership and policy had not yet jelled. Within a year or so the option of this kind of one-shot strategic defeat of the Soviet Union would vanish forever, as the Soviet "air-atomic" buildup (about which the Alsops had long cried alarm) would make such an attack prohibitively dangerous.

But there was a flaw in this logic that even Joe Alsop had to acknowledge: It was odd to argue that the hopes for a more moderate Soviet leadership and policy which accompanied Stalin's death could somehow be improved by armed attack. Indeed, the thinking of President Eisenhower's most influential advisers at the White House was that the time had come for a much more conciliatory approach. That advice, much more than surreal speculation about unprovoked strikes, seems to have set the tone of Eisenhower's reaction.

Moreover, as the Alsops surely knew, since they had reported the story in greater detail than most others, by failing to heed J. Robert Oppenheimer's pleas for a credible strategic defense system—which would soon be a key issue in the background of the Oppenheimer security case—the United States had left itself with a "glass jaw." Its defensive planning had been dominated by the jealousies of the Air Force's Strategic Air Command (SAC). As we will see in the next chapter, SAC believed that any resources added to defensive systems would necessarily be withdrawn from deterrent forces. Air defense had been "criminally neglected," Joe wrote in his column of June 13, which was inspired by the Oppenheimer case. "The American planners asking their rhetorical questions about Soviet atomic bombs already show the creeping paralysis of policy that Dr. Oppenheimer foresaw."[3]

It would soon become a self-evident premise of the atomic age that, moral issues aside, it could never be rational to fight a nuclear war for *any* objective, hence that some sort of rough parity between the nuclear powers would have to be accepted and maintained for the sake of stability. But even as late as the summer of 1954, this theorem was not yet obvious. Churchill, speaking on the news of the explosion of the first Soviet hydrogen-bomb device, noted the deadlock of the nuclear powers; and Oppenheimer, in a notable lecture of the time, compared the rivals to scorpions in a bottle, neither of which could sting the other without bringing death upon himself. But few then shared either Churchill's matchless rhetorical powers or Oppenheimer's sense of realism.

It was in this rather confused setting that Joe Alsop set out to test the climate of informed opinion on the "preventive showdown" option, even while conceding the "glass jaw." If he took the idea even half seriously, he cannot have been encouraged by the reaction. Arthur Schlesinger's was searching and skeptical; Paul Nitze's (as might have been predicted, had the then still-classified text of Nitze's NSC-68 memorandum been available) was withering.

From Cambridge, on June 1, Schlesinger wrote of his unease that Joe had been giving currency, in conversation and even in the column, to the preventive war idea — a "blind alley," the historian called it, entirely apart from the imaginable moral objections. No such "knockout blow against either Russia or China" could safely be anticipated, "and anything less would be fatal." Schlesinger did not view his caveat as an argument for weakness or passivity. He wanted "the best radar net . . . the most potent [bombers], the most advanced guided missiles, the most ghastly atomic weapons, the strongest and most prosperous allies." With these assets, war could be deterred "long enough for the whole relationship to pass into another historic phase."[4] This, of course, was perfectly orthodox Kennan containment doctrine, as enunciated seven years earlier in the famous Long Telegram and in the "Mr. X" article fashioned from it, in which Kennan, the government's ranking Sovietologist, had spelled out a long-term strategy for confronting Soviet power. Stewart Alsop always, and Joe in his less excited moments, accepted the premises of containment; and of course the strategy would eventually be fully vindicated. But it would require monumental patience, and all along there were those who considered a military showdown inevitable, as well as those — not a few — who advocated one. Joe seems unmistakably to have been for a time beguiled by their arguments, though to what degree we do not know. He could not have been altogether sold on them when he turned to his most respected friends for their views.

Having obtained Schlesinger's views, Joe then sent the correspondence on to Nitze, the former State Department policy planning chief. With the advent of the Eisenhower administration, Nitze, the past and future star of many negotiations with the Soviet Union, had left the government and was now president of a lobbying group, the Foreign Service Educational Foundation. He expressed skepticism on every count. His "own experience"—the allusion was clearly to Nitze's participation in the Strategic Bombing Survey after World War II—had been that "few strategic bombing people . . . can give any reasonable analysis of the link between a given level of physical destruction and the economic, military, political and psychological results expected to flow from that level. . . . Their beliefs rest more on faith than analysis." Nitze guessed that "a level of destruction ranging from 50 to 75 percent of Russian cities and important industrial concentrations might be possible." But most of the cities would be evacuated, and the Soviet armies and air force would survive. Atomic retaliation against American cities and industries would certainly follow.

Nitze estimated that the Russians might have as many as 150 deliverable atomic weapons. If only 50 percent reached their targets in the United States, a "considerable percentage" of American population and industry would be wiped out. On the political side of the equation, "most of mankind" would be "properly alienated" by a sudden American attack, and the prospects for success in another round of warfare would be dim. But even assuming an optimum outcome—even assuming that the Soviet and Chinese regimes crumbled—"we would then have to run something very close to a Pax Americana in the world." "American democracy as we have known it" might not survive these imperial responsibilities, since democracy and imperialism "have rarely mixed well for long." Finally, Nitze noted, this radical idea enjoyed no support in the Eisenhower administration, in Congress, or among the public, and it was far too important an issue to be left to generals.[5]

That Nitze, the principal author of NSC-68, should deliver this annihilating response to Joe's romance with the doctrine of "preventive war" may have been the decisive stroke: the idea rapidly disappeared from the Alsop column and from Joe's private letters. Probably the romance had been Joe's impulsive and temperamental response to the "defeat" in Indochina. And even if Joe's assumption were true, as the Soviets moved toward nuclear parity, the window of opportunity for a showdown was narrowing and soon would close for good.

How seriously Joe took these lugubrious musings, or meant his friends to take them, it is now hard to say. In his memoirs, Joe names "the four men I know to have advocated preventive war . . . an improbable group" consisting of Churchill, Bertrand Russell, Curtis LeMay, and

John Paton Davies, "who does not admit it." He does not list himself among them. He names the four by way of recalling that Davies, early in the postwar period, had written a State Department policy-planning memorandum on the subject for Kennan. According to Joe's account, Kennan was so alarmed that he gathered all the copies of the memo and burned them.[6]

Although Joe habitually predicted dire outcomes for what he regarded as excessively timid American policies, his intellectual ties were almost all to the moderates in Cold War strategy—Kennan, Nitze, Dean Acheson, Charles "Chip" Bohlen, and others. Given that Joe enjoyed contention, his brief flirtation with the "preventive war" nostrum may have been designed to draw precisely the argumentative responses it did. In any case, "preventive war" made only veiled and muted appearance in any of the columns. No *Saturday Evening Post* article of the period mentioned it seriously. Joe openly raised the idea only in letters. Even a sympathizer with the idea, Frank L. Howley of New York University, believed, as he wrote to Joe, that the opportunity had passed by the mid-1950s. "We could have forced the [Cold War] issues" as late as 1949, Howley thought. But with the balance of power now equalized it probably was too late.[7]

This brief speculation forms a useful background to the other great major domestic security issue of 1954—the Oppenheimer security clearance case. As in no other episode, the issues of defense and domestic security were closely linked by the Eisenhower administration's decision to bar the great physicist's access to defense secrets. As much as McCarthyism, it was a representative saga of these years; and, as usual, the Alsops were in the thick of it.

ON THE MORNING of June 2, 1954, Joe Alsop wrote a blunt and brief note to Gordon Gray, a former secretary of the army who had been, more recently, the chairman of a special board of inquiry that had just recommended the lifting of J. Robert Oppenheimer's security clearance. "By a single foolish and ignoble act," he told Gray, "you have cancelled the entire debt that this country owes you."

Joe later claimed that he had written the letter for the wastebasket, but his secretary assumed otherwise, and the sharp words were soon on their way to Chapel Hill, where Gray now served as president of the University of North Carolina. As chairman of a three-man security board for the

Atomic Energy Commission (AEC), Gray had joined, not without reluctance, in recommending the permanent removal of Oppenheimer's clearance—the "foolish and ignoble act" to which Joe Alsop referred.

The letter permanently strained his relations with Gray, who suggested in reply that the use of the word "ignoble" was libelous. Gray continued to cite the letter as evidence of Joe's bias, even in an off-the-record talk to the Brook Club in New York, of which both he and Joe were members. The exchange was typical of the personal strains that grew out of this monumental and divisive episode.[8]

Coinciding more or less exactly with the Army-McCarthy hearings, the Oppenheimer case added yet another layer of intrigue to the issues of defense and domestic security and the critically important issue of how the government ought to deal with its most distinguished scientists, many of whom had, like Oppenheimer, overcome professional doubts to enlist in the wartime atomic bomb effort.

Oppenheimer, chief among them, had directed the construction of the first atomic bombs at Los Alamos between 1943 and 1945. A tall, spectrally thin New Yorker of legendary brilliance, Oppenheimer had been schooled at Harvard and, after postgraduate work at Cambridge and Göttingen, had imported the new theoretical physics to generations of students at Berkeley and the California Institute of Technology. A scientist with a gift for administering huge projects like Los Alamos, he was also a mystic and a student of Hindu poetry. Joe Alsop knew him as a fellow member of the Harvard Board of Overseers and of its visiting committee to the physics department. From his earliest government work, commencing with the organization of the Los Alamos project in March 1943, Oppenheimer had been shadowed by security investigations. No scientist was more deeply respected by his colleagues; yet none had been so closely watched over by security officials or more frequently accused of indiscretion and disloyalty.

In the Atomic Energy Act of 1947, Congress had ultimately placed the nation's atomic weapons program under civilian direction. It had hedged the program in secrecy. Oppenheimer had been the obvious choice to head the AEC's advisory committee, a Sanhedrin of great names in American physics and chemistry. In that post, he had presided over the crucial deliberations of the postwar period—including those in the autumn of 1949, which brought a unanimous recommendation that President Truman *not* pursue a "crash program" to develop the hydrogen bomb, or "super" as it then was known. Oppenheimer was understood to have opposed the H-bomb, but so had all but one of the other members of the advisory committee. A more sinister whisper had it that Oppenheimer had obstructed the project even after President Truman ordered it carried forward in January 1950, four months after the explosion of the Soviets' first atomic bomb.

THESE SUSPICIONS NOTWITHSTANDING, Oppenheimer had repeatedly been cleared to handle the nation's most sensitive nuclear and military secrets. But now, as political associations were increasingly imagined to have sinister implications, Oppenheimer's bred suspicion. As a West Coast academic before the war, he had contributed money to various Popular Front causes. His younger brother Frank, also a physicist, had been a Communist Party member. His wife Kitty had previously been married to a Communist firebrand and organizer. His former fiancée, Jean Tatlock, had been on the left, along with many of his friends, protégés, students, and professional colleagues — much in the fashion of California academic life during the Great Depression years.

But how, after so many years of worry about Oppenheimer's political reliability, had his security case now suddenly come to a showdown? The timing owed much to the national mood. When the Alsops broke the story of the Gray Board hearing on Oppenheimer in the *Washington Post*, they wrote that "political observers here have no doubt that Senator Joseph R. McCarthy had [allegations against Oppenheimer] in mind when he charged in a recent telecast [April 6] that there had been an 'eighteen-month deliberate delay' in making the American hydrogen bomb. . . . McCarthy is known to have been secretly building a case against Dr. Oppenheimer and other scientists since last summer. He is expected to make sensational charges in his speech scheduled for delivery in Texas on April 21." The hearings on McCarthy's fight with the army were scheduled to start the next day, April 22, and given McCarthy's methods, this timing seemed more than coincidental.[9]

The Alsops believed at the time that McCarthy's reference to an alleged "eighteen-month delay" in H-bomb development had inspired the Eisenhower administration to anticipate McCarthy. But the story was far more complicated. The administration's hand had indeed been forced, but not by McCarthy's threats. The suspicions arose in a far more reputable quarter.

As staff director of the congressional Joint Committee on Atomic Energy, William L. Borden had puzzled over the Oppenheimer security file for years. After leaving the committee when the control of Congress changed, Borden found that he could make sense of Oppenheimer's behavior only on the hypothesis that Oppenheimer had been a Soviet agent all the while. Having satisfied himself of that probability, Borden summed up his surmise on November 7, 1953, in a long and detailed letter to FBI director J. Edgar Hoover. Borden stated his "exhaustively considered opinion . . . that more probably than not J. Robert Oppenheimer is an agent of the Soviet Union." The circumstantial evidence was compelling: Oppenheimer had supported the H-bomb program until the bombing of Hiroshima, then had begun to urge fellow physicists to "desist." He had been "remarkably influential" in urging a long hiatus in "super" research from mid-1946 through January 1950. Borden thought his conclusions squared also with information "furnished by Klaus Fuchs," the British atomic spy at Los Alamos, "that the Soviets had acquired an agent in Berkeley."[10]

Borden was neither a demagogue nor a crackpot; and his letter to Hoover reached the White House just as Eisenhower's attorney general, Herbert Brownell, had stimulated an angry partisan controversy over President Truman's supposed failure to pursue leads in the case of Harry Dexter White, a former high treasury official who had died suddenly under suspicion.

When Borden's suspicions came to his attention, Eisenhower was strongly advised that he must "make a record" of action on Oppenheimer. Hence, just before Christmas 1953, he ordered that the Atomic Energy Commission place a "blank wall" between Oppenheimer and the nation's defense secrets and initiate a confidential review of the scientist's security status. It was not the first round of charges against Oppenheimer. Five years earlier, Paul Crouch, one of the professional ex-Communist witnesses, had told California's legislative Committee on Un-American Activities that he had once attended a Communist cell meeting at Oppenheimer's house in Berkeley. Oppenheimer, however, could show that during the time of the alleged meeting—July and early August 1945—he had been at his New Mexico ranch near Los Alamos. In their column, the Alsops had called Crouch's charges a lie. Crouch had threatened a libel action but died before it came to trial.[11]

WILLIAM LISCUM BORDEN'S ROLE in the Oppenheimer matter puzzled his old schoolmaster at St. Albans in Washington, where Borden had led the class of 1938. "So far as I can see," wrote the Rev. Charles Martin to Stewart Alsop, "Liscum, who is a very able, very intense young man, was possessed of devils [and] unable to bear up under the strains which were imposed upon him. . . . He lost a sense of balance and . . . [wrote] the letter . . . a part of the tragedy of suspicion and distrust which is our time."[12]

That Borden and others had felt the new anxieties of the atomic age was not strange. For the first time, people had begun to speak casually and credibly of the annihilation of the planet as the possible penalty of lax security. There had been documented cases of atomic spying, too. The Rosenberg spy case hinged on the charge that David Greenglass, Ethel Rosenberg's brother, had stolen the design for the triggering device of the plutonium bomb and passed it to the Russians. The stories of Bruno Pontecorvo, Alan Nunn May, and Klaus Fuchs were similar and reinforced the anxiety. Extreme secrecy seemed to be the only answer, especially after the Russians rejected the Baruch Plan for international control and regulation of atomic energy.

On December 10, a month after Borden's letter, the AEC voted to hold a formal inquiry. Oppenheimer was summoned to Washington and told by the commission's chairman, Admiral Lewis Strauss, that he was again under suspicion.

Thus the sequence of events clearly seems to have begun with the Borden letter. What further evidence led the Alsops to believe that it was largely motivated by Strauss's vendetta against Oppenheimer? For if McCarthy planned to exploit the same charges, as they had reported, the AEC and the Eisenhower administration could hardly afford to sweep them aside.

The story was tangled. Strauss and Oppenheimer, as the Alsops knew from personal familiarity with both men, were almost polar opposites. Strauss, though untrained in science, had taught himself much about atomic energy. The 1913 recession had almost ruined his father's shoe business in Richmond, Virginia, and the young Strauss had been forced to abandon his formal education at age nineteen and hit the road as a salesman. Strauss remained sensitive to the condescensions of more fortunate figures, especially Oppenheimer, who once had commented that Strauss was "not greatly cultured." Strauss certainly fell short of Oppenheimer's standards of learning, as most people did. When Strauss was an AEC commissioner and Oppenheimer was the AEC's most eminent adviser, the two men had occasionally clashed over policy. One such clash had left lingering aftershocks.

In the spring of 1949, the Norwegians—U.S. partners in the NATO alliance—were seeking iron isotopes for aircraft research. Influential Republicans in the Senate resisted the request, charging the AEC, then under the chairmanship of David Lillienthal, with mismanagement. When the export issue came before the Joint Committee on Atomic Energy, both Strauss, an AEC commissioner, and Oppenheimer, chairman of the AEC's advisory committee, were called to testify.

Strauss made his usual case for restricting isotope exports to those suitable for medical uses. Oppenheimer took a diametrically contrary view. He flippantly conceded that while isotopes might be used for atomic energy development, "you use a shovel for atomic energy development. . . . You can use a bottle of beer. . . . The fact is that during the war and after the war these materials have played no significant part, and in my own knowledge no part at all." Those who were present sensed that the proud Strauss, who was at hand for Oppenheimer's performance, took Oppenheimer's bantering testimony as a slap in the face. Strauss seemed enraged. Afterwards, the AEC's counsel, Joseph Volpe, told Oppenheimer, "Robert, you did much too well for your own good."[13] "Neither man accepted opposition easily," writes Strauss's biographer, Richard Pfau, "and both were arrogant."[14] Yet in this strangely involved relationship, Strauss had also done good turns for Oppenheimer. As chairman of the Board of Trustees of the Institute for Advanced Study in Princeton, he had been mainly responsible for hiring Oppenheimer as director.

WHEN THE three-member Gray Board convened its closed hearings in May, the questions raised in Borden's letter had been refined and elaborated and Oppenheimer had filed a formal reply. The preparations remained secret until early April, when the *New York Times*'s Washington correspondent, James Reston, broke the story—closely followed by the Alsops.

Oppenheimer's chief administrative judge, Gordon Gray—the old friend to whom Joe eventually wrote his angry letter—was the heir to a North Carolina tobacco and newspaper fortune. After cabinet service under President Truman, Gray had recently become president of the university system that included his alma mater, the University of North Carolina. Gray, a shy intellectual, had passed a gilded youth in his family's vast, rambling chateau called Graylyn, near Winston-Salem, and then led his class at Chapel Hill and at Yale Law School. He struck some of his classmates as unworldly. Fellow members of DKE, his Chapel Hill fraternity, remembered the young Gray reading books while noisy parties swirled about him — evidence of his celebrated powers of concentration. His powers of communication were less impressive and often assumed a legalistic form. When explaining his views on school traditions to undergraduates, Gray was apt to spend more time on what he was *not* saying than on what he *was* saying. But AEC regulations mandated a fact-finding process, not a trial; and Gordon Gray was nothing if not judicious. When the hearings ended, he complained in his report of the rigidity of the security system rules but voted to apply them, even with their grave defects, to Oppenheimer's disadvantage. He and another board member voted to suspend Oppenheimer's clearance permanently. The third board member, a retired academic chemist, dissented.

Reviewing the Oppenheimer case three decades later, McGeorge Bundy, a historian and the national security adviser for President Kennedy, wrote that Oppenheimer had been railroaded — that the AEC's chief counsel, Roger Robb, "fully understood that his assignment from his client [Strauss's AEC] was to bring Oppenheimer down if he could."[15] Robb indeed operated more as prosecutor than as fact-finder. And though it was not known at the time, Strauss had had Oppenheimer's phone tapped and was giving Robb "guidance" based on the wiretaps. (Robb later denied to Strauss's biographer that he had known about the wiretapping.) The Alsops, despite their intimate ties with Oppenheimer and his camp, did not know of the wiretapping. It would have been a crushing trump card in their case against Strauss.[16]

EVEN WITHOUT the wiretapping information, however, they were superbly equipped to grasp and explain the intricacies of the case. Every major security issue, of strategic planning and secret-keeping, had figured in their advocacy of strong American defenses. They had supported Truman's decision to proceed with the U.S. hydrogen bomb, and they maintained close ties with well-informed physicists. Stewart frequently collaborated with Ralph Lapp, who had worked on the early atomic bombs at Los Alamos; the two men joined forces on *Saturday Evening Post* accounts of the decision to build the H-bomb and on stories about the then-obscure hazards of radiation and radioactive fallout.

The Alsops believed that if the Gray Board's decision went against Oppenheimer it would demoralize key scientists and jeopardize their vital collaboration in government defense research that had begun with the Manhattan Project. The scientific revolution in warfare and the exponential growth of the importance of research made that cooperation essential. The lesson of both World Wars seemed to be that the nation which most effectively mobilized its scientific elite would win the new struggle for strategic supremacy. The new chemistry of munitions had been vital in World War I, and radar and atomic weapons had been decisive in the Second World War; it made no sense now, in the midst of an equally deadly struggle, to undercut scientific morale in the name of security. As they mordantly wrote in a Matter of Fact column on October 1, three months after Oppenheimer's clearance was permanently suspended, "The Eisenhower administration is likely to have to answer a short, highly practical question—'Do we really need scientists, or can we just make do with Lewis Strauss?'"[17]

Gray and Morgan eventually rejected the most damaging formal charges, rebuffing Borden's suspicion that Oppenheimer was "probably" a Soviet agent. Oppenheimer had been, they affirmed, both loyal and discreet. But his political associations and duplicities were troubling. Indeed, Gray and Morgan blundered into a morass from which the full AEC would later seek to retrieve them. They suggested that Oppenheimer had been unenthusiastic about the hydrogen bomb and, while not actually opposing it, had chilled the enthusiasm of his fellow scientists. More "enthusiastic support" from him "would perhaps have encouraged other leading scientists to work on the program." His skepticism had "an adverse effect on the recruitment of scientists and the progress of the scientific effort."[18]

Since the Gray Board proceeding itself probably damaged the scientific effort far more than Oppenheimer could ever have dreamed of doing, this was a strange conclusion. The Gray Board's choice of words was certainly ominous, implying that what the nation needed from its key scientists was not their best professional judgment but emotional commitment to whatever the political leadership ordered. It was true that Oppenheimer had loathed the H-bomb, for strategic and military as

133
*Oppenheimer,
The Bomb, and
Survival*

well as for ethical and temperamental reasons. So had the other scientists on the AEC advisory board. But Oppenheimer had assumed all along that the "miserable thing" would be built if the theoretical problems could be surmounted. What he had specifically opposed in 1949, along with James Conant, Isidor Rabi, Enrico Fermi, and the others, was a so-called crash program, which at the time made no scientific sense.

Gray and Morgan apparently failed to grasp the technical problem as it had appeared five years earlier, in October 1949, when the scientists under Oppenheimer's leadership were called upon to advise the AEC and Truman. The Gray Board's criticism implied that Oppenheimer was being disqualified to share the nation's nuclear secrets on the grounds that he had held politically incorrect views—grounds more familiar in totalitarian states. In its ratification of the Gray Board finding a few weeks later, the AEC discreetly passed over the "lack of enthusiasm" charge and turned to other grounds, some altogether new, for sustaining the judgment on Oppenheimer's Q clearance, the highest category.

IN A BRILLIANT series of columns that began on June 4, the Alsops demanded, "Just what the devil is national security?" If, as the Gray Board declared, the nation was indebted to Oppenheimer for "loyal and magnificent service," and if he had been neither disloyal nor indiscreet, what could possibly be the sense of security rules that forced his removal from trust? Gordon Gray, in deploring the security rules he reluctantly enforced, had come near asking the same question. He had spoken of the possibility of reaching a very different conclusion but for the "rigid circumscription" of the security rules.

"The real threat to the security of this nation," the Alsops wrote, using the Oppenheimer case to reinforce an old complaint, "is that we are in danger of losing the air-atomic supremacy that has been this country's whole defense in the post-war years." It was self-defeating to look "at the little things and not the big things." The security proceeding had "sacrificed the bell-wether of the scientific flock . . . to satisfy the personal spite of . . . Admiral Lewis Strauss." The columns continued one after another, in a rolling barrage, throughout the month of June. Their gist was that Oppenheimer was a victim of officious stupidity and Strauss the instigator of his downfall. In later years, Joe Alsop would explain the truly extraordinary, almost obsessive focus on the case by telling friends that he had been "goddamned angry."[19]

But were the Alsops right in assuming that Strauss was acting as Oppenheimer's persecutor? It is time to look more deeply into this charge, which lay at the center of their argument.

Like his mentor and idol, Herbert Hoover, Lewis Strauss had made an early personal fortune (in investment banking) and turned to public service and philanthropy. He had taken an unusually early interest in nuclear research—his mother had required radiation treatment for cancer—and personally subsidized the researches of Leo Szilard and other pioneer investigators. As the Alsops acknowledged in rare moments of generosity to Strauss—who otherwise, like Louis Johnson, had the misfortune to qualify as an irredeemable bête noire—Strauss had made useful contributions. He had pushed for the deployment of air-sampling devices that enabled the United States to monitor early Soviet developments in atomic bomb research; that was how the first Soviet atomic test had been detected in 1949.

Strauss's biographer, Richard Pfau, views the Alsops' theory of Strauss's role in the Oppenheimer affair as a "caricature."[20] But almost everyone who knew both Strauss and Oppenheimer and had observed their relationship over the years believed that personal animus had crept into the balance. It was far from unthinkable, for instance, that the famous 1949 hearing on isotope exports had been a "crystallizing event," as the Alsops wrote. In their pamphlet *We Accuse*, the Alsops returned again and again to their belief that the isotope issue had incited Strauss's rage and later his retaliation: "With such a man as Strauss Oppenheimer was fated from the first to get on badly. . . . [Oppenheimer] has high intellectual standards. He insists on them, with more than a trace of intellectual snobbery and sometimes with cold scorn for those who fall short. . . . He is not patient with obtuseness, and his tongue can be very cutting . . . faults [which] were bound to exaggerate and indeed to inflame the faults of Strauss."

Even Strauss's sponsorship of Oppenheimer as director of the Institute for Advanced Study had very possibly caused tension, since Strauss imagined that "he had placed Oppenheimer under an obligation," while Oppenheimer acted independently and occasionally rejected Strauss's judgment in making some appointments. Oppenheimer, the Alsops wrote, assumed "he had been given a job because he was worthy of it." In offering this fairly basic analysis, the columnists may have passed up an inviting opportunity to explore the complex relationship between two supreme egotists. But in 1954 the issues were more political than psychological; and their business was more polemic than novelistic art.[21]

WHATEVER THE ultimate origins of Oppenheimer's fall from political grace, it galvanized the atomic scientists, especially at Los Alamos. On their angry reaction to Oppenheimer's condemnation, the Alsops could write authoritatively. They had an excellent source of information about the commotion at the weapons lab in New Mexico: Alvin Glanzberg, the Los Alamos correspondent for the *Santa Fe New Mexican*, forwarded big bundles of annotated newspaper clippings, documenting the seismic shock of Oppenheimer's suspension.[22] J. Carson Mark, director of the Los Alamos theoretical division, had told journalists that the AEC must be suffering from a "Salem witchcraft delusion." As Glanzberg noted, the comment was the more significant in that Mark was a close friend of Edward Teller, the only great American physicist who had testified against Oppenheimer before the Gray Board.

Teller's role in the affair had generated great bitterness. Teller shared top credit for the technical breakthrough that had made a deliverable American hydrogen bomb possible. He had been as enthusiastic for it as Oppenheimer and others had been cold to it, and in his testimony before the Gray Board he had sharply questioned Oppenheimer's judgment.

Yet it was hard to believe that Teller was as hostile to Oppenheimer as some journalists thought. A year earlier, Joe Alsop had undertaken to relieve Teller of his suspect role in the anti-Oppenheimer cabal. *Fortune* had published an unsigned article (written by Charles Murphy, an editor who had served in the office of the secretary of the air force) that outlined a popular devil-theory of H-bomb delay.[23] Murphy's piece reflected the view within the air force that Oppenheimer, its number one enemy in the scientific establishment, had plotted to delay the development of the thermonuclear weapon on which deterrence depended. Murphy hinted at Teller as his source. Joe, scenting a story, placed a call to the prickly Teller to ask if the article was accurate. Teller bristled. In a letter of August 10 he pronounced the query useless and warned Joe that "if your statement [presumably in some future column] is other than strictly factual, I might have to hold you legally responsible." Joe was shocked. He had written only to let Teller know that "your name was being widely used to give color of truth to a story which . . . is an ugly slander." He had heard that Teller did not approve of the *Fortune* piece—the first notable source of the charge that Oppenheimer had been insufficiently "enthusiastic" about the H-bomb.[24]

Because it so perfectly reflected the air force version of Oppenheimer's role, the *Fortune* account of the H-bomb delay is worth examining. In time the Alsops attacked the *Fortune* story with as much relish as they attacked the Gray Board report a year later. *Fortune* purported to tell the story of a "hidden struggle" over hydrogen bomb development in 1950. It was billed as no less than "the story of Dr. Oppenheimer's persistent campaign to reverse U.S. military strategy." The writer, a former aide to General Hoyt Vandenberg, wove an elaborate conspiracy theory. Oppenheimer and an anti-H-bomb cabal ("a group calling themselves ZORC—Z for Jerrold R. Zacharias, an MIT physicist; O for Oppenheimer; R for Rabi; and C for Charles Lauritsen"), a high-level scientific team, sought "a near perfect air defense" as an alternative to the H-bomb. Such a defense would render deterrence less important. The conspiracy, which developed in a summer study of air defense, took place at MIT's Lincoln Laboratory and "suggested a jet-propelled, electronically hedged Maginot Line" that would offer "a more moral solution to the dilemmas of cold-war strategy" than deterrence by the Strategic Air Command.[25]

It was true that the Lincoln summer study performed under Oppenheimer's direction had reached gloomy conclusions about U.S. exposure to enemy bombing, conclusions that found numerous echoes in the Alsops' columns. It was estimated that within three years—by the mid- to late 1950s—the Soviet Union would have the capacity to cripple the United States in a surprise attack, with 80 percent of the attacking planes getting through to target. An adequate continental defense would make such a sneak attack far less tempting—assuming that it really was a risk worth taking on any terms. But such a defense would require heavy investment in sophisticated radar, fighters, and interceptor missiles. Stewart Alsop's 1952–53 columns on the "air gap" clearly drew on the Lincoln study, and their use of this data showed that the Alsops had been in touch with Oppenheimer. The Alsop columns spoke of "a great emergency project like the Manhattan District," costing the then-colossal sum of $25 billion over two or three years. The columns supporting strategic defense had enraged the air force and did not improve its opinion of Oppenheimer's influence. Secretary Thomas Finletter told Murphy, the author of the *Fortune* article, that while Oppenheimer might not be a Communist, "he is the cleverest conspirator in America."[26]

Later, the ZORC theory was elaborated at book length by two other *Time Inc.* writers—James Shepley, chief of *Time*'s Washington bureau, and Clay Blair, a special writer on military affairs. Their book *The Hydrogen Bomb* zeroed in on Oppenheimer as the leader of the obstructionists and extolled Teller as the heroic defender of the air force. Teller was depicted as "increasingly dissatisfied" and as believing "that the AEC, under Oppenheimer's influence, was trying to postpone, if not stifle," the development of the H-bomb, which would greatly strengthen deterrence.[27]

THE *Fortune* article foreshadowed, and may indirectly have influenced, the Gray Board's decision. The charge that Oppenheimer had been insufficiently zealous for the hydrogen bomb and had backed a search for defensive alternatives was the theme. As the Alsops would write in *We Accuse*, Murphy's piece was "full of snide hints about Oppenheimer's motives." But if the ZORC theory tantalized Gordon Gray and Thomas Morgan, it was regarded by most physicists as a malicious fairy tale, replete with scientific and technical absurdities. The Alsops had good reason to know that. In an eleven-page October 1 letter solicited by the Alsops, Hans Bethe, the former head of the theoretical division at Los Alamos, patiently explained why the Murphy-Shepley-Blair theory

was wrong. Its most basic flaw was historical. When President Truman decided to move ahead with the H-bomb program, Bethe said, theory was primitive—"comparable," wrote Bethe, "to that of the atomic bomb in 1939 when Fermi and his collaborators started their work." Not even the basic theoretical calculations had been done. "It was for this reason that the work got off to a slow start. Purely theoretical work may seem slow . . . but there was simply no basis for building hardware until the theory had been clarified. . . . High-speed computers came into existence only in 1952, and somewhat less advanced machines were made in 1951. It has often been said rightly that our H bomb could not have been developed without the use of these machines." It was only in the winter and spring of 1951, Bethe explained, that Teller had developed a "new concept" that erased theoretical doubts that a "deliverable" super-bomb could be built. "It is to the credit of the General Advisory Committee," Bethe went on, "that they were immediately convinced by this 'new concept.'"[28]

That was the real story of the H-bomb delay, and it made nonsense of the melodramatic conspiracy-theory notion that the ZORC cabal had plotted to delay the bomb. No such thing had happened or could have happened. When they challenged and ridiculed the Murphy-Shepley-Blair story, the Alsops relied on their correspondence with Bethe, who knew infinitely more about the bomb's technical history than the generals who were feeding *Fortune* and *Time* the official air force line.

When *Time*, in its issue of November 9, 1954, named "the brothers Alsop" as the most "violent and sustained" detractors of the Shepley-Blair book, the Alsops repeated a challenge they had made in earlier columns: "Some time ago, we . . . offered Messrs. Shepley and Blair to retract our entire criticism of their book, if they could find a single leading physicist or official of the Atomic Energy Commission who would defend *The Hydrogen Bomb* as fair, honest and accurate. The offer has not been taken up." *Time* suppressed the Alsop letter, and apparently Shepley and Blair found no witnesses to support their version of the H-bomb story.[29]

BY MID-JULY 1954, Oppenheimer's cause was plainly lost. The AEC had dismissed the charge that Oppenheimer had delayed or obstructed the hydrogen bomb. But it made a third finding: that "defects of character" disqualified Oppenheimer from government trust. That damaging judgment relied, in the main, on the most tangled element of the story — Oppenheimer's wartime association with Haakon Chevalier, a Berkeley colleague and professor of romance languages. At an Oppenheimer dinner party one evening in 1943, as Chevalier and Oppenheimer stood casually talking in the kitchen, Chevalier mentioned that George Eltenton, an English-born engineer of left-wing sympathies who worked in the Bay area, had offered himself as a conduit for passing atomic information to the Soviets. Oppenheimer immediately rebuffed Chevalier, who seems to have been at most a half-hearted go-between. But Oppenheimer failed to report the overture to the security officers in California or at Los Alamos. When he finally did so eight months later, he compounded his error of omission. He substituted a "cock and bull story" (his own later description to the Gray Board) in which he mentioned no names, apparently to protect Chevalier, and implied that there had been several such overtures. The fabrication was to haunt him in the Gray Board proceedings. Yet the Chevalier affair — the overture from Eltenton—had been relayed to General Leslie Groves, the army's director of the Manhattan Project, and had been known to the AEC in 1947 when the commission renewed Oppenheimer's security clearance. Strauss had joined the clearance vote. If it mattered so little then, how could it matter so much now? Certainly not, as Strauss's biographer has suggested, because "new evidence" had turned up; it hadn't.[30]

In their book *We Accuse*, the Alsops admitted the seriousness of Oppenheimer's laxity and failure of candor in the Chevalier matter. Yet the revival of the episode seven years after it had been considered and dismissed in the 1947 security clearance seemed to them to be additional proof that the Oppenheimer proceeding could be explained only as the result of Strauss's personal grudge. What obviously had changed was that the fight over isotope exports to Norway, featuring Oppenheimer's smart-alec rebuff to Strauss, had intervened. In the Gray Board hearings, wrote the Alsops, the Chevalier affair had been "worked like a mine to produce thirteen admissions of lying" from Oppenheimer, and the cumulative result was "as big and ugly an untruth as Oppenheimer ever told" the army security people during the war.[31]

THOUGH THE Alsops had already written at least a dozen daily newspaper columns deploring the Oppenheimer proceeding and warning of its consequences for the national defense, they did not drop the matter there. In July, Joe wrote a long article for *Harper's*; later he expanded it to book length. He and Stewart entitled the article "We Accuse," echoing Emile Zola's immortal pamphlet on the Dreyfus treason case in late-nineteenth-century France, another episode in which an official institution—the French army—had been slow to do justice to a patriot falsely charged with disloyalty. Joe was cheered on in this extra effort by a number of eminent Washington figures, all Oppenheimer sympathizers, including Justice Felix Frankfurter of the Supreme Court. Frankfurter's interest is clear from several letters of advice and counsel. Writing on July 27, Frankfurter urged Joe to consider "two things of which I have seen little or no mention." One was that part of the record on the basis of which Oppenheimer had been condemned was secret, open to neither public checking nor cross-examination. The other was the distinct possibility, as the justice saw it, that the AEC's verdict had been tainted by the Gray Board's theory that Oppenheimer had dragged his feet on the H-bomb. Even if that theory had later been repudiated by the AEC, the

140
Oppenheimer,
The Bomb, and
Survival

situation was "the kind of thing," commented Frankfurter, "that happens in courts when evidence is allowed to come improrperly [*sic*] before a jury but is subsequently struck out with the admonition to the jury to disregard it."[32]

The Frankfurters, the Archibald MacLeishes, and other friends read and commented on early drafts of the *Harper's* piece. MacLeish reported that he had read it aloud at his summer house in Conway, Massachusetts, and commended Joe on his "passion" and "persuasion." Both these eminent preliminary readers thought the draft needed to be toned down. "The color of your adjectives came off on your nouns," wrote MacLeish, who speculated that Joe would have squirmed at some of the purple passages if he had been present to hear the piece read aloud. Frankfurter likewise found the piece "powerful" but urged Joe to prune "adjectives that one uses around the table but are unworthy of the height of your great argument. . . . It takes very little blueing to color a whole tub of water."[33]

The article, duly chastened of adjectives, appeared in the October *Harper's*, which, to Joe's chagrin, paid only $1,000 for it—less than a third of the usual *Saturday Evening Post* rate. Faced with Joe's plea for more money, Russell Lynes, the managing editor of *Harper's*, apologized. But he pointed out that this was four times the usual *Harper's* fee.

The AEC, forewarned, was ready with a rebuttal, which Robb's deputy, Charles Rolander, circulated in mimeographed form to sympathetic journalists—though not, oddly, to the Alsops themselves. Stewart, who wrote a point-by-point answer, was indignant that the columnists had not been sent a copy in advance. The AEC was after all a public agency, and he found it "a bureaucratic landmark . . . that a government agency can prepare, at public expense, a document attacking private citizens, and that the citizens attacked can then be denied access to the document or to the names of those who have received the document."[34] The slyness of the AEC counterattack was a foretaste of disappointments to come. *We Accuse*, in its book form, fell dead. It went against the grain of public opinion, which, to judge by both polls and newspaper editorials, overwhelmingly approved the findings of the Gray Board and endorsed the suspension of Oppenheimer.

As a study of bureaucratic folly and legalistic obstinacy, the *Harper's* article and the nearly identical book are worthy of their 1898 namesake. Its impact can be measured in part by the dismay it caused at the AEC, which went to great lengths to rebutt the charges. But otherwise, the Eisenhower administration never responded. An even dimmer fate awaited the publication of *We Accuse* as a dollar-a-copy paperback. In early February 1955 Stewart wrote Gerard Piel, noting that Piel's review in *Scientific American* was, "so far as I know, the only review which has thus far appeared."[35] *Library Journal* added the ultimate insult by comparing *We Accuse* unfavorably with the "superior reportage" of the Shepley-Blair book on the hydrogen bomb, which, as has been seen, could not withstand serious historical or scientific scrutiny. Even the *New York Times*, the nation's newspaper of record, boycotted the book. The Alsops were curtly informed by Sunday editor Lester Markel that the *Times* did not review "pamphlets." In England, meanwhile, the *Times Literary Supplement* commissioned a review by Hugh Trevor-Roper, soon to be Regius Professor of Modern History at Oxford. Trevor-Roper's admiring piece was set in type but unaccountably not printed. Eventually, it appeared in *The Spectator*.

In *The Progressive*, however, the Alsops' loyal friend Arthur Schlesinger, Jr., called *We Accuse* "an obvious tribute to the courage of the Alsops [and] also a tribute to what one can only call their gallantry. For on one of the major issues . . . the question of building the H-bomb—the Alsops were vigorously on the other side of the debate from Oppenheimer." This was a generous point that needed emphasis. Schlesinger took note of other instances in which the Alsops had defended the loyalty and integrity of men with whom they had bitterly differed on issues of policy, and hailed "the grace of spirit which moves people to defend those with whom they disagree."[36] As for the Oppenheimer case itself, most of the nation's newspapers—even the *New York Times*, whose James Reston had first broken the story of the Gray Board hearings—agreed with the AEC that Oppenheimer had forfeited the nation's trust. The Alsops had made a powerful case, early and often, but apparently it had persuaded almost no one. It was one of those instances in which daily journalism must await the verdict of time, which indeed has vindicated the Alsops' judgment.

THE SEQUEL was full of irony. Thirteen years later J. Robert Oppenheimer died a sad and diminished man, never rehabilitated by the AEC but revered as a philosopher of science. (His friend George Kennan recalls that Oppenheimer's later lectures were both mesmerizing and, often, indecipherable.) In May 1956, the AEC formally altered its security clearance procedures, silently conceding that the Gray Board's encasement in over-rigid regulations might have led it into error. Boards of inquiry in security cases might now use "common sense" in judging political associations—a standard that clearly implied the AEC's recognition that common sense had been lacking in the Oppenheimer case.

Two years later, when Lewis Strauss was no longer chairman of the AEC, there was some congressional pressure to review the case. The internal evaluation of the findings by the AEC's general counsel, Loren Olson, again seemed to vindicate the Alsops and other critics. The record, Olson reported, was "messy . . . from a legal standpoint. . . . the charges kept shifting . . . the evidence was stale and consisted of information that was twelve years old [and] was a punitive, personal abuse of the judicial [*sic*] system."[37]

But the Eisenhower administration was by now on the way out, and nothing came of Olson's report. McGeorge Bundy, writing about the case many years later in *Danger and Survival*, his magisterial study of nuclear policy, registered his surprise that Eisenhower had relied on Strauss ("an accomplished twister of truth") and never reviewed the record for himself. It was odd, Bundy thought, that Conant, John J. McCloy, and Rabi, who were all esteemed by Eisenhower, testified without effect in Oppenheimer's behalf. "What Eisenhower could have learned in an afternoon with [the three] is what he never learned from Strauss: that all three had seen [Oppenheimer] tested and repeatedly proven clear-headed on the subject of Soviet behavior."[38] The day of Oppenheimer's symbolic rehabilitation finally came in November 1963, when he became the first recipient of the Enrico Fermi award, which was presented at the White House to mark the anniversary of the first chain reaction in Fermi's lab in Rome. Even then, there was widespread grumbling that the Kennedy administration was reversing a valid decision.

Meanwhile, the Alsops' warnings about the alienation of science from government had quickly begun to look prophetic. The launch of the Soviets' Sputnik space satellite in 1957 was widely taken as an implicit indictment of Eisenhower administration complacency. Soon, scientists were again lionized as they had not been since the security mania of the McCarthy years warped the nation's sense of the soundness of their judgment.

As for the strategic issues, that outcome was also ironic. The Eisenhower administration pushed on with its big-bomber strategy, relying on a form of deterrence described by Dulles as "massive retaliation." Eventually, the idea of "mutual assured destruction"—a concession of mutual U.S.-Soviet nakedness to nuclear attack, a state of being en prise to total destruction—became established strategic doctrine. Then, after thirty years, the idea of strategic defense was suddenly revived and elevated to political prominence by Ronald W. Reagan, than whom a more distinct antithesis to J. Robert Oppenheimer could hardly be imagined. Reagan probably had never heard of the Lincoln summer study, the symposium that had persuaded the U.S. Air Force that Oppenheimer's advocacy of strategic defense constituted a menace to national security. It is one of history's ironies that the scientist most influential in persuading Reagan to adopt his Strategic Defense Initiative, or SDI, was the same Edward Teller who had opposed the Lincoln study and had seen in it the seeds of gross scientific misjudgment.

Chapter Eleven Last Years of a Partnership

W ith the three great crises of the spring and summer of
1954 now behind them, the Alsops could look back on
one clear victory and two grave losses. Joe McCarthy had
hurled himself headlong into a showdown with the army
and its canny counsel, Joseph Welch, and had emerged severely crippled and discredited. Millions had watched him on television
for the first time and disliked what they saw. McCarthy's approval ratings
in the polls plummeted; he would not again terrorize the American
political world as he had done for four years. Meanwhile, the defeated
French were quitting Indochina, a strategic defeat for the West that by
Joe Alsop's reckoning was sure to topple the dominos elsewhere in Asia.
And the suspension of Robert Oppenheimer's security clearance had angered and demoralized the nation's most gifted scientists just as the
threat to American freedom, and the freedom of its allies, most required
their cooperation.

PROFESSIONALLY, though, the column was prospering. Stewart Alsop, writing to their *Herald Tribune* syndicate manager Sylvan Barnet, Jr., in New York suggested that the time had come for "a little tooting of the Alsop horn." As Stewart saw it, the triumphs to be celebrated were not in advocacy but in reporting—above all in the "air-atomic field." Stewart went through the list of claims. He and Joe claimed to have scooped all their colleagues on the various stages of Soviet and U.S. rocket development and on early intercontinental ballistic missile development. In March 1955, more than two years before the Soviet Union launched Sputnik, they had written "the first story of the plan to launch an earth satellite." Earlier, they had been the first journalists to describe, for a mass newspaper and magazine audience, a nuclear-age phenomenon that would soon become an element of common knowledge and fear: the toxic clouds of radioactive dust and debris, called "fallout," which settled back to earth after a nuclear explosion. Their accounts of the behind-the-scenes struggle within the Truman administration over the development of an American hydrogen bomb at the beginning of the decade had "produced a major public uproar."[1]

THESE PREOCCUPATIONS, we shall see, did not diminish by mid-decade; indeed, they would shortly become bigger stories than they already were. But from the Alsops' perspective, the focus of the national security issue seemed at the moment to be shifting sharply toward the developing regional conflicts in the Middle East—especially in Egypt, where a corrupt monarch had been expelled by nationalist army officers and their leader, Colonel Gamal Abdel Nasser, had come to power. Nasser, in turn, was in the process of expropriating the European shareholders in the Suez Canal, still a crucial shipping link in the transport of Middle Eastern oil to Western Europe. Almost three decades later, the absorbing Suez crisis of 1956 has been largely forgotten except by foreign-policy specialists and historians. But to the Alsops, as to most observers in that very different world of familiar but decaying colonial empires, it marked a monumental transition. And in combination with the exactly contemporary revolt against oppressive Communist rule in Hungary, the Suez crisis was instrumental in persuading Joe Alsop that he ought to shift his base of operations to Paris—a move which, in turn, would bring lingering tensions in the brotherly working partnership to the surface and lead to its dissolution.

BY MID-OCTOBER 1956, just before the Suez crisis came to a head, Joe was complaining to his friends Bill and Susan Mary Patten about the boredom of Republican Washington. "Nothing worth recording ever seems to happen in Washington . . . a very dull city nowadays, since the Republicans for some strange reason are rather seldom agreeable and congenial people. The Eisenhower official world is stuffy and self-satisfied, in a degree that I sometimes find rather hard to credit. . . . If it weren't for the Bruces, the Walkers, the Wisners, Stew and Tish, and half a dozen cozy old friends of the same sort, I could not bear to live here for a week."[2] This had been a constant theme of Joe's correspondence in the preceding three or four years. For one whose love of foreign travel amounted to a kind of wanderlust, it seems, in retrospect, unsurprising that such remarks heralded a wish to change anchorages.

Within days of writing that letter to the Pattens, Joe Alsop witnessed the debacle he and Stewart had been warning against for months. The British, French, and Israelis, after elaborate conspiratorial planning from which the election-conscious Eisenhower administration had been wholly excluded, raced across the Sinai Desert in an attempt to retrieve the Suez Canal. The canal had been nationalized during the previous spring by the rebel Egyptian army officer who then seemed the most charismatic of the new nationalist insurgents of the ancient Middle East —Gamal Abdel Nasser, the Middle East's boldest, most daring, and most effective challenger of the tenuous European colonial legacy.

Part of that colonial legacy, from the Arab point of view, was the State of Israel. The UN's establishment of Israel in 1947 required a wrenching partition of mandatory Palestine. This action ignited a war against Israel which was destined to smolder, with brief and bloody flare-ups, for another four decades and more. From the outset, the Alsops were strong partisans of Israel. But as a student of Middle East history—indeed, at times a romantic one—Joe Alsop was clear on the trauma Israel had occasioned for Arab opinion. For Joe, who was the team's anointed expert on the Middle East and who therefore wrote most of the columns on the subject, the issue of Israel became and remained a part of the larger Cold War picture. It was his much-reiterated premise that the Arab-Israeli dispute weakened Western solidarity by offering the Russians an opportunity to divide the oil-sufficient U.S. from its oil-dependent European allies and thus to acquire leverage for mischief. This theme echoed through almost every column touching on Middle East politics. Beyond that, Joe's occasional on-the-scene inspections left him indignant over the lingering refugee problem left by Israel's war of independence. The refugee camps were "horrifying." Joe recalled, "If you see them once you can never forget your indignation against the Israelis for their callousness about the . . . problem; against the Arab leaders, who have made political capital of the refugees' misery; against the Western nations and the UN, because the provision for the refugees is so pitifully inadequate; and against the very world we live in, for producing such horrors."

The Alsops were equally far-sighted in their view of the dilemma of the "unfortunate Palestinian Arabs, who are not refugees because they still have their homes, but are destitute because their fields have been taken from them."³ These lines, written almost four decades ago, still have not lost their resonance.

By 1955, a resurgent Arab nationalism, with Israel as its kindling, was the message of Nasser's revolt. But the economic issue—access to oil— preoccupied French and British minds. Since the British departure from India a decade earlier, it seemed clear that colonies could safely be part- ed with; but fuel was indispensable, and a threat to its safe supply raised ultimate issues of national survival, or certainly seemed to. The super- tankers of the 1970s were then far in the future—indeed, in large part they would be a by-product of the continuing struggle over the Suez Canal and other strategic waterways. The century-old canal, the gem of

Benjamin Disraeli's imperial acquisitions, was regarded as Western Eu- rope's lifeline. Nasser, by seizing it, had applied a choke hold. The Alsops had reported and warned all summer long of the seething impatience in London and Paris over Nasser's challenge. Heedless of these warnings, the United States kept its closest allies at arm's length, proposed various compromise measures, and coolly pursued its leisurely preoccupation with the approaching presidential election campaign, a duller rematch between Eisenhower and Stevenson. The Eisenhower administration's response to the gathering crisis was to seek to restrain its allies from rash action. Secretary of State John Foster Dulles, whom Joe would soon de- scribe as "the most hated man in Western Europe since Josef Stalin," proposed a "user's association" of maritime powers united to apply leverage against Nasser, but the idea was not taken seriously outside the United States.

The exasperated governments of Anthony Eden in London and Guy Mollet in Paris secretly plotted an operation designed to regain Anglo-

French control of the canal but disguised to look like something very different. It would at first be made to appear that the Egyptians and Israelis were engaged in another of the periodic wars that were destined to continue until the Yom Kippur War of 1973 finally yielded peace. Then, as if spontaneously, the Anglo-French forces would launch an intervention to "separate" Israeli and Egyptian forces in a battle to be initiated by the Israelis.

Few observers thought the British and French acted prudently, and Dwight D. Eisenhower turned in fury on his old comrades in arms and applied brutal economic pressure to call them off. The Alsops thought the British and French had been amply provoked by Nasser's high-handedness and Dulles's feckless attempts to devise a temporizing solution to what the Allies could only view as a deadly threat. And while the Allies were engaged in this elaborate exercise in mutual deception, Nikita Khrushchev sent Soviet troops and tanks into Budapest to crush a liberalizing tendency in Hungary's Communist regime. Whatever its arguable merits, it was clear that the Suez operation had provided a smokescreen behind which the Soviet Union could work repressive mischief elsewhere.

As the Suez crisis subsided in mid-December, Joe laid out his views to Hugh Gaitskell, the leader of the British Labour Party, who had vehemently criticized the Suez operation. "You could not deal with Nasser's brand of Arab nationalism by mere appeasement. . . . The [Anglo-French-Israeli] operation was as badly conceived, as badly planned in all its details, and as badly executed as any operation I have ever heard of. The object of giving the Arab nationalists a good sharp lesson, like the slap on the face that brings the victim of hysteria back to talking sense, was the only aspect of the operation with which I sympathized." Nevertheless, neither the Eisenhower administration nor Gaitskell and the other opposition leaders in the European capitals had "made the best of a bad business which involves the vital interests of the West. . . . Instead, after a humiliating military defeat by the Israelis, Humpty-Dumpty Nasser has been put right back on the wall again." And even though Nasser was not a Communist—was even, in fact, an anti-Communist—"what he wants to do in the Middle East, which is utterly to destroy the remaining British positions everywhere in the Arab world, is exactly what the Soviets want him to do."[4]

After the Suez debacle—and its exploitation by the Soviet Union as a cover for its reimposition of Communist Party orthodoxy in rebellious Hungary—Joe Alsop was not alone in believing that the West had not only suffered a serious defeat but, by seeming to appease and resurrect the damaged and humiliated Nasser, had also compounded the appearance of weakness.

The Suez crisis was only the beginning, not the end, of a long struggle between East and West for the soul of Israel's most important and powerful Arab neighbor, which would culminate twenty years later in the peace treaty with Israel signed at Camp David by Nasser's brilliant understudy and successor, Anwar Sadat. By that time, the canal had long since ceased to be a critical strategic waterway. But gloomy apprehension, more than imaginative foresight, was Joe Alsop's predictable reaction. He indulged in the usual luxury of fearing the worst, and by December 28 he was writing to Chip Bohlen, U.S. ambassador in Moscow, that "the realistic consequences will be little less than appalling." Because of the events surrounding Suez, "one can now foresee that the Western Alliance will tend to be weakened and even to be dissolved during the next two or three years. And our only preparation for this fairly alarming development is to repeat the assertion . . . that 'We must base our strategy and policy on the United Nations.'"

"Do you think this is foundation enough?," he asked Bohlen, who was soon to welcome Joe on his first visit to the Soviet Union. Joe clearly thought the question answered itself.[5] But the most important and immediate consequence of these cosmic forebodings was personal and professional: Joe decided to leave Washington and establish his reporting base abroad. Writing to Bill and Susan Mary Patten "for your eyes only," he portentously announced that the world crisis "has reached the stage where one of us [either Stewart or himself] must follow developments continuously on the spot. If one has to spend ten or eleven months abroad anyway, it seems a little foolish to maintain an enormous and expensive base in Washington." He would soon be coming to Paris, where he would live for as long as the "world crisis" persisted.[6] Joe leased the private wing of his house to Oatsie Leiter and, after a fateful visit to the Soviet Union, took quarters at the Hotel St. James and Albany in Paris. For the next year or so his life would be comparable, by his own description, to that of a "commercial traveler." In December he explained it in this way to a correspondent soliciting a progress report on his life for the forthcoming twenty-fifth reunion of his Harvard College class:

"As a fireman must go where the fires are, so newspapermen must go where the crises are; and in order to do this more easily I am transferring my base abroad. My headquarters will be in Paris, but I shall not be there much longer than . . . to catch my breath and pick up a few clean shirts from time to time."[7]

FOR THE ALSOPS, it was no novelty to be on the official Moscow hit list. They could boast the honor, for instance, of having been denounced at the United Nations as "homicidal" by Andrei Vichinsky—Stalin's ambassador to the UN organization and, many years earlier, Stalin's infamous special prosecutor of the Old Bolsheviks in the Moscow Trials. Stewart Alsop had merrily exploited the supposed insult, recalling in a column that, whatever Vichinsky meant, the alleged tendency was perhaps hereditary: One of their ancestors, a Harvard University professor of chemistry named John Webster, had been convicted and executed in 1850 for the notorious murder of George Parkman, the uncle of the historian Francis Parkman.

The special insults continued. An editor's note appended by the *New York Herald Tribune* to Joe's first dispatch from the Soviet Union in early 1957 noted that *Komsomolskaya Pravda* had recently denounced both Alsop brothers in vivid terms. "Assassins, robbers, pirates and rapists of all nations," said the Communist youth newspaper, "have been put to shame by the Alsops." Their friend Chip Bohlen in Moscow told them they had also been characterized in the Soviet press as "troubadours" of the ruling American capitalist circles.[8]

Just what prompted this elaborate attention, apart from the columnists' advocacy of strong Western defenses, it is hard to guess. But in retrospect, the words of ideological insult formed an ominous overture to a visit that ended, a few weeks later, with a sinister episode that would cause Joe Alsop lasting pain.[9]

JOE PREPARED for his first journey to the enemy's lair with his usual industry. Not long before leaving to take up his new quarters in Paris, he invited Soviet embassy officials in Washington to lunch at Dumbarton Avenue and tried to loosen their tongues with what turned out to be an astounding volume of good wine and brandy. Of these invitations and meetings, he kept friends at the CIA informed. He reported that one Soviet visitor, the minister-counselor at the embassy, "cheerfully finished a quarter of a bottle of brandy after polishing off about a bottle of red and white wine and a cocktail; and this visitor talked very freely indeed" — about the Middle East, Yugoslavia, the "satellite" nations of Eastern Europe, and about George Kennan, whom he wanted to meet.[10]

In his visa-application letter to the Soviet ambassador in Washington, Georgi N. Zarubin, Joe acknowledged that "you and your government may well hold that my political viewpoint is unsound, to put it rather mildly." But he could "claim to be a reporter above all." One of his chief motives in traveling there, he said, diplomatically but disingenuously, "is the fear that I may have misjudged the Soviet Union's present world role."[11] There is no evidence at all that Joe, who tended to be very sure of his judgments, was worried in the least about the opinions he had formed from afar about the Soviet Union. Still, it was a different Soviet Union now that Stalin had been dead for three years and Nikita Khrushchev, as would shortly be revealed, had told the Twentieth Party Congress at great length about Stalin's crimes and illegalities. And as a first-hand observer, Joe was usually at his journalistic best.

HAVING DROPPED OFF most of his baggage in Paris, Joe arrived in Moscow in mid-January 1957. It was now the height of the post-Stalin thaw. He discovered, to his surprise, a jolly, almost celebratory mood. The physical setting, he noted with his usual attention to climate, mood, and architecture, was by no means so grim as he had expected it to be.

The Kremlin was not the gray fortress he had imagined (this was of course before satellite transmissions in color had made every distant cityscape intimately familiar). The scene stimulated Joe's descriptive powers. The Kremlin, he wrote, was "unimaginably pretty . . . a rich dark strawberry red," its interior rich in "ancient churches ris[ing] to happy riots of colored and gilded domes" and "palaces painted a bright butter yellow." It reminded him of "a particularly gay decoration by Bakst for one of Diaghilev's earlier ballets."

He found the company colorful as well. One afternoon, along with several hundred other visitors, Joe pressed into St. George's Hall in the Kremlin for a reception honoring a delegation of visiting Bulgarians. He couldn't help noticing the strikingly short stature of the members of the prevailing "collective leadership"; he speculated that Stalin, a short man himself, had wanted no tall men around him.

The Soviet Union had now become a "high technical society" and, in spite of the police repression, had bred a literate middle class with an interest in the arts and "things of the mind," although it was obviously a society deadened by an excess of officious "governessy" rule. Stalin's terror was gone, but the sense of being watched survived the old terrorist's passing. And a certain Victorian primness of taste was so pervasive that it was a treat, he reported, to visit an art exhibit which, however mildly and indirectly, defied socialist-realist conventions.

The Russians seemed to Joe to have split personalities. They were lively in personal conversation about anything but politics. When the talk turned to government or to East-West relations, they seemed to go on automatic and sounded like "gramophone records." In his Kremlin office, Nikita Khrushchev, who was clearly on his way to unchallenged first among equals, spoke to him in a long interview—featured on the front pages of many of the Alsops' client newspapers—of the mutual withdrawal of United States and Soviet forces from their advance positions in Europe. This was the era of the Rapacki Plan, the proposal of Poland's foreign minister that the great powers "disengage" their hostile forces from central Europe and form a belt of neutrality. George Kennan, as Eastman professor at Oxford University, would support a variation on Rapacki's idea in his 1957 Reith Lectures on the BBC. More cautious analysts like the Alsops did not fail to notice that in some versions of the plan favored by the Russians, the United States would have to withdraw its forces some three thousand miles, and across an ocean, while the Russians would be withdrawing overland a tenth that distance and, unlike the Americans, putting no ocean between them and a possible line of collision.

But on the whole, Joe was encouraged by what he saw. On this firsthand look, his first and only one, the Soviet Union seemed touched in an indefinable fashion with the promise of change for the better. Joe took a side trip to Siberia, where, fulfilling the promise he had made in his visa application, he conscientiously interviewed industrial managers and tried to interpret for his readers the structure of the new Soviet economy and its strange mixture of enterprise and state planning.[12]

IF JOE needed reminding of the darker side of the Soviet Union, however, he did not have to wait long. He had written ebulliently of the convivial company of singers, talkers, and drinkers gathered at his hotel from all over Europe. They were to be encountered at all hours. Among them there had been planted an agent provocateur from the secret police (later the KGB), who was aware of Joe's long-concealed homosexuality. One night in Moscow he and this companion were photographed in a sexual act in his hotel room, and he was soon confronted with the photographs and the threat of blackmail and was urged—unsuccessfully—to become an undercover agent.

The details of the episode, which was to haunt Joe to the end of his life, remain shadowy to this day, though many of Joe's oldest and closest friends in Washington had heard accounts of it, usually garbled and often strikingly inconsistent. By one such account, Joe reacted to the entrapment with his usual bluster and bravado. He was not to be put off his stride by it, and having taken care to inform a friend at the British embassy, he set out for Leningrad for the continuation of his tour. By this account, Chip Bohlen, one of Joe's closest friends, soon learned of the incident and, sensing the danger, quickly recalled Joe from Leningrad and rushed him out of the country. By a slightly different account, Joe was crushed and distraught, humiliated. As he set out for Leningrad, he handed Bohlen a sealed envelope and explained that if he had not been heard from in five days the envelope was to be opened. "Chip was no fool," recalled another old friend who had heard the story from Bohlen himself. "Curiosity soon got the better of him. Chip opened the envelope and found an account of the incident and a suicide note. He lost no time running Joe down and getting him out of the country and beyond reach of the NKVD."[13]

Both accounts, though inconsistent in major respects, are consistent with the small fragments of documentary evidence that survive in the Alsop Papers at the Library of Congress—which are themselves significant only if one happens to know, or guess, what they pertain to. An undated telegram, addressed to Joe at the Astoria Hotel in Leningrad, reads: "Have urgent personal message for you which ambassador saw before departure. He suggests you return immediately Moscow. Please call me on return. s/David, Embassy."[14]

The other is a cryptic allusion in an April 2 letter to Bohlen, a month after Joe's hasty departure. He apologizes that his last letter went to Moscow by open mail, "not that it matters so desperately, after re-reading the carbon." Joe's secretary, he explained, had not understood that "all Moscow letters" should be sent by the diplomatic pouch through the U.S. embassy in Helsinki. "I have heard no word from Frank [clearly a reference to his CIA friend Frank Wisner, to whom he had turned for advice and help regarding the Moscow incident]: and I am therefore acting on what seems to me the only possible assumption, that he does not want me to do anything further about the matter we discussed."[15]

Considerably more can now be said about this glancing reference. On Wisner's instructions, Joe had prepared a detailed account of the Moscow incident and a relevant narrative history of his sex life. Wisner, following standard practice in counterintelligence matters, forwarded the document to the FBI. This was the usual operating procedure, designed to forfend blackmail. But FBI director J. Edgar Hoover, a master at the art of transmuting base gossip into the gold of bureaucratic influence, had quickly grasped the material's possibilities for ingratiating himself with members of the Eisenhower administration who had been repeatedly stung and irritated by Alsop's columns. By mid-April of 1957, which could not have been very long after the arrival at the FBI of Joe's "confession" (as the bureau would refer to it in confidential files), Hoover was recording in private memoranda to himself how he had spread the word both internally and externally. For example, here is part of a memorandum dated April 17:

> Today following a conference in Governor Adams' office at the White House, I remained behind and told Governor Adams briefly of the developments in the Joseph Alsop case. He had not previously been advised of this situation, and I told him that as I understood it, the information had been held quite closely and that I knew that the Secretary of State and the Under Secretary of State had been advised of this by Mr. Allen Dulles, the Director of CIA, and that I, in turn, had advised the Attorney General and the Deputy Attorney General. . . . I stated that I thought it was desirable for the White House to be informed of the Alsop case in view of the implications involved in the same. Governor Adams expressed his appreciation.[16]

It had been a busy time for Hoover. Three days earlier, he noted a morning call from the attorney general, William Rogers. Rogers related that he had been the first to tell Secretary of Defense Neil McElroy about the Moscow incident. Rogers was "amazed" that McElroy hadn't heard, Hoover noted in his memorandum of April 14, and "thought we should get together what we have on Alsop as he believed very few people knew of this and he was not sure that the President was aware."

Rogers asked if Joe's "confession" had been signed and, assured that it was, "then commented that he was going to see that certain individuals were aware of Alsop's propensities." His list included President Eisenhower and, among others, Gordon Gray, with whom Joe had been at odds over the Oppenheimer case. From other accounts, it appears that some of Joe's targets within the administration relished the information they were getting from Hoover and the FBI. Hoover's official excuse for disseminating the contents of the confidential file was that three very low-level clerks in the White House mail room, themselves homosexuals, had told the FBI of having seen previous Hoover correspondence regarding the columnists.[17]

IT IS NATURAL to ask, these many years later, whether the lurking presence of this sordid episode in the FBI files and in the Washington gossip mills might have affected Joe Alsop's views—on the Soviet Union, on the issue of homosexuals in government, or in other ways.

In the 1950 *Saturday Evening Post* article on the "miasma of fear" which had aroused Senator Joe McCarthy's ire, the Alsops had lamented the attempt of the Senate Republican minority leader, Kenneth Wherry of Nebraska, "to elevate the subject of homosexuality [in the State Department] to the level of a serious political issue on the ground that sexual perversion presents a clear and present danger to the security of the United States." It was a bold if not daring criticism, given Joe Alsop's vulnerability; and McCarthy was quick to seize upon it in veiled, insinuating language. In his letter to Ben Hibbs, the *Post*'s editor, he spoke slyly of the "morally perverted and degenerate" Roman empire. "I can understand," McCarthy wrote, "why [Wherry's remarks on homosexuality] would be considered 'vulgar' or 'nauseating' by Joe Alsop." As Edwin R. Bayley notes in *Joe McCarthy and the Press*, "this insinuation that Joe Alsop ... was a homosexual, was underlined in another paragraph in which McCarthy said Alsop had never been in his office and that the only person from the [*Saturday Evening*] *Post* who had ever been there was a photographer who seemed to be 'a fine normal young man.'"[18]

What this earlier brush with McCarthy suggests—it was, of course, a prelude to much else—is that the secret of Joe's hidden sex life seems not to have inspired caution, even in the face of McCarthy's threats. Indeed, this writer has reviewed the body of Joe Alsop's post-1957 journalism without finding a trace of evidence that it ever did so—after the Moscow

156
Last Years
of a
Partnership

incident or earlier. In three postmortem columns from Paris, where he returned to set up his base at the Hotel St. James and Albany, Joe summed up his impressions of the Russian journey. These columns offer conventional sentiments and observations but no detectable clue to Joe's thoughts about his harrowing and humiliating Moscow experience—unless it is the understated characterization of the journey as "rather intense." For a man trapped in the toils of the Russian secret police that would be a mild way of putting it. There is no evidence that the incident changed—hardened or softened—Joe Alsop's assessment of the Soviet Union. He ostensibly hoped for change. But his humiliation in a Moscow hotel could only have reinforced his normally pessimistic outlook on things and perhaps clouded his initially optimistic belief that the Russians would someday transcend their police-state habits.

In his case, the Soviet Union persisted. More than a decade and a half after the Moscow episode, a number of Joe Alsop's colleagues in the upper levels of Washington opinion journalism received prints of the explicit and compromising photographs in the mail. Those who were singled out to receive these embarrassing materials still remember the dilemma they presented. Should they be reported to investigative or intelligence agencies? Or to Joe himself? Or ignored?

Shocked to find the salacious and explicit photographs in his mail, anonymously sent, one popular syndicated columnist immediately telephoned Phil Geyelin, then editorial page editor of the *Washington Post*, on whose op-edit page Joe's column regularly appeared. They needed to talk, he told Geyelin, and the two agreed to meet for lunch at the Sans Souci, the capital's most popular restaurant at the time. The recipient of the unwelcome materials had no political or intelligence specialty and could only surmise that he had been sent them because he and Joe Alsop were known to have had a comic quarrel over a wholly unrelated matter. When they had seated themselves and ordered a drink, the columnist showed Geyelin the pictures. They brainstormed as they ate; then, leaving lunch half-eaten in their agitation, they walked for almost an hour around and around the block, trying to think what to do. "We finally decided that the best thing was to do nothing," Geyelin later recalled.[19]

The responses varied, but Joe Alsop himself was aware of the campaign. One day in the early 1970s, when he had learned from their recipients that the photographs were once again in circulation, he summoned an old friend with high connections in the U.S. intelligence community who was fully aware of the story. When the two had sat down, Joe announced that he was tired of the demeaning game the KGB was playing and proposed to make a public declaration of his homosexuality and thus bring the matter conclusively to an end. Friends he trusted already knew about the episode anyway. He was dissuaded on various grounds, including embarrassment to younger members of his family. His friend also told him that it would be unnecessary, and so it was. It appears that stern representations were soon made to the Soviet KGB that its persistence in the distribution of the materials would bring retaliation, and the campaign ceased. One very definite effect lingered, however. Never again in his lifetime did Joe Alsop feel that he could safely travel behind the iron curtain as he had once many years earlier, going on a lark to Leipzig. He was emphatically advised not to run the risk, and for once he took the advice.

BOTH PARTNERS had agreed that the new transatlantic working arrangement, with Joe stationed in Paris and Stewart in Washington, was an experiment. It went smoothly enough for a few months. But then strains began to develop. The first was symptomatic—an argument, not without petty aspects, over column scheduling. It sounds like a mundane matter, but its importance could be considerable for whoever was in the dark about what the other was writing, and when. There were immovable deadlines to meet, and when the two partners were separated by an ocean it was not always clear who was to write for any given release date. Schedules had been easy to shape when the brothers were working from a common office in the basement of Joe's Dumbarton Avenue house, and even when one or the other was off on a brief reporting trip. Now scheduling became an irritant, made no easier by their demanding commitments to the *Saturday Evening Post*. Both Alsops usually had a *Post* article in the cooker.

Who should take on the tedious job of schedule-keeper? Joe insisted that it must be Stewart in Washington, for he was in regular touch with the syndicate and with the march of events. Stewart found scheduling a nuisance. He certainly did not wish to attend to scheduling chores as regularly as Joe demanded. "The reason I want you to keep me regularly and completely informed about scheduling is simple," Joe wrote from Warsaw in September 1957. "It helps me. Maybe it is unreasonable that I should find it easier to plan my own work when I know what columns have been printed and what columns you have in mind. . . . Don't let's argue about it any longer." But the argument continued. Stewart, replying on September 30, complained that the eight scheduling messages he had sent in three weeks were hardly "inadequate." "I suggest you compare the way I have kept you informed . . . with the way you kept me informed when I was abroad, when it was your custom to hold my columns in reserve for as much as three weeks and to reply to my inquiries . . . either by total silence, or by such messages as, 'do not worry about scheduling.'"[20]

It was a sharp response; but, then, Joe's recent Warsaw letter had been abrasive for other reasons. In that letter he had questioned Stewart's investment of time in Little Rock, Arkansas, where he had been among the scores of reporters covering the biggest school integration crisis of that era. The central issue was a question of compliance with the Supreme Court's May 1954 decision in *Brown v. Board of Education of Topeka, Kansas*, which seemed to require at least a token break in the racial segregation of southern public schools. Governor Orval Faubus, on pretext of preventing a race riot, had ordered the Arkansas National Guard to Central High School and then had used it to block the scheduled entry of black children. It was the first really serious and direct collision between federal judicial power and claims of state sovereignty and authority over local public education since the Supreme Court's decision three years earlier. Those who followed the segregation story—and they were many, especially in Washington and the southern states—understood that Little Rock was a story of historic proportions, and that assumption had drawn Stewart Alsop to Little Rock. The crisis that Faubus had gratuitously provoked quickly deepened when President Eisenhower seemed, at first, to take an almost casual view of Faubus's obstruction. (Eisenhower's own private doubts about desegregation would later be revealed but, during the crisis, were not yet known.) He sent other southern governors to act as intermediaries with Faubus in an attempt to negotiate some sort of face-saving compromise—to no avail. Finally, caught (he believed) between an irresistible Supreme Court mandate and an immovable state government, Eisenhower at last federalized the Arkansas Guard and sent U.S. Army troops to maintain order and carry out the court's integration orders.

Stewart had gone to Little Rock to report what he correctly regarded as one of the major stories of the 1950s. One result, however, was that he was not at hand in Washington to keep Joe posted on scheduling. Joe, as he shuttled from place to place through the troubled Europe of the time, had also complained that Stewart's comments on the Eisenhower administration—then reaching a low ebb of prestige and popularity—were bland. Stewart reciprocated by confessing that Joe's comments had always struck him as too shrill and by observing that in any case he had no gift for trying to imitate Joe in tone or approach. In Stewart's words, Joe had been designed by God as a columnist; he had not.[21]

As they grew in bluntness, these transatlantic exchanges probably went further in saying the unsayable than either partner intended. The barrier of distance had become a buffer permitting both brothers to air old grievances freely. They hit a sore spot with Stewart, who thought that Joe, dashing about and playing foreign correspondent in Europe and the Middle East, was losing his sense of the American scene. "After some months abroad," Stewart wrote in December, "one loses a feel for the home audience . . . [and] for the real nature of the situation in Washington and in the country. . . . I believe strongly that we will only be able to work successfully in harness if you will agree to return to Washington for a sort of refresher course in the domestic scene." Stewart also wondered whether "this wandering Jew performance, however stimulating and rewarding, . . . can be satisfactory as a way of life."[22]

Having reached this level of candor, the transatlantic argument soon descended to an even more sensitive issue: money. Under their joint financial agreement, all income from their writing, except for fees Stewart earned in his yearly lecture tours, was initially pooled. (By late 1957, gross income for the partnership had reached the impressive sum of $90,000, which in constant dollars would of course be perhaps five times that amount now.) Expenses were deducted from the gross, then the balance was split 55 percent to 45, with Joe, as senior partner, getting the larger cut. But Joe was still unmarried, while Stewart had a wife and four children to support. Stewart now found himself so strained financially that he was thinking of accepting a Groton scholarship for his oldest son. Moreover, Joe seemed unable to grasp Stewart's lecture-tour plans and, it seemed to Stewart, continued to insinuate in his letters that those lectures would somehow interfere with the projected Washington meeting at which they planned to argue out the future of the partnership.[23]

THERE WAS ALSO the matter of books. Joe, an insatiable reader and book buyer, had the habit of ordering scores of books at a stroke from Blackwell's in Oxford. By agreement, books related to the column or used as background for *Saturday Evening Post* articles were treated as a common expense and deducted from gross income. They were, by Stewart's reckoning, assets of the partnership. But these books often found their way to Joe's private library shelves, even though they were supposed to be jointly owned, like the camera they had bought before Stewart's first trip to the Soviet Union. Joe scoffed at the complaint. Stewart, after all, was also free to buy books and put them on his shelves. Joe wrote that he had no intention of "breaking up" his library. By April 1958, three months of these wrangles had gradually led to a decision—an inevitable decision, it seems in retrospect—to dissolve the partnership. But even then, echoes of the book quarrel lingered. Surely, Joe said, the issue had been conclusively settled "by the *Saturday Evening Post* article on Chinese history, which was wholly the result of the historical reading I had done." The same was true of some newspaper columns. "The books I have bought in this way have never been entered as partnership assets; and of course I do not mean to divide up my library."[24]

It is unlikely that either Joe or Stewart foresaw, as they argued over books, money, and column schedules, that they were gradually approaching a conclusion that the partnership had run its natural course. The decision to part transpired over a space of months; and its inevitability is perhaps apparent only to a reader of these letters who knows the eventual outcome. Since their first column together, late in 1945, Joe had acted as a mentor to his younger brother, and this brotherly relationship had often been ruffled by extreme difference of temperament and manner. Joe was officious, combative, and domineering, "a genius, in the correct meaning of that word," as Stewart wrote in his memoirs, "and like most geniuses . . . not easy to work with. He seems to feel a psychic need for at least one shouting, foot-stamping row per week."[25] Stewart discovered that to cope with the stress of the partnership he needed frequent retreats to his rustic country place, Polecat Park—a "necessary refuge" from the strain of working in the same office with a genius. Tish Alsop still recalls evenings after a day's collaboration with Joe when the before-dinner martini served a therapeutic need for Stewart. In the complementary temperaments and talents that made the partnership work, there was of course the natural tension of a big-broth-

161
Last Years of a Partnership

er-to-younger-brother relationship and other seeds of strain and irritation. When Joe went abroad, the grievances piled up and spilled out.

Aside from money worries, Stewart felt that his talent had matured. He had less need of a partner and mentor now; he wanted to escape the shadow of his famous and bossy brother and strike out on his own. He liked writing magazine articles better than he liked the constant grind of the column, while for Joe the opposite was true. When Joe wrote to Isaiah Berlin in March that he and Stewart for the past five or six years "have been bumping on the ceiling of what we could accomplish together," he made the separation seem almost mechanical.[26] But it hadn't been quite that cut-and-dried. It had been prompted by personality clashes and by a relationship which, however affectionate, was strained from the first by Joe's imperious manner, his dogmatism, and his tendency to view Stewart as his junior and apprentice.

But while it lasted the partnership had made the Alsop brothers as well known in the newspaper trade, and among habitual readers of journalistic commentary, as the Smith brothers and Wright brothers were, respectively, in cough remedies and aviation. Unlike Walter Lippmann, neither had yet inspired a famous *New Yorker* cartoon. Joe's enshrinement by that peculiar form of American journalistic immortality would come later. But among literate and informed readers their collaboration was familiar. On March 27, 1953, a clue (to 32 Across) in the *New York Times* crossword puzzle was "Writers Joe and Stewart"—"fame indeed for a *Tribune* man," as George Wheeler of NBC remarked in calling Stewart's attention to the puzzle.[27] They had won two Overseas Press Club awards for the best foreign correspondence of the year. But not even strong lobbying by Frank Kent of the *Baltimore Sun* and others had secured them a Pulitzer Prize—not even in 1954, the year of their gallant campaigns against Senator Joe McCarthy and for J. Robert Oppenheimer. Their omission from that honor at a time when distinctly lesser talents and accomplishments won it remains a mystery; perhaps Joe's notoriously abrasive personality had something to do with the slight. On the other hand, the Pulitzer Board had not yet established "commentary" as an award category.

When they began to realize that their transatlantic correspondence was leading to a breakup, both the brothers felt a bit "weepy," as they confessed to one another. On the other hand, both could look forward to making more money, and each would be doing what he really liked. Joe would continue writing the column, perhaps recruiting someone else as a junior partner. He would also go back to writing books, as he had done in two notable collaborations before the war. Stewart now had a lucrative contract to do ten or twelve articles a year for the *Saturday Evening Post*—an assignment that would eventually evolve into a widely read column in that publication and, after the *Post*'s collapse, in *Newsweek*. They agreed that the breakup of the collaboration would be described to friends as the result of an irresistible offer from the *Post*, though in fact Stewart had solicited the offer.

In a final joint appearance titled "Hail and Farewell," written for release on March 12, 1958, they announced the end of "a long and happy brotherly partnership." For practical reasons, they wrote, "it has become desirable to divide the functions of newspaper reporting and magazine writing."[28] (The text of this column is reprinted in the appendix.)

More candidly, the junior partner, recounting his conversations with the *Saturday Evening Post*, told Joe that he had explained the breakup on two grounds:

> First, I said, we were a bit like a pair of middle aged cart horses, who had been in harness together for a long time, and although we had a deep affection for each other, the harness was inevitably beginning to chafe a bit. Second, I said that while you were chosen by God and nature to be a newspaper columnist I was not, and that I enjoyed magazine work far more. Both statements are of course quite true. But I also made a major point of the fact . . . that we had had no row, that there had been no break between us. I intend to underline this point to the world by giving you a large ball on your return.[29]

The reference was to a running series of black-tie dinner-dances for friends and family which had become known as "the Alsop ball" and which on more than one occasion stirred their guests to satirical poetry. On this occasion the ball punctuated an era, and afterward, while they remained friends, professionally the two brothers went their separate ways.

Chapter Twelve Was There a Missile Gap?

The decision to break up the partnership freed Joe Alsop from his younger brother's more cautious instincts. He was now at liberty to be alarmist as never before and lost no time being so. No previous indulgence in Cassandra-style journalism left longer repercussions than his famous series of columns written in January 1960 on the "missile gap"—a term which, like "domino effect," he later claimed to have coined.

With the Eisenhower tide at its final ebb, 1960 was quickly becoming a critical election year. When Joe turned to his missile-gap series, he had already signed on as a sort of unofficial adviser—in print and in person —to the developing campaign of John F. Kennedy. Kennedy, who shortly took up the cry that American strategic supremacy was under threat, later became the principal political beneficiary of the missile-gap campaign. There would be those, in fact, who later considered this episode a cynical canard, invented to promote the Kennedy candidacy. The story, as usual, was more complicated than that.

Both Alsop brothers, as their letters show, had been closer over the years to Lyndon Johnson, Kennedy's major rival for the 1960 nomination. Joe had known Kennedy only casually during the years since Kennedy had arrived as a young congressman from Massachusetts not long after the war. At that time, Joe had been invited one night to a get-acquainted dinner at the Georgetown house Kennedy then shared with two of his sisters. At the appointed hour, Joe rang the doorbell, heard no answer, and entered through the unlocked door to behold a scene of cyclone-struck dishevelment. The house was a scene of jolly disorder. Neither his host nor anyone else was to be seen. Kennedy soon appeared with apologies, and the dinner went ahead as planned. But the scene of confusion lodged in Joe's memory.[1]

After Kennedy's marriage to Jacqueline Bouvier and Joe's own decision to move to Paris, there had been protracted discussions of leasing his Dumbarton Avenue house to the Kennedys. But the Kennedys planned to do extensive remodeling to Joe's house if they did lease it. Their plans had so frightened Joe's Filipino servants, Jose and Maria, that the project was called off. Another friend, Oatsie Leiter, took the lease instead.

Their political friendship grew with Kennedy's presidential ambitions. Joe at first assumed that Kennedy's ambitions for 1960 went no further than another bid for the vice presidential nomination, which had narrowly eluded him four years earlier, when Adlai Stevenson opened the choice to the Democratic convention. But Kennedy one day told Joe, "I'm completely against vice in all forms," signaling to Joe's surprise that he meant to try for the presidential nomination itself.[2] Weary after eight years of Eisenhower, Joe welcomed Kennedy's ambition and soon became an unabashed Kennedy partisan, and the alliance intensified after the young senator became a sounding board for the missile-gap theory Joe had been trumpeting since January of the election year. Along with his friend Philip Graham, the publisher of the *Washington Post*, Joe would also claim credit for the brilliant stroke of persuading Kennedy, at the Los Angeles party convention, to choose Lyndon Johnson as his running mate—a choice that probably made the difference in the narrow election result.[3]

Variations on the story, some mythic and others self-serving, emerged in profusion. After his brother's assassination, Robert Kennedy would persuade himself, and seek to persuade others, that the selection of Lyndon Johnson had been an accident—a misunderstanding brought on by the fatigue of the nominee and his circle on the night they clinched the presidential nomination. Robert Kennedy had hotly contested the choice and had even embarked on a daring mission to Johnson's hotel suite, where he tried to persuade the powerful Senate majority leader to withdraw his name. The normally sedate Sam Rayburn, who was there with Johnson, spoke for the Johnson circle: "Shit, little man," he said contemptuously to Robert Kennedy's suggestion that Johnson withdraw. The episode was the beginning of an enmity between Johnson and the younger Kennedy that intensified after the president's November 1963 assassination. Joe assumed, however, that Jack Kennedy had been persuaded by the strong argument he and Graham had made for a southern strategy. Joe's theory was that Kennedy's appeasement of his brother and of the angry labor leaders had been an act, a cover-up. In his careful investigation of the Johnson choice, the columnist Jules Witcover acknowledges the persistent variety of memories but notes that when Joe and Phil Graham called on Kennedy on the opening day of the convention they both found it hard to believe how receptive the prospective nominee was to Johnson. "Joe and I were a bit shaken by his positiveness," Graham later recalled in a memorandum he wrote for his own files.[4]

Visiting the Kennedy compound at Hyannis Port, Massachusetts, in August, after the convention, Joe was happy "to see Jack going into the hardest campaign of the century with his rather special combination of a hard, realistic grasp of his problems and a high heart."[5] Once again, as he had so often done before, Joe was wearing the hats of commentator and insider at once. He had huddled with the Kennedy strategists, and when he returned to Washington afterward, he even found himself doubling as an unofficial social adviser to Jacqueline Kennedy. She was agitated by the threatening glare of press publicity and agonized about what it might mean for the Kennedys' daughter Caroline, "whom [the photographers] want to chase around with flashbulbs and turn into a ghastly little Shirley Temple if I'd let them." Joe counseled equanimity and urged Jacqueline Kennedy to take it in stride and bear in mind the example of Mrs. Robert Taft, "who found the most stylish and most effective solution" to the publicity demands of Washington:

> She never did the oddly humorous and even downright fantastic things that Cousin Eleanor did—such as appearing as a model at a

Democratic fund-raising fashion show. She didn't indulge either in the little ad man's phoninesses, the false homey touches, that I'm afraid I think Pat Nixon indulges in. But she did everything that could be useful and that involved no fakery or real loss of dignity . . . things, of course, she would never have done if she had been plain Mrs. Taft of Cincinnati, Ohio, and this I suspect is the standard you are applying.[6]

Joe topped this counsel with the advice that Mrs. Kennedy, who was then expecting the Kennedys' son John, ought to buy, and be seen buying, maternity clothes at Bloomingdale's rather than at the usual expensive Manhattan boutiques—Bloomingdale's apparently represented Joe's notion of democratic shopping, not altogether surprising in one whose suits, shirts, and shoes were handmade for him in London and Milan. "I can see no very great difference," he wrote her, "between this kind of piece on the woman's page, and the other kind of piece, accurately stating that the beautiful Mrs. Kennedy looks just dandy in her new Givenchy ball dress. It's the kind of thing . . . that can be done for public purposes without any overture from or falsification of your private self." Jacqueline Kennedy accepted the advice. She would be going to Bloomingdale's, she informed Joe, and David Dubinsky, the head of the garment workers' union, would be going with her, presumably to amplify the common touch.

AFTER KENNEDY'S ELECTION, Joe and his new wife Susan Mary, the widow of his old friend Bill Patten and an intimate pen pal for years, were often guests at the White House. (They had married in the election year, not long after Joe had astonished Susan Mary by proposing to marry her and support her two children.) There was no doubt of Joe Alsop's partiality to Kennedy; and that partiality would eventually nourish the view that the missile-gap series had essentially been propaganda in the Kennedy cause. A major social news item from the evening of January 20, 1961, reinforced that impression. In the small hours of the morning, as the inaugural balls were winding down, Kennedy had appeared in white tie and top hat at Joe Alsop's door—the only private residence other than his own which he visited on that historic night—and stayed for hours, visiting with a miscellany of guests and having a very late supper of terrapin soup.

With Kennedy's arrival, a drastic transition began in the capital, one that Joe Alsop had eagerly awaited. He had never really liked the business-oriented men who arrived with Eisenhower. He found them both dull and self-serving and soon found that he missed the Truman years. He had observed the latter with such patronizing condescension that he eventually wrote a letter of apology to Truman. Kennedy, six years younger than Joe but of the same generation, became the first American president to be born in the twentieth century. Joe's late-ripening friendship with him became the most intense of his many political enthusiasms, brief and passionate.

BUT THAT is to get a bit ahead of the story, which really begins with the missile-gap series itself, Joe Alsop's most elaborate journalistic engagement in a subject since, six years earlier, he had thrown himself into his defense of J. Robert Oppenheimer. In five consecutive columns, which appeared between January 25 and January 29, Joe proclaimed that, short of major emergency measures to redress the balance, the United States would soon be exposed to the danger of annihilation by Soviet intercontinental ballistic missiles (ICBMs). Three years earlier, in the autumn of 1957, the Russians had gained a lead in the race to thrust an artificial satellite into space; and the rocket thrust and calibration required for the Sputnik success implied a capacity to launch ICBMs at a faraway target with considerable accuracy. Joe's imagination, never less than lurid at such moments, soared; he conjured up visions of apocalypse.

That, at any rate, was the lingering impression afterward. The truth was that notwithstanding the doomsday premise, the missile-gap series took a considerably more sober, understated, and analytical tone than Joe's usual writings on the dangers of Soviet aims. To be sure, the subject itself was intrinsically alarming and needed little theoretical or rhetorical embellishment. The January series could be seen as a continuation of earlier Alsop alarums of approaching strategic disadvantage. With the sudden appearance in the mid-1950s of swarms of new Soviet bombers (which the Pentagon called "Bisons"), the air force had begun to speak of a bomber gap and the term found echo in Joe Alsop's column. That worry eventually subsided, however, as the new American B-52s became available and were deployed to Strategic Air Command bases in England and placed on round-the-clock alert.

The Alsops had established their credibility earlier in the decade by

scooping their competitors on the timing of the decision to make the hydrogen bomb and on the story of radiation fallout and the health men-
aces it produced.[7] The missile gap of 1960 drew, in addition, on a mood
of restlessness in the country, a feeling that the Eisenhower administration had become complacent about the Soviet strategic threat.

As his point of departure for the missile-gap series, Joe relied on an
address to the New York Economic Club by General Thomas Power,
Curtis LeMay's successor as head of the Strategic Air Command. "With
only some three hundred missiles," the general warned—the words had
been italicized in the text from which he spoke—"the Soviets could virtually wipe out our entire nuclear strike capability within a span of thirty
minutes." Power's disturbing estimate was based on a standard calculation. If the U.S. assumptions about their average accuracy were correct,
three missiles aimed at each of the hundred-odd U.S. strategic bases
would "assure" their destruction. Since the Soviet Union was thought to
have about 150 intermediate-range missiles in stock and deployed—and
presumably targeted on American bases in England and elsewhere—the
only question was whether, and how soon, the Soviets would undertake
a crash program to build and deploy additional intercontinental-range
missiles capable of reaching bases in the continental United States. "That
number [of additional missiles] is not large," Joe Alsop wrote on January
26 in the second piece of the series, "only ten months of the productive
capacity of our own Atlas ICBM plant." In the worst case, it meant that
without timely U.S. countermeasures the Soviet Union would have a
deadly advantage within a year or two. The years then ensuing would be
the years of the "gap"—a time of maximum danger of sudden, annihilating attack.[8]

As followers of the long strategic nuclear weapons debate will notice,
this was one of the first appearances in the popular press of that mythic
"window of vulnerability" whose dangers were heatedly debated throughout the 1960s, 1970s, and 1980s. Weapons systems changed, but the
"window" never seemed to close. The idea of a "window of vulnerability" was finally laid to rest in 1983–84 by the Scowcroft Commission, a
strategic study panel appointed by Ronald Reagan to seek an answer to
the basing dilemma of the projected new American ICBM, the so-called
MX missile.[9]

The supposed American vulnerability of which General Power and
Joe Alsop were speaking rested on the wholly theoretical calculation that

one nuclear superpower striking the other suddenly and unexpectedly, with overwhelming force, would do such damage that the stricken foe would have no rational alternative but to sue for peace terms. Even if segments of its deterrent force survived, it would be too weak and demoralized to risk a counterattack. It would, in the parlance of strategic risk, lack a "second-strike capacity." These calculations rested, in turn, on a larger analysis, equally theoretical, of the nature of nuclear deterrence. It had been worked out and refined at the Rand Corporation and other strategic think tanks, which had arisen as prominent by-products of the nuclear age, heavily subsidized by Pentagon research contracts. These theoretical studies, clad in all the esoteric jargon of nuclear weaponry, were seldom openly accused of bias; but it would have been surprising if any such study failed to find reasons to worry and, of course, reasons to spend more to relieve those worries. If one accepted the initial premise, the logical implications were hard to get around.

For Americans with even the shortest memories of wartime, moreover, there was another element in this dread of sudden, annihilating attack. While the Soviet military neurosis reflected its historic memories of overland invasion, French or German, across the northern European plain and its lack of natural defensive barriers, the American military neurosis plainly reflected the memory of Pearl Harbor, the Pacific navy base caught sleeping on the early morning of December 7, 1941, by Admiral Yamamoto and his Japanese host. Any warning or anxiety, however far-fetched and however dependent upon esoteric and unverifiable strategic theory, was unlikely to be dismissed out of hand by Americans or their representatives in Congress.

With the comparatively primitive state of detection—by radar surveillance of Soviet missile test sites from Turkey—it was left to the mandarins of the National Intelligence Estimates boards to assimilate the raw information about Soviet capabilities and calculate the dangers. It was on this very point—the difficulty of predicting what the Soviets might do—that the Eisenhower administration appeared to be divided. Unlike General Power, who spoke for the Strategic Air Command, other high military and defense officials took the view in public testimony that a missile gap was a remote danger. Secretary of Defense Thomas Gates, in appearances before congressional committees, had dismissed the risk as negligible. Joe took care to admit, for the sake of argument, that the question could not easily be resolved.[10] But it seemed to him now, as it had in the Louis Johnson era at the Defense Department, that economy-mindedness and penny-pinching rather than strategic concerns were dictating defense budget levels. To Joe's mind, that explained the Eisenhower administration's willingness to play Russian roulette with U.S. safety and survival.

Such gambles, Joe argued on January 27, had been tried before and had proved perilous. "The record shows a consistent series of gross American underestimates of Soviet weapons achievements from 1946 onward. From the atomic bomb, to the first Soviet jet engine for aircraft, to the first Soviet long-range jet bombers, to the ICBM itself, the estimators went on making the same kind of error. On average, the Soviets were always expected to make such major advances a good two years later than the actual moment when the advance was made." Finally, Joe argued, the "shocking" fact was that intelligence estimates were now being gauged by "intentions" rather than capabilities. He suspected that this shift in the basis of estimation was being driven by political and budgetary concerns.[11]

Joe was confident enough of the importance of his basic case on the missile gap to have the series reprinted in pamphlet form and sent, along with a personal note, to every member of the Senate and to all the key members of House defense or preparedness committees. The response was more than perfunctory, especially among the Democrats, for there was no doubt that the country was jittery about Soviet missile technology and not unwilling to assume the worst. There was blood in the water, the Eisenhower administration was on the defensive, and within a few months Kennedy, in particular, would echo Joe Alsop's claims in Senate speeches.

As few knew or could know at the time, and as Joe Alsop apparently did not know, the missile-gap outcry was to serve as an object lesson in the limitations of journalistic perspectives. The keen reportorial nose that had often served Joe so well—in the McCarthy controversy, for instance—failed him here. Whatever their capacity might have been (and as late as August 1959 the CIA had not yet spotted a single "operational" Soviet ICBM) the Russians clearly had not raced along with the crash program that strategists had warned against. In this respect, Nikita Khrushchev's frequent boasts about his capacity to rain remote destruction on NATO cities was largely hollow, a bluff. The U.S. surveillance satellites would soon prove so conclusively. Had the fears expressed by General

Power and echoed by Joe been more solidly grounded, it is doubtful that Khrushchev would have precipitated the Cuban missile crisis two years later—a reckless enterprise, giving rise to the most dangerous nuclear crisis of the Cold War period. Khrushchev sought to bootleg intermediate-range missiles into Cuba in October 1962, in a transparent attempt to compensate for the superiority of U.S. strategic striking power.

How then had the missile-gap delusion prospered? It was brassy even by Joe Alsop's standards—and Joe's impatience with less brilliant mortals was well known—to pit his strategic military judgment so vocally and stubbornly against that of General of the Armies Dwight D. Eisenhower, the man in the White House. Eisenhower was forced to stew silently under press and partisan charges that, for the sake of a balanced budget, he was putting American survival at risk. As later studies of Eisenhower have shown, defense economies were close to the top of his list of priorities, and that concern was certainly related to his administration's exceedingly conservative fiscal and monetary policies. But Eisenhower was justifiably unhappy with the insinuation that he would parsimoniously expose the nation to attack. "Privately," writes Michael Beschloss in *May Day*, an account of the U-2 shoot-down and its aftermath, "the President pounded his desktop and threw offending magazines and newspapers against the Oval Office walls: Alsop was 'about the lowest form of animal life on earth.'"[12]

In fact, Eisenhower held an intelligence trump that was known only to him and to a few high White House aides: his national security adviser, Gordon Gray; his military adviser, General Andrew Goodpaster; his secretary of state, John Foster Dulles; and his son John, who served as a military aide. Since July 4, 1956, the United States' U-2 surveillance aircraft, operated in the deepest secrecy by the CIA and equipped with extraordinarily powerful cameras that could read an automobile license plate from twelve miles up, had been overflying the Soviet Union and delivering filmed intelligence on Soviet strategic developments. This was no secret at the Kremlin. Long before Captain Francis Gary Powers's U-2 was shot down over Sverdlovsk in May 1960, half a year after Joe's series concluded, the Soviets had maintained the conspiracy of silence for reasons of prestige.[13]

As pressure mounted for an official response to the recommendations of the 1959 Gaither Report, a post-Sputnik document that drew conclusions almost as alarmist as Joe Alsop's, Secretary of State Dulles suggested to Eisenhower that the U.S. surveillance capacity be declared openly. Eisenhower's judgment was better; he demurred, and probably was wise to do so. Even later, with the deployment of surveillance satellites—a development that further reassured U.S. officials and stabilized the situation—American presidents and diplomats went on speaking guardedly, in coded and indirect language, of "national technical means" of intelligence-gathering, avoiding the naked claim that the air space of another nation was now subject to U.S. penetration at will, with or without that nation's permission. Of all this intelligence Joe Alsop apparently had no inkling until Powers's plane was shot down on the eve of the Paris summit in June 1960. Joe hailed the existence of the spy planes as "wonderful news."[14] U-2 surveillance, though less comprehensive or reliable than satellite photography later would be, offered solid evidence that the Russians were hardly rushing to build an ICBM knockout punch —even if it lay within their technical capability to do so. But even confronted with evidence that Eisenhower might know more than he did about Soviet rocketry, Joe did not retract his scary columns about the missile gap.

YEARS LATER Joe Alsop would defend the missile-gap series, even while acknowledging that the fears were exaggerated and unwarranted. Such was the ongoing nature of the "historical process," he maintained, that in some crucial matters of national life and death no risk-taking whatever could be morally justified. For the first time in history, a modern state could make mistakes of omission that could literally be fatal to national survival; not many mistakes of this sort were possible, perhaps, but a few were. In the face of intelligence uncertainties, it was better in these matters to be safe than sorry. It was, Joe argued, a bit like buying fire insurance for a house. The insurance could be costly, and the chances of fire might be infinitely remote. But one fire without insurance would be ruinous and absolutely unaffordable, so one had to buy the policy.[15] It was an arresting analogy, but the fact was that Joe had been warning that the arsonists were firing up their torches to burn the house down when, in fact, there was no evidence of such an intention. After the embarrassment of the Cuban missile crisis in October 1962, the Soviets did apparently attempt to achieve what looked from time to time like a commanding advantage in land-based ICBMs. But whether a missile gap ever was a real danger, even then, remains a matter of speculation.

WHAT LINGERED in the public and political memory about the missile-gap controversy was not the complexity of the art of intelligence estimating but the belief that Joe had been carrying water for John Kennedy and that, once safely elected, Kennedy had lost no time in repudiating what from the first had been a cynical campaign gambit. This was unfair both to Joe, who did not know the U-2 story, and to Kennedy, who even as a certified presidential candidate was denied full and candid briefings on the missile balance and was left to guess and speculate. As memories dimmed, the missile gap, along with Vietnam and Watergate, took on the murky properties of historical myth, and the mythic story was undoubtedly damaging to Joe's reputation as a public commentator.

Whatever role Joe's missile-gap series played in setting the stage for Kennedy's election, Kennedy's brief term was for Joe Alsop an era of stylish fun and also of the danger and excitement he relished—the missile crisis (about which Stewart Alsop would write a famous *Saturday Evening Post* piece in collaboration with Charles Bartlett, another of the Kennedys' journalist friends), the Berlin crisis, and the building of Nikita Khrushchev's Berlin wall (Joe thought the wall had probably prevented World War III).

The sense of at last being near the center of power was so exhilarating that after the young president's death in Dallas on November 22, 1963, Joe began to realize that these thousand days—as Arthur Schlesinger, Jr., would call them in his memoir—had been the most interesting years of his life.[16] His had been the sort of relationship with the administration that lends validity to the notion, proposed by the British historian Sir Dennis Brogan, that being in Washington was a bit like being at the court of Louis XIV in the times chronicled by the Duc de Saint Simon. The term *courtier* isn't used in Washington; but in this brief and luminous interval Joe came as close to being a true courtier as he ever did. After Kennedy's death, he summed up his sense of the experience in a letter to his friend Isaiah Berlin, who was spending the academic year in California:

> You are quite right in saying that things will never be the same. For me, it is a very odd sensation indeed, to discover quite abruptly, without any prior realization, that I have lived the best years of my life between the ages of forty-eight and fifty-three. Thank God, I have everything still that makes life worth living, conspicuously headed by Susan Mary and the children, and with friends like you and Aline to

make the cup brim over. But it will never be as exciting, as satisfying, as interesting again. . . . I had never known I loved the President (for one does not think of this kind of relationship in those terms) until I felt the impact of his death. To me, this was his most inexplicable quality. With the sole possible exception of Harry Hopkins, FDR did not command love from those who were close to him; he was loved by the poor who did not know him. . . . Kennedy, in contrast, was genuinely loved by astonishing numbers of the people who served him.[17]

It was, Joe wrote to friends, a "phenomenon" beyond easy or rational explanation that he could find the death of Kennedy bitterer than the death of his own father. Years later, as he groped for terms adequate to the elusive Kennedy quality that had entranced him, he would recall lines from the English poet Andrew Marvell's "Ode to Cromwell," Marvell's elegiac tribute to the doomed King Charles I on the day of his beheading: "He nothing common did or mean / Upon that memorable scene."

Epilogue

I n Joe Alsop's case, it sometimes was hard to see where the panache ended and the bedrock of serious and brilliant character began. As I knew him in the last fifteen years of his busy life, Joe was a prickly and ornate relic of a more individualistic past, a true eccentric. But as his peer and contemporary James Reston suggested to me in the course of a long afternoon's discussion, the American system probably couldn't afford very much eccentricity of the Alsop kind. If we indulged in the luxury of more Joe Alsops, Reston said, the melting pot, which has rarely melted as advertised, would hardly have melted at all.

In any case, Americanization in its superficial sense would have been a repugnant idea to Joe Alsop. He resisted all of its conventions and cults. As the midnight hour approached at one of his formal dinners one New Year's Eve, someone suggested that a television set be brought in so that his guests could watch the festive rituals of the evening in Times Square. A television set? Joe Alsop barely conceded that television existed—he had once written that if he could disinvent one great twentieth-century

176

menace, it would be television rather than the atomic bomb. He had none under his own roof, he insisted. But after whispered consultations, his housekeeper Gemma produced from somewhere below stairs an ancient wooden relic of the 1940s with a miniature screen. When it was turned on, the strains of "Auld Lang Syne" wheezed tinnily from the ancient speaker. Joe put down the oversized Oriental teacup from which he took his after-dinner coffee and covered his face in a characteristic gesture of mock despair.

"What is that ghastly sound?" he demanded, with apparent innocence.

"Guy Lombardo," someone said.

"Who the hell is Guy Lombardo?" he roared. (There is evidence that this little ritual served to entertain more than one New Year's Eve gathering.)

IT IS CLEAR that Joe, and perhaps Stewart as well, wished to be remembered. Their extensive papers at the Library of Congress suggest no shyness of biographers and historians, although Joe's touchy reactions to the efforts of various friends and acquaintances to write humorously about him suggest that he would not always have relished their findings. The Alsop Papers fill over two hundred boxes and span a rich and interesting stretch of the recent American past, from the late 1930s, when Joe first became a successful newspaper reporter and columnist, well into the late 1970s.

The Alsop partnership described in this book flourished during the golden age of the syndicated newspaper column, when the canons of "objective" journalism left the privilege of analysis and interpretation almost entirely to columnists. Joe and Stewart Alsop traveled the world to interview leaders of state and opinion on nearly every continent and to report local situations in intimate and often colorful detail. A *Time* report of June 1956, entitled "Alsop's Fables," admiringly describes Joe's triumphant eleven-week tour of the Middle East. *Time*, which had had its differences with the Alsops, hailed his "dramatic flair as a reporter in foreign lands seiz[ing] on color, incident, history and personality to bring a situation crackling to life." At a dinner for four hundred thrown by King Saud for the Imam of Yemen, Joe drew on depths of literary allusions. The Imam "waggles his big, richly turbaned head like a teetotum in a sort of passion of politeness," while, as the guests drank orange pop, "a court bard, descended straight from the poetic line that sang before

Agamemnon at Mycenae . . . recites a long poem in praise of the King and Imam into a deafening loudspeaker system." This vivid reportage was the product of their "go and see for yourself" rule.

The literary strengths of the Alsops' journalism are easier to pinpoint, however, than its "influence," at least if one measures influence by things done or left undone in direct response to a newspaper column or magazine report of the sort they specialized in. Joe believed that it was fact, not opinion, that sways the world, though perhaps the distinction between the two is not always so obvious as he supposed. Joe's "reporting" often seemed very opinionated.

When they dissolved their partnership in 1958, Joe and Stewart Alsop attempted an interim assessment of their collaboration in *The Reporter's Trade*. The book was not a publishing success; it appeared during the New York newspaper strike and lost readers it might otherwise have reached. But the book throws a revealing light on what they thought their big stories had been; and these almost all had to do with national defense and security.

At that time there had been no major turn in what Joe liked to call the "historical process"; few of the national security issues they addressed had reached closure. Three decades later, we can begin to see more clearly how the story turned out, and the outcome has in some important ways vindicated their judgment in people and causes. George F. Kennan and other architects of the "containment" doctrine, whether in its political or militarized variations, have been vindicated. And in the face of the Soviet menace, theirs was the guidance in world strategy that the Alsops adopted and advocated.

In their prime, the Alsops had an aura of "influence," and while that influence was real it was also intangible and eludes quantitative measurement. One might ask whether the critical American decisions the Alsops applauded—President Truman's bold decisions to push ahead with a U.S. hydrogen bomb in the face of scientific doubts, and to fight the North Korean invasion of South Korea—or even those they strongly opposed—Eisenhower's decision to make a compromise peace dividing Korea at the 38th Parallel, and his reluctance to intervene in support of the French in Indochina in 1953–54—might have differed if their views had differed. That would be a hard case to make: It is difficult to think that columns and magazine articles could have made so fundamental a difference. But the test may be too stern for mere journalism, which by definition is of its day and evanescent.

Joe was right in his instinctive belief that events and decisions are usually driven by facts, or what decision-makers take to be facts. That remained his journalistic creed, even when he was at his most opinionated. But comment may have other more gradual and incremental effects. A timely and well-wrought newspaper column may modify or reinforce a public mood, rendering the public more receptive, or less so, to a contemplated line of official policy. Both the Alsops, especially Joe, believed that it was their function to be brokers of vital information, reported at a high level of sophistication. That was the case they repeatedly pressed on friends who worked at high policy-making levels in government: Without the facts, the American public could not understand policy objectives or govern itself well; and without the candid collaboration of responsible officials who were really in the know, reporters like themselves couldn't get the facts out. The Alsop Papers reveal several lengthy appeals addressed to friends in power, such as Paul Nitze, Chip Bohlen, and Dean Acheson, in which the case for privileged briefings was carefully elaborated, often with unrewarding results.

Sometimes, as in the painful case of Dean Acheson, the reaction was not merely uncooperative but also obstructive. To be sure, Joe's appeals for the facts, while genuine enough, often represented a quest for reinforcement of what he already thought and believed. One high intelligence official decided, reluctantly, to accept Joe's invitation to luncheon, expecting to be pumped for information. Not at all. It was Joe who talked, he who listened. But the ambience was agreeable and the wines and food excellent.

Probably no accumulation of facts, however compelling, would have curbed Joe's urge to promote deeper American involvement in Indochina in 1953–54, nor have persuaded him that the Truman administration was spending enough on defense before the invasion of South Korea in June 1950 so quickly wrought a revolution in defense budgeting. Moreover, as Joe's ventures into archaeology and art history show, he delighted in second-guessing experts, whatever their field. He felt he often knew more than they did, and often enough he was right. There are few examples in his writings and behavior—the situation was a bit different with the milder Stewart—of deference to the judgment of any but those he regarded as truly great figures: Forrestal, Marshall, Bohlen, Kennan. They, and few others, were usually (but not always) presumed to know what they were doing. But a man like Lewis Strauss, as head of the Atomic Energy Commission, was entirely capable of wasting "half an hour of our valuable time."

The Alsops' journalistic impact can be observed more visibly in their campaign to curb the savagery of McCarthyism and the lunacies of the Truman and Eisenhower "security" and "loyalty" programs, which resulted in the discharge or ruin of valuable and unoffending public servants. The exposure of McCarthy's lies, along with Joe's inside reports on the true extent of his and his staff's boorish behavior in the Schine affair, had a marked effect. On occasion at least, so did the intercession on behalf of the State Department's much-abused China Hands, though neither Joe Alsop nor anyone else managed to save good men like John Paton Davies from early obscurity at a time when the country could have used their services. In the end, so did Stewart Alsop's valuable exposés of the abuses connected with the FBI's paid witness programs.

One consequence of U.S. isolation from China after 1949 was the Chinese intervention in Korea. Having no diplomatic channel to Washington, Chou En-lai recruited the Indian ambassador to Peking, V. N. Pannikar, to warn the American government against threatening the Chinese border along the Yalu River. The Alsops made the serious mistake of discounting Pannikar's warning, dismissing the Indian envoy, they ruefully admit, as "Mr. Panicker." Read more closely than they usually have been, Joe's noted *Saturday Evening Post* articles on the "loss" of China conceded —as did some later Matter of Fact columns—that almost any policy would have been better than the policy of trying, after Chiang's flight to Formosa, to isolate China. Davies was shown to have been far-sighted in advocating a "Titoist" solution in China, even before Tito gave his name to the phenomenon in Yugoslavia. But in the embittered Korean War years, Communist China was thought of as the obedient puppet of Stalin. The Alsops can be faulted for adopting that view, but it was the conventional wisdom of the time.

We began with a possible paradox: Did the Alsops, by dwelling upon, and perhaps intensifying, the sense of menace from the Soviet Union and its allies, contribute to the domestic disorder called McCarthyism, which they passionately deplored? Any connection between the two seems speculative. The revisionist historians of the Cold War, who flourished briefly during the Vietnam War years and were so clearly an aspect of the reaction against it, were quick to find imagined continuities between Communist-baiting at home and the Cold War abroad; but they persuaded very few. In displaying what Arthur Schlesinger, Jr., called "grace of spirit"—the grace to vouch for the integrity, loyalty, and honor of officials whose policies they vehemently opposed—were the Alsops fighting fires they had helped set, or fan? The case for that thesis, closely examined, is not persuasive.

The Communist threat abroad was severe, and it was at once psychological, military, and political. Subversion was among the familiar techniques of Communist penetration; and as Schlesinger has shown, there were real conspiratorial cells in Washington, especially in the 1930s. But at no time in the late 1940s or 1950s could the threat to American national security be usefully defined in domestic terms. By the time Senator McCarthy and the other congressional inquisitors discovered the issue and went into their war dance, the battle against Communist penetration in labor unions, in Hollywood, and in a few leftist publications and so-called fellow-traveling organizations was mostly over and had been won in instances both appropriate and inappropriate. Where confusion remained, it was hardly of the Alsops' making. They patiently explained, not once but often, how the political divisions at home, worsened by partisan exploitation, incivility, and irresponsibility, weakened the national effort to cope with the real security threat abroad. This view was not popular on the fringes, left or right, but it was common to those who would later be called, often with no flattery intended, "Cold War liberals." It was unfortunate that Joe's *Saturday Evening Post* series contributed a headline—"How We Lost China"—and a dubious proposition (the idea that China had been ours to "lose") to the debate and perpetuated a divisive myth. But as we have seen, "lost" was a term of journalistic shorthand, not an assertion of literal historical fact.

In trying to balance the gains and losses of the fifties, and the Alsops' role in the decade, we now have the considerable advantage of seeing the landscape as neither of them lived to see it. The "historical process" has suddenly taken an unexpectedly favorable turn that was foreseen by no one, least of all Joe, in his chronic gloom. The Alsops were history-minded; they knew that history had its great discontinuities. But their invocations of history were largely backward-looking and drew upon the "lessons of the past" as they understood them. The main lesson came from the immediate pre–World War II period, the overwhelming experience of their formative years; and it was that weak or half-hearted responses to aggressive behavior invite more of the same. Fortunately, their gloomier forebodings turned out to be not so much incorrect as inconsequential.

Joe and Stewart Alsop were splendidly positioned by education, heritage, and sense of history to articulate an enlarged vision of American responsibility. Their own attitudes, appropriately updated, did not differ materially from those embraced half a century earlier by their great-uncle, Teddy Roosevelt. A sense of civility mandated certain restraints in domestic politics; a sense of national responsibility mandated a strong hand abroad. These two strands were only apparently, and exceptionally, in conflict. For the most part they were mutually sustaining and complementary, equally indispensable if the United States was to play a strong and honorable role in a dangerous world. There could be no honor in a brute strength that was vitiated by violence to tolerance and liberty at home, and little security in a world where the strong were left to prey with impunity on the weak. So the causes they espoused were equally important; and in the end, the paradox was no paradox at all.

Appendix

Three milestones in the Alsop collaboration follow. The first column marks its tenth anniversary, the second its breakup, and the third Joe Alsop's retirement from full-time journalism.

ANNIVERSARY REPORT

WASHINGTON—Exactly ten years ago today, the first column by these reporters appeared in a handful of American newspapers. It is an odd experience, entertaining in a way and sad in another, to flip over the pages of that first year's scrapbook of columns, and to note how times have changed—and how they have not. There is a nostalgia, which the reporters may be pardoned for indulging in at this season, in the yellowed clippings and the dated words.

The first column begins with the remark that "The most conspicuous single fact in Washington today is Harry S. Truman," and concludes that "It is still an open question whether Truman can master his job." The question is still open and will no doubt remain so for many more decades. The columns that follow are filled with names which are already dim in the memory, and political rows which it is an effort to recall at all. There is much about "the President's cronies"—Ed Pauley, Vardaman, Vaughan, Steelman, Snyder, and the redoubtable George Allen, who has managed to retain his role as a Presidential crony until the present day.[1]

The rows about the President's appointment of Pauley to be Under-Secretary of the Navy, and Allen to be head of the Reconstruction Finance Corp., are analyzed in detail, and one wonders a little why these dusty battles seemed so important at the time.

Then there are the other engrossing struggles of the era, like Chester Bowles' fight with John Snyder over the O.P.A. (remember the O.P.A.?), Henry Wallace's break with Truman, and John L. Lewis's homeric battle with the administration. There is the contest between John Snyder and Lewis Schwellenbach (remember Schwellenbach?) for control of labor relations, and there is the great steel strike of that year, and the battle between the pro-Communists and anti-Communists for the soul of the C.I.O. and the liberal movement.[2]

There is much, indeed, about the Communist threat (at a time when the internal Communist danger was hardly recognized by those who now proclaim themselves its first discoverers). "It is not easy to shake Communists loose," one column remarks, "but if this country is to have the independent and vigorous liberal movement it so badly needs, it must be done."

There are surprising hints of things to come and many echoes of a forgotten past. But what stands out . . . is not how much, but how little, the really important things have changed. The cold war started ten years ago, although, again, it was not at all fashionable to admit it at the time. The third column these reporters wrote noted flatly that the nation was "without a basic policy for dealing with the basic problem of current international relations—the new Soviet imperialism." Omit the adjective "new" and the sentence would be as accurate today as it was ten years ago.

A few weeks later, another column remarks that the weakness of American foreign policy arises from "the unwillingness to use our vast economic power to the full and with all energy in order to cure the terrible ills which weaken all nations in Europe and Asia, and thus encourage Soviet expansionism . . ."

Toward the end of that year, these reporters succumbed to a fit of over-optimism, which has not frequently been repeated since. "The Soviet foreign policy which has plagued the whole world," a December column stated, "seems to be in process of basic revision. It is too early to cheer, but not too early to hope." Within a matter of weeks it proved to be a great deal too early to hope. It still is.

Yet there may be ground for hope of a sort in something else that stands out from the yellow pages of the decade-old scrapbook. There was much, even then, about the new weapons, which (as the six or seven persons who are believed to read this column fairly regularly may have noted), have been something of an obsession with these reporters.

"Even now," one of the first columns remarked, "no one has grasped the fullness of the change in world power relationships wrought by the scientists of World War II." The end result of the new weapons, another column reported, was to "make possible that war among the continents which must haunt the imagination of every informed and imaginative man."

And yet, even now, ten years later, despite small wars and great crises, missiles and jets and hydrogen bombs, the worst has not happened. Is it to succumb to another fit of over-optimism to hope that, if only we keep our guard up, it never will? —*New York Herald Tribune*, January 1, 1956

HAIL AND FAREWELL

WASHINGTON—At the end of the month the above joint byline, the symbol of a long and happy brotherly partnership, will cease to appear in its accustomed place. For various highly practical reasons, it has become desirable to divide the functions of newspaper reporting and magazine writing which our partnership has always combined.

A parting in which personal feelings pull one way and practicality pushes the other way is always a sentimental business. So maybe it is sheer sentimentality on our parts, to want to mark the announcement of this oncoming parting with a sort of retrospect of our twelve years and more of work together.

We formed our partnership when we had barely put our wartime uniforms in mothballs, in the first peacetime months of the first Truman administration. If you want a measure of how incredibly long ago that was, there is the odd fact that we ran into our first trouble as columnists because of insufficient faith in the high and noble purposes of the Soviet Union.

The first Azerbaijanian crisis was just on the horizon; and in analyzing Stalin's grab for Persia, we followed the line of the exceptionally brilliant Soviet experts that the government had in those days. (One of them is in exile now; another has been driven from the public service; and we now seem to rely on the Secretary of State's direct wire to the Almighty for the functions the experts used to perform. But that is another subject.)[3] Having followed the line of our expert friends, we were denounced as hard-nosed, maliciously anti-Soviet pessimists by an impeccably Republican publisher of great importance to us, who later indulged in more than a little appeasement of Sen. Joseph R. McCarthy.

Being a newspaper columnist is a little like being a Greek chorus. You report, you analyze, you comment and you describe the parts of the drama that do not take place on the open stage. Since irony is a principal ingredient of the political drama, anyone who spends much time in the chorus is bound to remember a good many ironical episodes, like the episode of the indignant publisher.

The business itself has its own ironies. You find you bore people till their teeth hurt when you are most right, as we did with our angry reports on the Truman-Johnson disarmament program before the Korean War, and with our similar reports on the Eisenhower disarmament program that has been only a little modified by the Sputnik. You also find that the things you have to drive yourself to do very often end by being no more than wryly funny, as when one of us rather queasily decided to go in with the first wave at the Inchon landing, and was vaguely, peacefully deposited on quite the wrong beach. You find, too, that you are sometimes most popular when what you are writing is most wrong or most empty of real content.

The ironies of the business underline the cardinal rule that a newspaper man's feet are a lot more important than his head. But there is another rule as well. A newspaper man must never forget that the drama in which he is one of the chorus is a real drama—no mere sock-and-buskin fraud but a real-life drama of national and human destiny. And in this respect, how splendidly exciting, how full of movement and suspense, how often tensely stirring these last twelve years have been!

"The American lead" was a fact beyond imaginable questioning when we two went to work together. The question was, rather, whether this great technical and economic lead would be transformed into American leadership in freedom's bitter struggle to survive in a divided world.

Every American political tradition was against the transformation. The wisest and most experienced Americans regarded the transformation as utterly impossible—for instance, one of us can remember that very experienced man, James F. Byrnes, inveighing against the first proposers of the Marshall Plan as feather-witted visionaries who did not "know Congress."

Yet this great transformation of American lead into American leadership none the less took place; and there followed years that were troubled, certainly, but heroic, too. Maybe it was the unaccustomed effort of peacetime heroism that caused the subsequent welling up of poisonous mutual suspicion and quick hatred among Americans.

At any rate, the poison has been neutralized now. But the "American lead" has been lost too, and the future seems more doubtful today than one could have thought remotely possible twelve years ago. Maybe, indeed, our particular section of the chorus is separating just as the drama reaches its climax, which is another reason why we regret the separation.

But the separation has been decided, and this retrospect has gone on long enough. — *New York Herald Tribune*, March 12, 1958

AFTER 42 YEARS, A DECISION TO RETIRE

Rather soon—next New Year's Day, to be precise—the series of reports that have been appearing in this space will come to an end at long last. It has been very, very long. I went to work as a reporter in July, 1932. I went to work as a columnist in November, 1937. When you are not awfully far off half a century in the same job, it is time to stop.

There is the heart of the matter, but old friends and friendly readers may wish to know a bit more. To begin with, it has not been an easy decision. Starting with my long-term employers, the *Los Angeles Times* and the *Washington Post*, a contrary decision has been vigorously urged; and it has been generously urged as well in the two cases named.

To go on, if you have been a reporter for forty-two years plus and have been doing a column for just under thirty-seven years, it begins to seem downright unnatural to call a halt. But the plain truth is, alas, that the reporter's trade is for young men. Your feet, which do the legwork, are nine times more important than your head, which fits the facts into a coherent pattern.

The time spans already noted tell most of the rest of the story, although not all of it. Retirement, to be blunt and practical about it, always requires a man to cash in his savings. My savings, somewhat eccentrically, have gone into a much-loved house and garden and the house's endless pleasurable contents.

Long ago I concluded that I should probably do better buying the things I know about and could use and care for instead of all the conventional things that people put their savings into. Mercifully, this has turned out to be quite true. But leaving a house I designed myself, built myself and have enjoyed since the Truman times has also turned out to be a bit like a hermit crab abandoning its shell.

All the same, I long ago began to hear the voice of the barman (or is it the subway conductor?) in T. S. Eliot's "Waste Land"—the mysterious figure who calls out, "Hurry up, please, it's time." To be precise, the voice first called me when another Alsop brother, so long my partner, also vanished from the reportorial scene, leaving this city a sadder, poorer place.[4]

By a chance that I count my great good fortune, my brother needed me when he lived. Only when he died, therefore, could I do just as I chose. And at that moment I felt not just the pain of loss and the decrepitude that is natural if you were born in 1910; I felt further a final failure of all the zest and gusto and eagerness to know what will happen next that are the impelling motives of any good reporter.

It was a problem my brother and I had already begun talking about in that last year of his life, when it was again my great good fortune to see so much more of him. Oddly, he who was doomed to die felt no loss of zest at all. He diagnosed my different feeling on the main grounds. "You belong to the past much more than I do," he said.

I am now sure that he was right. I was formed in the wonderful years of President Franklin Roosevelt, when this city was still a village, yet a village full of responsibility and hope. I reached maturity during the second great war. My heyday was the postwar period that extended from 1945 until just the other day.

The postwar period, as I believe, was a time for all Americans to be proud of. Great world-wide tasks of reconstruction were undertaken by this country. Other toilsome burdens were assumed, and costly wars were even fought in order to prevent the postwar period from merging into a prewar period. All the American leaders of that time remembered how the British and French had not done particularly well in this respect; and how the postwar period that began in 1918 almost instantly merged into a prewar period about 1930.

The great Americans of the postwar period were the leaders I followed. Theirs were the ideas I shared (and still share). But all that is over now, for the postwar period is clearly at an end; and we have to find new bearings.

So I must close with a fervent prayer that this time the new bearings will be found so that the postwar period will not again merge into another prewar period. What happened last time does not have to be repeated; the past merely conveys a warning. To this prayer, I must also add an explanation, however. As noted, I shall carry on as usual until the New Year. But I am writing this report today because my plans have begun to be discussed by a few people, and I do not like being beaten on my own story. — *Washington Post*, 1974

Notes

PROLOGUE

1. Joseph Alsop, *The Rare Art Traditions: The History of Art Collecting and Its Linked Phenomena* (New York: Princeton University Press and Harper & Row, 1982).

2. Paul Hyde Bonner to Joseph Alsop, October 25, 1949, Box 5, Alsop Papers, Library of Congress (hereafter cited as APLC).

3. Neil Sheehan, *A Bright Shining Lie: John Paul Vann and America in Vietnam* (New York: Random House, 1988), 9–10.

4. "So the fact has got to be faced: newspaper reporting is a craft or trade, like undertaking, which it sometimes resembles." Joseph and Stewart Alsop, *The Reporter's Trade* (New York: Reynal & Company, 1958), 4.

5. Joseph Alsop, *From the Silent Past: A Report on the Greek Bronze Age* (New York: Harper & Row, 1964).

6. Henry James, preface to *The Aspern Papers* (1888; New York: Oxford University Press, World Classics Edition, 1983).

7. Cf. Frederick Marks III, *Velvet on Iron: The Diplomacy of Theodore Roosevelt* (Lincoln: University of Nebraska Press, 1979), and John Milton Cooper, Jr., *The Warrior and the Priest: Woodrow Wilson and Theodore Roosevelt* (Cambridge: Belknap Press, Harvard University Press, 1983).

8. Douglass Cater, *The Fourth Branch of Government* (Boston: Houghton Mifflin, 1959), 99.

9. Author's interview with a confidential source.

10. Joseph W. Alsop with Adam Platt, *"I've Seen the Best of It"* (New York: Norton, 1992).

CHAPTER ONE

1. George F. Kennan, *Memoirs, 1925–1950* (New York: Pantheon, 1967), 296–97.

2. George Kennan ("Mr. X"), "The Sources of Soviet Conduct," *Foreign Affairs* (July 1947).

3. Joseph and Stewart Alsop, "Must America Save the World?," *Saturday Evening Post*, February 21, 1948.

4. Author's interview with Peter Jay, London.

5. Joseph and Stewart Alsop, *The Reporter's Trade* (New York: Reynal & Company, 1958), 134.

6. Joseph Alsop to Clark Clifford, December 1, 1948, APLC.

7. Joseph and Stewart Alsop, "Enter Baldwin's Ghost, Mewing," *New York Herald Tribune*, December 3, 1948.

8. Joseph Alsop with Adam Platt, *"I've Seen the Best of It"* (New York: Norton, 1992). See also Alsop to Rex Barley of the *Los Angeles Times* Syndicate, February 8, 1979, APLC: "I don't regard myself as being in competition with the large thinkers who do not stay with the news or bother with factual reporting. . . . I regard myself as being in competition, rather, with the reporter-columnists like David Broder on the *Post* or Tom Wicker and Scottie [*sic*] Reston on the *Times*, who are in the happy situation of writing today for tomorrow morning." Alsop to Frederick J. Mersbach (a University of Illinois student then writing a term paper on him), May 23, 1949, Box 4, APLC: "Facts alone in the long run possess influence. . . . If a member of my trade forgets this important truth, and begins to think his readers will be guided by his personal opinion, it is time for him to think about retiring."

9. Arthur Schlesinger, Jr., to Joseph Alsop, May 25, 1953, APLC: "One thing happened during the weekend which I feel I should acquaint you with. I had a long talk with Nancy Wechsler, who said, inter alia, that Jimmy had been terribly hurt and disappointed over the silence of the Alsops regarding his tangle with McCarthy." Alsop to Schlesinger, May 29, 1953, APLC: "I am horrified that Jimmy should feel as he does. . . . The reason we did not write about Jimmy, of course, is that we have an almost unbreakable rule against straight editorial comment. And in Jimmy's case, the writers of tomorrow morning's papers were continuously ahead of us, so that we felt that we had nothing new to add."

10. Alsop and Alsop, *Reporter's Trade,* 42.

11. Joseph Alsop to Paul Nitze, December 10, 1949, APLC: "There is no use telling our people what ought to be done. You must also tell them why it ought to be done. There is no use telling them what is being done. You must also tell them how it is being done. . . . The raw material of a positive policy is public opinion. There is no way to secure a favorable public opinion . . . except to inform the public. The best medium for informing the public is through the press. Thus the official does no favor to a newspaperman when he takes some of his hard-pressed time to explain a complex subject; instead, he is serving his own interests, and the interests of the policy he is working for." See also Joseph Alsop to Felix Frankfurter, draft letter dated January 6, 1950, APLC.

12. Alsop and Alsop, *Reporter's Trade,* 12–13.

13. "*Daily Express* Libel Suit," Box 148, APLC. In 1962, Joe Alsop consulted London solicitors when the *Daily Express* incorrectly reported that Lord Home had refused to see him. Joe claimed that he had merely insisted that John Russell, press spokesman for the Foreign Office, not be present during his interview with the foreign secretary. The interview was granted, but Alsop was reprimanded by Lord Home.

14. Alsop and Alsop, *Reporter's Trade,* 65–69.

15. Ibid.

16. Stewart Alsop, *The Center: People and Power in Political Washington* (New York: Harper & Row, 1968), 194–95.

17. Charles E. Sergis to Stewart Alsop, November 1, 1956, APLC; Joseph Alsop to Sergis, November 7, 1956, APLC.

18. Buchwald's droll account of the affair, including the quote from Stewart Alsop's review, is in his book *Counting Sheep* (New York: Putnam, 1970), 58–65.

19. Author's interview with Philip L. Geyelin.

20. Joseph and Stewart Alsop, "A Dark Lesson," *New York Herald Tribune*, May 25, 1949.

21. Alsop and Alsop, *Reporter's Trade*, 15.

22. Alsop and Alsop, "Dark Lesson."

23. Joseph Alsop, "About Mr. Johnson's Credibility," unpublished column, carbon copy, Box 166, APLC. See also Alsop and Alsop, *Reporter's Trade*, 73–74.

24. Ibid. See also Louis Johnson, "What Are the Communists' Objectives?," *U.S. Air Services*, September 1955, p. 12: "What is the job of the [American] Legion? . . . Be vigilant to see to it that we are putting more energy, more resources and more skill into the atomic air race than the Russians. It is better for us as a group to err on the side of calling for more defense than to err on the side of calling for too little." A reader who sympathized with their anti-Johnson blasts had clipped the article and sent it to the Alsops.

CHAPTER TWO

1. Joseph Alsop with Adam Platt, *"I've Seen the Best of It"* (New York: Norton, 1992), 306–8. See also Dean Rusk (as told to Richard Rusk), *As I Saw It* (New York: Norton, 1990), 161.

2. Sarah Booth Conroy, "The House that Alsop Built: A Man and His Taste," *Washington Post*, September 29, 1974, K1.

3. Arthur Schlesinger, Jr., to Joseph Alsop, November 10, 1949, APLC.

4. Joseph Alsop to Anderson & Sheppard Ltd., January 4, 1966, APLC.

5. Douglass Cater, conversation with author, July 1990.

6. Joseph Alsop to B. H. Blackwell's Ltd., October 29, 1964, Box 92, APLC.

7. Joseph and Stewart Alsop, *The Reporter's Trade* (New York: Reynal & Company, 1958), 2.

8. Joseph Wechsberg, "Caviar for the Comrades," *Reader's Digest*, May 1953; Wechsberg to Alsop, February 14 and 28, 1953; Alsop to Wechsberg, February 23 and March 2, 1953, APLC. Alsop to Wechsberg, April 28: "I have heard nothing but compliments on your . . . piece, which has evidently made me a hero. Equally evidently, I was silly to be so fussed about it and I apologize herewith."

9. Stewart Alsop, *Stay of Execution: A Sort of Memoir* (Philadelphia: J. B. Lippincott, 1973), 110.

10. Ibid., following 160.

11. Joseph and Stewart Alsop, "Lament for a Long-Gone Past," *Saturday Evening Post*, January 26, 1957, 17ff.

12. Alsop and Alsop, *Reporter's Trade*, 1.

13. Joseph Alsop, *FDR: A Centenary Remembrance* (New York: Viking Press, 1982). Joseph Alsop with Adam Platt, "The Wasp Ascendancy," *New York Review of Books*, November 9, 1989.

14. "A President's Family Album," draft manuscript for *Life* (1939), Box 90, APLC.

15. Author's conversation with Joe Alsop.

16. Author's interview with Corinne Alsop Chubb, Highland Farm, Chester, N.J., March 16, 1991.

17. Joseph Alsop to Mrs. Oates Leiter, December 21, 1956, APLC.

18. "How It Feels to Look Like Everybody Else," unpublished ms. (1937), Box 49, APLC.

19. Stanley Walker to an unidentified addressee, APLC.

CHAPTER THREE

1. Joseph and Stewart Alsop, "How Not to Make Policy," *New York Herald Tribune*, August 30, 1948.

2. Joseph and Stewart Alsop, "The Lesson of Korea," *Saturday Evening Post*, September 2, 1950.

3. Writing from the Air Ministry in Whitehall, Slessor repeatedly cautions Alsop against provocations by MacArthur's forces near the Chinese border, which in his view "would bring in the Soviet Air Force" and compromise MacArthur's unchallenged air supremacy over Korea. As for the talk of using atomic weapons, "anything more crazy . . . I cannot imagine." "There is one thing about this terribly worrying situation, which worries me more than most things. Whatever happens, nothing must be done to weaken Anglo-American solidarity—the one great hope in a not yet hopeless world. . . . Times are hard, but never mind, we shall come through all right so long as we keep stout hearts and level heads and keep *together*" (emphasis in original). Air Marshal Sir John Slessor to Joseph Alsop, December 3, 1950, Box 6, APLC.

4. Nikita Khrushchev, *Khrushchev Remembers*, translated and edited by Strobe Talbott with commentary and notes by Edward Crankshaw (New York: Bantam Books, 1971), 400–407.

5. Carl Mydans to Joseph Alsop, July 9, 1952, Box 8, APLC: "I still picture you in a disgracefully dirty set of field greens and a sweaty face, reaching from time to time into some kind of medicine kit."

6. Joseph Alsop, "Business-As-Usual War," *New York Herald Tribune*, August 18, 1950.

7. Ibid.

8. Joseph Alsop, "Farewell to the Battalion," *New York Herald Tribune*, September 11, 1950.

9. Joseph Alsop, "Crossing the Han," *New York Herald Tribune*, September 25, 1950; "The Conquerors," ibid., September 27, 1950.

10. Lincoln Kirstein to Joseph Alsop, September 18, 1950, Box 6, APLC.

11. George F. Kennan to Joseph Alsop, October 20, 1950, APLC.

12. Joseph Alsop, "The Deadly Parallel," *New York Herald Tribune*, September 29, 1950.

CHAPTER FOUR

1. Dean G. Acheson, *Present at the Creation: My Years in the State Department* (New York: Norton, 1969), 303.

2. Joseph and Stewart Alsop, "Oh, What a Tangled Tale," *New York Herald Tribune*, January 23, 1950.

3. Joseph Alsop, "The Feud between Stilwell and Chiang" (part one of a three-part series, "Why We Lost China"), *Saturday Evening Post*, January 7, 1950, 17.

4. Quoted in Barbara Tuchman, *Stilwell and the American Experience in China, 1911–1945* (New York: Macmillan, 1971), 300.

5. David Halberstam, *The Best and the Brightest* (New York: Random House, 1972), 115–16. Halberstam describes Joe's series as "the first assault on the [State] Department . . . in the *Republican* [my emphasis] *Saturday Evening Post*. . . . An important organ like the *Post* was looking for conspiratorial answers, and it had exactly the right author . . . and it was not a serious bit of journalism . . . but rather a creation of the Chennault-Chiang Line. . . . The Alsop articles emphasized the conspiratorial nature of events." This is the Alsop series read, and severely bent, through the antiwar lens of the late sixties, correct in only one particular: that Joe Alsop was indeed a partisan of Chennault. Otherwise, as an examination of the articles shows, they are not an "assault" on the State Department but an assault on General Stilwell and his wartime China strategy; they did not advance a "conspiratorial" theory of events, which Alsop in fact believed to be nonsense, as his strenuous intervention in behalf of Davies and other State Department China Hands shows; they reflect Alsop's view that alternative China policies emphasizing closer cooperation with Mao and Chou En-lai were, in retrospect, quite defensible. As journalistic works, the Alsop articles were at least as "serious" as *The Best and the Brightest*, if not in some ways somewhat more so. Finally, as the Hibbs-Sommers-Alsop correspondence shows, the allegedly "Republican" and conspiratorially minded editors of the *Post* were at pains to persuade Joe to be fair to Generals Marshall and Stilwell.

6. Martin Sommers to Joseph Alsop, October 21, 1949, APLC.

7. Ben Hibbs to Joseph Alsop, September 12, 1949, APLC.

8. Joseph Alsop to George F. Kennan, September 21, 1949, APLC.

9. Kennan to Alsop, September 27, 1949, APLC.

10. Herbert Feis, *The China Tangle* (Princeton: Princeton University Press, 1953).

11. John Paton Davies, *Dragon by the Tail* (New York: Norton, 1972), 243.

12. John King Fairbank, *The Great Chinese Revolution* (New York: Harper & Row, 1987), 213.

13. "Secret" Joe Alsop to T. V. Soong, July 12, 1943, APLC. In this influential thirteen-page letter, which Soong passed along to Harry Hopkins, Joe reports that in a recent visit to Kunming "I chanced to find two or three old friends who have high places in Stilwell's ground force organization. . . . As you can imagine I pumped them for all they are worth . . . [for] depressing data on the character and utility of Stilwell's personal set-up. . . . I distrust the old gentleman so much that I hardly trust my own judgment where he is concerned." Joe Alsop's behind-the-scenes lobbying against Stilwell, technically his superior officer, has drawn caustic reviews in Tuchman, *Stilwell and the American Experience in China*, and in Eric Larrabee, *Commander in Chief: Franklin D. Roosevelt, His Lieutenants, and Their War* (New York: Simon & Schuster, 1987), chap. 9.

14. Larrabee, *Commander in Chief*, chaps. 9 and 10.

15. George F. Kennan, *Memoirs, 1950–1963* (Boston: Little, Brown, 1972), 203–6.

16. Joseph Alsop, "Investigate Everybody," *New York Herald Tribune*, September 5, 1951.

17. Joseph Alsop to Brig. Gen. Conrad E. Snow, July 18, 1951, APLC.

18. Joseph Alsop, "Before the Loyalty Board," *New York Herald Tribune*, August 23, 1951.

19. Kennan to Joseph Alsop, July 25, 1951, Box 6, APLC; John P. Davies to Alsop, ibid.

20. Alfred Kohlberg to Joseph Alsop, July 25, 1951, APLC; Alsop to Kohlberg, July 27 and August 15, 1951, APLC.

21. Joseph Alsop to John Foster Dulles, February 27, 1954, APLC.

CHAPTER FIVE

1. Joseph and Stewart Alsop, "Why Has Washington Gone Crazy?," *Saturday Evening Post*, July 29, 1950, 20ff.

2. Richard Rovere, *Senator Joe McCarthy* (New York: Harcourt Brace and Company, 1959), 103–4: "It was in the working-class wards that [Sen. Robert La Follette] lost, and it has often been said that he was defeated because the Communists wanted him out of the way. The Communists despised . . . La Follette because he . . . regarded Communism as totalitarian. . . . McCarthy was reported to have said, when accused of having Communist support, 'Communists have the same right to vote as anyone else, don't they?'"

3. Joseph and Stewart Alsop, "Sense about Security," *New York Herald Tribune*, August 6, 1948.

4. Rovere, *Senator Joe McCarthy*, 122. See also Adrian S. Fisher (Legal Adviser to the Department of State) to Stewart Alsop, September 20, 1950, with attachments, APLC.

5. Stewart Alsop, "Senator McCarthy and His 'Big Three,'" *New York Herald Tribune*, March 5, 1950.

6. Rovere, *Senator Joe McCarthy*, 160: "[McCarthy] had set himself the formidable task of putting an end to Millard Tydings' long career in the Senate. . . . Tydings lost in the fall to John Marshall Butler, who was the beneficiary of large sums of money raised by McCarthy, of tons of anti-Tydings literature—featuring a faked picture of Earl Browder tête-à-tête—prepared by McCarthy's staff."

7. Joseph and Stewart Alsop column, *New York Herald Tribune*, December 3, 1953.

8. Alsop and Alsop, "Why Has Washington Gone Crazy?," 60.

9. Joseph R. McCarthy to Ben Hibbs, August 24, 1950, APLC.

10. Stewart Alsop, "We Might as Well Confess," *New York Herald Tribune*, August 11, 1950.

11. Richard Hofstadter, *The Paranoid Style in American Politics and Other Essays* (New York: Vintage Books, 1967), 3–40. The historical accuracy of Hofstadter's association of McCarthyism, as an American political phenomenon, with late-nineteenth-century varieties of American Populism has been strenuously disputed by, among others, C. Vann Woodward; see Woodward, *The Burden of Southern History* (Baton Rouge: Louisiana State University Press, 1959).

12. Rovere, *Senator Joe McCarthy*, 3.

13. Herman Phleger to Joseph Alsop, November 2, 1954, APLC; Alsop to Phleger, November 12, 1954, APLC. In his reply to Phleger, Alsop wrote, "There is as good a case for the view . . . that Bob Taft was a secret communist as for most other interpretations of the human mind, which is unknowable." Phleger quotes Lord Justice Brown in an English law case: "The state of a man's mind is as much a fact as the state of his digestion."

CHAPTER SIX

1. Hearings before the Internal Security Subcommittee of the U.S. Committee of the Judiciary, August 23, 1951.

2. Prepared testimony of Joseph W. Alsop to the McCarran Committee (undated), Box 64, APLC.

3. Joseph Alsop to Gen. Albert C. Wedemeyer, September 23, 1951, "China" folder, APLC.

4. Alsop to Wedemeyer, October 11, 1951, APLC; Wedemeyer to Alsop, October 8, 1951, APLC. When the War Department's so-called Victory Program

was leaked and published by the McCormick newspapers in Chicago and Washington on December 4, 1941, three days before Pearl Harbor, "Wedemeyer was suspected by some of making the leak, because of his intimate knowledge of the program, his German training, his America First views." Eric Larrabee, *Commander in Chief: Franklin D. Roosevelt, His Lieutenants, and Their War* (New York: Simon & Schuster, 1987), 124–25. This is the episode to which Joe Alsop refers in prodding Wedemeyer to step forward in defense of the unjustly impugned China Hands.

5. Wedemeyer to Alsop, October 8, 1951.

6. Albert Wedemeyer, *Wedemeyer Reports!* (New York: Henry Holt, 1958), 312.

7. Joe Alsop comment to Tom Braden and Patrick Buchanan, radio interview on the publication of his *FDR: A Centenary Remembrance*, WRC Radio, Washington, D.C., 1982.

8. Joseph Alsop to Ben Hibbs, October 10, 1951, APLC.

9. Joseph Alsop, McCarran Committee testimony.

10. Ibid. Joe Alsop was well aware of the stark military impropriety of his out-of-channels role in the backstairs intrigue against Stilwell, which he describes three years earlier as "a somewhat illicit but nonetheless fairly important part in the rather sordid transactions of that period." Joseph Alsop to Elliot Bell, August 12, 1948, Box 3, APLC.

11. Henry A. Wallace to Joseph Alsop, August 18, 1952; Alsop to Wallace, August 20, 1952, APLC.

12. Joseph Alsop to S. H. Levitas, December 3, 1951, APLC.

13. Joseph Alsop, "Lattimore and Vincent," *New York Herald Tribune*, December 21, 1952.

14. Draft letter, Joseph Alsop to Sen. Pat McCarran, February 27, 1952, APLC.

CHAPTER SEVEN

1. John Alsop told his brother Stewart that the term "egghead" was suggested to him by the domed forehead typical of intellectuals.

2. Taft's foreign-policy views are discussed by his biographer James T. Patterson in *Mr. Republican: A Biography of Robert A. Taft* (Boston: Houghton Mifflin, 1972), chap. 31.

3. Joseph Alsop, "The Desperate Act," *New York Herald Tribune*, May 28, 1952.

4. Joseph Alsop, "Theft in Texas," *New York Herald Tribune*, May 30, 1952, and "Skulduggery in Texas," *New York Herald Tribune*, June 1, 1952.

5. Orville Bullington to Joseph Alsop, June 7, 1952, APLC; Alsop to Bullington, June 17, 1952, APLC.

6. Patterson, *Mr. Republican*, chap. 34.

7. Ibid., 559–60.

8. Joseph Alsop, "He'd Rather Not Be President," *Saturday Evening Post*, June 28, 1952.

9. Ibid.

10. Joseph Alsop to Martin Sommers, April 21, 1952, APLC.

11. Joseph Alsop with Adam Platt, *"I've Seen the Best of It"* (New York: Norton, 1992), 340.

12. Joseph Alsop and Stewart Alsop, "How Stevenson Responded," *New York Herald Tribune*, July 24, 1952.

13. Joseph Alsop, "Go Down, Little Daniel," *New York Herald Tribune*, August 29, 1952.

14. Joseph Alsop to Adlai E. Stevenson, February 27, 1952, APLC.

15. Joseph Alsop to Carl McGowan, July 31, 1952, APLC.

16. Joseph Alsop to Isaiah Berlin, October 20, 1952, Box 8, APLC.

17. Stewart Alsop and Charles Bartlett, *Saturday Evening Post*, December 8, 1962. Recent revelations concerning the settlement of the missile crisis indicate that President Kennedy secretly promised Nikita Khrushchev to withdraw U.S. Jupiter missiles from Turkey, in effect accepting the implicit bargain that Stevenson had been pilloried for proposing.

CHAPTER EIGHT

1. Fred Greenstein, *The Hidden-Hand Presidency: Eisenhower as Leader* (New York: Basic Books/Colophon, 1982), 169–70.

2. The text of the Fifth Amendment provides that "no person shall be compelled in any criminal case to be a witness against himself," and, taken literally, would not necessarily apply in a congressional hearing ostensibly convened, as McCarthy's hearings were, to gather information pertinent to a legislative matter from witnesses who are not facing criminal charges. But there had been instances—notably the Alger Hiss case—when criminal perjury charges grew out of such hearings. It was therefore an advance in civility and due process, in the view of many constitutional lawyers, when the Fifth Amendment privilege was extended to benefit witnesses called for congressional testimony. But it is long-standing Fifth Amendment doctrine that once one accused of wrongdoing waives his right to stand silent, he may not answer questions selectively; and that rule was carried over to congressional hearings. The reason is that it would be patently one-sided to permit a witness, once he or she had decided to testify, to answer favorable questions but to decline to answer hostile ones. (Author's telephone interview with Prof. William Van Alstyne of Duke University School of Law, April 12, 1994.)

3. Joe Alsop may have confused the security status of some research at the Radiation Lab with its technological significance in the war effort. The latter was unquestionably of "the highest importance."

4. Joseph Alsop to Paul Cabot, April 15, 1953; Cabot to Alsop, April 22, 1953; Mark DeWolfe Howe to Alsop, April 27, 1953; Alsop to Charles Coolidge, May 12, 1953; Coolidge to Alsop, May 14, 1953; Alsop to Coolidge, January 22, 1954; Coolidge to Alsop, January 26, 1954; Alsop to Coolidge, January 29, 1954; Kenneth T. Bainbridge to Joseph Alsop, September 1, 1954; Alsop to Bainbridge, September 10, 1954, all in Box 153, APLC.

5. Joseph Alsop to William L. Marbury, April 15, 1953; *Atlantic Monthly*, April 1953.

6. Greenstein, *Hidden-Hand Presidency*, 164.

7. On September 6, 1946, in an early Matter of Fact column, the Alsops charged that "In the disorganized period at the close of the war, considerable numbers of American Communists and fellow travelers infiltrated the military government [in Germany], and there became the most passionate advocates of pastoralization, as well as assisting Soviet policy in other ways. The chief center from which the infiltration was accomplished seems to have been Camp Ritchie, Maryland, where German and other language officers were trained for military intelligence. . . . The fact is uncontested that a considerable number of American Communists found posts in the economic division, the information-control division and even the counter-intelligence branch of the military government." On May 14, 1954, Joe Alsop wrote to Melvin Lasky in Berlin, seeking more information "on the heavy communist infiltration in the Eisenhower and early Clay headquarters in Germany." He explained to Lasky that since, in the Oppenheimer security case and others, "the administration's security rules are being applied in an outrageous manner . . . I want to be able to prove that bad judgment . . . and a foolish tolerance of communists were not limited to our wholly a-political scientists. Under the present rules, Eisenhower himself would be a bad risk." Joseph Alsop to Melvin Lasky, May 14, 1954, APLC.

8. William Bragg Ewell, Jr., *Who Killed Joe McCarthy?* (New York: Simon & Schuster, 1984), 220.

9. William C. Chanler to Joseph Alsop, March 19, 1954, APLC.

10. Flanders quoted in Robert Griffith, *The Politics of Fear: Joseph R. McCarthy and the Senate* (Lexington: University Press of Kentucky, 1970), 273.

11. Ibid., 247.

12. Ewald, *Who Killed*, which draws on the unpublished papers of Fred Seaton, is an invaluable inside account of behind-the-scenes maneuvering within the Eisenhower administration.

13. Joseph and Stewart Alsop, "After Munich What?," *New York Herald Tribune*, March 3, 1954.

14. Ewald, *Who Killed*, 242.

15. Joseph and Stewart Alsop, "The Tale Half Told," *New York Herald Tribune*, March 15, 1954.

16. Ewald, *Who Killed*, 278.

17. Ibid., 374–78.

18. Testimony of Robert T. Stevens before the Senate Permanent Subcommittee on Investigations, April 22, 1954.

19. Joe Alsop testimony, "Executive Session—Confidential," May 7, 1954, manuscript transcript, Box 156, APLC. See also Joseph Alsop to Douglas Hamilton (counsel for the *New York Herald Tribune* Syndicate), March 21, 1954, APLC; Joseph Alsop to Thomas R. Prewitt, draft letter, May 21, 1954, APLC.

20. Hamilton to Joseph Alsop, March 24, 1954, APLC: "Cohn told Milton Lewis on the telephone the other day that when this matter blows over he is going to sue you but Milton was inclined to discount what he said. We will have to wait and see."

21. Joseph Alsop with Adam Platt, *"I've Seen the Best of It"* (New York: Norton, 1992), 358–59.

22. Douglass Cater, *The Fourth Branch of Government* (Boston: Houghton Mifflin, 1959), 72–73.

CHAPTER NINE

1. Author's interview with Ambassador Peter Jay, London, July 1990.

2. Bernard Fall, *Hell in a Very Small Place: The Siege of Dien Bien Phu* (Philadelphia: J. B. Lippincott, 1966).

3. Joseph Alsop, "French Want More Help in Indochina," *Washington Post*, January 4, 1954. *Foreign Relations of the United States 1952–54*, vol. 13: Indochina (Washington: Government Printing Office, 1982), part 1 of 2. The author is grateful to Don Oberdorfer, former diplomatic correspondent for the *Washington Post* and a close student of U.S. policy in Southeast Asia in this period and after, for guiding him to this treasury of documents on one of Joe Alsop's bolder behind-the-scenes intrigues.

4. *Foreign Relations*, 940–41, 994.

5. Ibid., 996. The same U.S. diplomatic records show that after a January 26 luncheon in Berlin, Counselor of Embassy Arthur MacArthur (General Douglas MacArthur's son?) noted in a secret "Memorandum for the Record," "Neither we nor the French are ready to throw American or Korean battalions into the breach at this time. Yet if we all had the nerve to take this action, this war [in Indochina] could be brought to a fairly quick close. I do not think China would intervene militarily, and from my personal point of view, if she did, so much the better. We would then take up the war where we left off with the unfortunate armistice in Korea, and we would win it. That is, we would put Chiang Kai-shek back on the mainland in southern China and shake, maybe even destroy, the power of the Chinese Communist government, which is only stalling for time to march on, later, to the absorption of Southeast Asia" (ibid., 1028–29). The optimism that underlay the U.S. intervention in Indochina ten years later was, it would seem, already entertained among some influential American diplo-

mats. As he indicated in his column of June 13, 1954, Joe Alsop emphatically agreed.

6. Ibid., 1029.

7. Joseph and Stewart Alsop, "End at Dienbienphu?," *New York Herald Tribune*, April 30, 1954.

8. Joseph and Stewart Alsop, "Measuring Disaster," *New York Herald Tribune*, June 11, 1954.

9. Joseph Alsop, "Two Who Were Right: General and Scientist," *New York Herald Tribune*, June 13, 1954.

CHAPTER TEN

1. John Lewis Gaddis, *Strategies of Containment: A Critical Appraisal of Postwar American National Security Policy* (New York: Oxford University Press, 1982), 48–49.

2. Ibid., 149, 174.

3. Joseph Alsop, "Two Who Were Right: General and Scientist," *New York Herald Tribune*, June 13, 1954. Six months earlier, at the request of Sen. Stuart Symington, Joe had laid out what he regarded as "a minimum program to avoid an eventual world war and surrender. . . . An all-out effort to build an effective air defense, at whatever cost, combined with an equally strong effort to increase Curt LeMay's [Strategic Air Command] striking power. If we have a complete glass jaw defense-wise, our striking power will be valueless, for we shall not dare to use it for fear of retaliation." The "double effort" was "essential in order to correct the air-atomic power balance, which is now turning so rapidly against us." Alsop to Stuart Symington, January 25, 1954, APLC.

4. Arthur Schlesinger, Jr., to Joseph Alsop, June 1, 1954, APLC.

5. Paul Nitze to Joseph Alsop, July 1, 1954, APLC. See also McGeorge Bundy, *Danger and Survival: Choices about the Bomb in the First Fifty Years* (New York: Random House, 1988), 251.

6. Joseph Alsop with Adam Platt, *"I've Seen the Best of It"* (New York: Norton, 1992), 271–72.

7. Frank L. Howley to Joseph Alsop, July 30, 1954, APLC.

8. Joseph Alsop to Gordon Gray, June 2, 1954, APLC. Gray's irritation with Alsop's letter was sharpened by what he regarded as an inappropriate telephone inquiry in which Joe had asked about a point of board procedure without mentioning his displeasure with the board's verdict. Joe, while declining to yield on the substance, apologized for the tone of the letter, which he said was "written in the first heat of my shock and indignation [and] . . . signed . . . unintentionally, in the middle of a batch of routine mail." Gray to Alsop, June 4, 1954, APLC; Alsop to Gray, June 10, 1954, APLC.

9. Joseph and Stewart Alsop, "A-Scientist Under Probe in Security Risk Case,"

Washington Post (undated). In April 1994, as the manuscript of this book was being prepared for final editing, Pavel Sudaplatov, an eighty-seven-year-old survivor of Stalin's secret police apparatus, published a memoir entitled *Special Tasks: The Memoirs of an Unwanted Witness—A Soviet Spymaster*. Sudaplatov, who at one time had been given major responsibility for Soviet espionage in the nuclear weapons field, alleges that J. Robert Oppenheimer, Enrico Fermi, and Leo Szilard—along with Klaus Fuchs and Bruno Pontecorvo, long identified as atomic spies—knowingly collaborated with the KGB to obtain secrets of U.S. atomic research at Los Alamos and elsewhere. Knowledgeable scholars in the field promptly, and with virtual unanimity, challenged Sudaplatov's allegations as undocumented, plainly misinformed as to who was where at what time, and unreliable—a view I share. Negatives, however, are difficult to prove conclusively. Pending the production of probative materials, the best to be said for Sudaplatov's charges is that they are unfounded; the worst to be said is that they constitute an outrageous libel upon Oppenheimer, Fermi, and Szilard. In his similar allegations regarding Nils Bohr, Sudaplatov (or his ghostwriters) clearly misunderstood the great Danish physicist's effort to interest Winston Churchill and President Roosevelt in the "internationalization" of control of atomic energy.

10. John Major, *The Oppenheimer Hearing* (New York: Stein & Day, 1971), 28–33.

11. Joseph and Stewart Alsop, "Information on the Informer," *Washington Post* (undated), "Crouch Libel Suit" folder, Box 81, APLC.

12. Charles Martin to Stewart Alsop, October 1, 1954, APLC.

13. The crucial isotope hearing incident is related by Major, *Oppenheimer Hearing*, 245–46. See also Philip M. Stern, *The Oppenheimer Case: Security on Trial* (New York: Stein & Day, 1969), 128–30; and Nuel Pharr Davis, *Lawrence and Oppenheimer* (New York: Simon & Schuster, 1968), 288–91.

14. Richard Pfau, *No Sacrifice Too Great: The Life of Lewis L. Strauss* (Charlottesville: University Press of Virginia, 1984), 93.

15. Bundy, *Danger and Survival*, 306.

16. Pfau, *No Sacrifice*, 162.

17. Joseph and Stewart Alsop, "Do We Need Scientists?," *New York Herald Tribune*, October 1, 1954.

18. Quoted in Major, *Oppenheimer Hearing*, 181.

19. Joseph and Stewart Alsop, "What Is Security?," June 4, 1954; "Behind Those Curtains," June 14, 1954; "The Scientific Hornets," June 18, 1954; "Security Risk Griggs?," June 23, 1954; "Super and Security," July 1, 1954; "Operation Spill-the-Beans," July 12, 1954; "Operation Don't Argue!," July 14, 1954, all in the *New York Herald Tribune*.

20. Pfau, *No Sacrifice*, 181.

21. Joseph and Stewart Alsop, *We Accuse* (New York: Simon & Schuster, 1954), chaps. 2, 9.

22. The clippings are in Box 158, APLC.

23. Anonymous article, "The Hidden Struggle for the H-Bomb," *Fortune*, May 1953.

24. Edward Teller to Joseph Alsop, August 10, 1953, APLC; Alsop to Teller, August 14, 1953, APLC.

25. Major, *Oppenheimer Hearing*, 255, provides additional light on the Lincoln summer study.

26. Stern, *Oppenheimer Case*, 193–96.

27. James Shepley and Clay Blair, *The Hydrogen Bomb* (New York: David McKay Co., 1954).

28. Hans Bethe to Joseph and Stewart Alsop, October 1, 1954, Box 82, APLC.

29. Joseph and Stewart Alsop, unpublished letter to the editors of *Time*, November 18, 1954, Box 82, APLC.

30. Pfau writes, "[The Alsops] ignored the new evidence developed at the [Gray Board] hearing, evidence that Oppenheimer lied to security officers, that he continued his association with Chevalier, and that his clearance in 1947 was not routine. Under the rules of the AEC in 1954, Oppenheimer's character and associations made him a security risk even if he was loyal" (*No Sacrifice*, 181). On Pfau's own evidence, what had changed between 1947 and 1954 was not the evidence, all of which had been known and weighed in earlier clearances, but the Eisenhower administration's security regulations, of whose extreme rigidity even Gordon Gray complained.

31. Alsop and Alsop, *We Accuse*, 14.

32. Felix Frankfurter to Joseph Alsop, July 27 and August 13, 1954, Box 165, APLC. The quotation is taken from the second letter.

33. Archibald MacLeish to Joseph Alsop, undated but early or mid-August 1954, Box 165, APLC; Frankfurter to Alsop.

34. Stewart Alsop, "New Debate on the Oppenheimer Case," *U.S. News & World Report*, December 24, 1954, 87.

35. Stewart Alsop to Gerard Piel, February 1, 1955, Box 165, APLC.

36. Schlesinger to Stewart Alsop, March 1, 1955, enclosing carbon copy of draft *Progressive* review, Box 165, APLC.

37. Robert Donovan, *Eisenhower: The Inside Story* (New York: Harper & Brothers, 1956), 297–99.

38. Bundy, *Danger and Survival*, 317.

CHAPTER ELEVEN

1. Stewart Alsop to Sylvan Barnet, Jr., September 6, 1957, Box 129, APLC.

2. Joseph Alsop to William and Susan Mary Patten, October 17, 1956, APLC.

3. Joseph and Stewart Alsop, *The Reporter's Trade* (New York: Reynal & Company, 1958), 296.

4. Joseph Alsop to Hugh Gaitskell, December 12, 1956; Gaitskell to Alsop, December 5, 1956 (referring to a previous "card" from Alsop, now apparently lost); and Gaitskell to Alsop, December 21, 1956, "Suez" folder, all in APLC.

5. Joseph Alsop to Charles E. Bohlen, December 28, 1956, APLC.

6. Joseph Alsop to William and Susan Mary Patten, November 29, 1956, APLC.

7. Typescript dated December 11, 1956, and annotated "Mailed—with completed form," APLC.

8. Bohlen to Stewart Alsop, March 26, 1955, Box 20, APLC.

9. Some of the sources consulted for this chapter have held high positions in the U.S. intelligence community and wished to speak on background without identification, and from personal recollection. I am indebted to Professor Athan Theoharis of Marquette University, who has made a special study of the personal files of J. Edgar Hoover. He generously supplied documents and citations illustrating Hoover's circulation of confidential information about Joe Alsop's entrapment in Moscow.

10. See the memorandum dated November 6, 1956, apparently forwarded to Robert Amory at 2430 E Street N.W., in Box 129, APLC.

11. Joseph Alsop to Ambassador Georgi N. Zaroubin, August 8, 1956, APLC.

12. Joseph Alsop, Matter of Fact columns, *New York Herald Tribune*, January 16, 18, 21, 25, 28, 30, February 6, 10, 11, 13, 15, 18, 20, 21, 22, 1957.

13. Author's interview with a confidential source.

14. Undated telegram from David [?], U.S. Embassy, to Joseph Alsop, Box 129, APLC.

15. Joseph Alsop to Bohlen, April 2, 1957, Box 129, APLC.

16. Memo, Hoover for the Personal Files, April 14, 1959; "Alsop, Joseph," Folder 26, Official and Confidential File of FBI Director J. Edgar Hoover. It is of ironic interest that a recent book by Anthony Summers purports to describe Hoover's participation in homosexual and transvestite affairs at the Plaza Hotel in New York City and elsewhere. The report is delicious but implausible. I agree with Arthur Schlesinger, Jr.'s recent evaluation of the Summers book: "I would dearly love to believe that J. Edgar Hoover wore fluffy black party dresses with flounces, but the 'evidence' adduced in the recent book . . . is far from convincing." "The Perils of Pathography," *New Republic*, May 3, 1993, 37.

17. Memo, Hoover for the Personal Files, April 14, 1959.

18. Edwin R. Bayley, *Joe McCarthy and the Press* (Madison: University of Wisconsin Press, 1981), 161–62.

19. Author's interview with Philip L. Geyelin, Arlington, Va.

20. Joseph Alsop to Stewart Alsop, September 8, 1957, APLC; Stewart Alsop to Joseph Alsop, September 30, 1957, APLC.

21. Stewart Alsop to Joseph Alsop, December 27, 1957, APLC.

22. Ibid., November 25, 1957, APLC.

23. Ibid. See also Stewart Alsop to Joseph Alsop, November 29, 1957, APLC.

24. Joseph Alsop to Stewart Alsop, April 1 and 10, 1958, Box 14, APLC; Stewart Alsop to Joseph Alsop, April 12, 1958, ibid.

25. Stewart Alsop, *Stay of Execution: A Sort of Memoir* (Philadelphia: J. B. Lippincott, 1973), 97.

26. Joseph Alsop to Isaiah Berlin, March 20, 1958, Box 14, APLC.

27. George Wheeler to Stewart Alsop (undated, but probably March 27, 1953), Box 20, APLC.

28. Joseph and Stewart Alsop, "Hail and Farewell," *New York Herald Tribune*, March 12, 1958. See the appendix.

29. Stewart Alsop to Joseph Alsop, December 27, 1957, APLC.

CHAPTER TWELVE

1. Joseph Alsop with Adam Platt, *"I've Seen the Best of It"* (New York: Norton, 1992), 410.

2. Ibid., 406.

3. The best account of the much-disputed choice of Lyndon Johnson is in Jules Witcover, *Crapshoot: Rolling the Dice on the Vice Presidency* (New York: Crown, 1992), 140–58.

4. Ibid.

5. Joseph Alsop to Mrs. John F. Kennedy, August 4, 1960, Box 130, APLC.

6. Mrs. John F. Kennedy to Joseph Alsop (undated but obviously in response to Alsop's letter of August 4, 1960), and Joseph Alsop to Mrs. John F. Kennedy, August 4, 1960, Box 130, APLC.

7. Joseph and Stewart Alsop, *The Reporter's Trade* (New York: Reynal & Company, 1958), 69–70.

8. Throughout the long years of strategic rivalry between the United States and the Soviet Union, an esoteric debate raged within the American intelligence community over the appropriate criteria for measuring the balance of power. Joe Alsop stood emphatically on the side of those who believed that capacity, not presumed intentions, was the only prudent standard of measurement. His passionate interest in intelligence estimates was driven home to me by a personal experience. In 1976, some fifteen years after the missile-gap controversy of 1960–61, George Bush, as director of the Central Intelligence Agency in the Ford administration, ordered a competitive, or comparative, evaluation of Soviet strategic capabilities by an "outside" group of experts and scholars, headed by Prof. Richard Pipes of Harvard, a distinguished historian of czarist and Bolshevik Russia. The outside team, designated "Team B," came up with distinctly gloomier assessments than the CIA's in-house estimators. When word of the contest leaked out, a stormy controversy ensued, having partly to do with the merits of the argument and partly to do with the fury of CIA professionals at being second-guessed by what some of them regarded as a rigged and political-

ly biased inquiry. As the storm raged, one day Joe Alsop came to the *Washington Star* as my luncheon guest. Ignoring others at the table, who included both the editor in chief and the publisher of the newspaper, he focused an embarrassingly single-minded attention on correcting what he viewed as my own insufficient attention to the importance of capability, as opposed to intentions, in estimating intelligence. Like a terrier shaking a rat, he would not let the subject go. Even after we left the table, walked to the elevator, and descended four floors to the lobby and walked out to his waiting taxicab, Joe continued to lecture me on the importance of capabilities.

9. Author's interview with the Hon. James Woolsey, in 1984 a member of the Scowcroft Commission, and since 1993 the director of the Central Intelligence Agency, Washington, D.C.

10. Michael R. Beschloss, *Mayday: Eisenhower, Khrushchev and the U-2 Affair* (New York: Harper & Row, Perennial Library, 1987), 237: "In his diary, [George] Kistiakowsky [White House science adviser] wrote . . . 'In fact, the missile gap doesn't look to be very serious.'"

11. Joseph Alsop, *New York Herald Tribune*, January 27, 1960.

12. Beschloss, *Mayday*, 5.

13. Ibid., 9.

14. Ibid., 258.

15. "Is There a Strategic Arms Race? (II)," *Foreign Policy* 16 (Fall 1974): 83–88.

16. Joseph Alsop, Kennedy Library interview with Elspeth Rostow, Box 82, APLC, p. 36.

17. Joseph Alsop to Isaiah Berlin, December 11, 1963, Box 19, APLC.

APPENDIX

1. These now largely forgotten figures were, as the Alsops indicate, a very visible part of President Truman's personal entourage and frequented the poker games at the White House, and on the presidential yacht, which were the president's chief relaxation. Edwin Pauley, a Californian, had made his fortune in the oil business and gave generously to the Democrats. He served for a time as chairman of the Democratic National Committee. General Harry Vaughan, the president's military aide, was an old comrade in arms from Battery D, President Truman's World War I artillery unit. John Steelman, a professor of labor relations at the University of North Carolina, frequently advised Truman in that field. Both Snyder, who was secretary of the treasury, and James K. "Jake" Vardaman were Missouri bankers by origin, old Truman friends from home. Vardaman, with the rank of captain, served as Truman's naval aide. Allen, originally a North Carolina tobacco executive, dispensed confidential advice as a kind of all-purpose confidante—not only to Truman but later to President Eisenhower, a

mark of his political flexibility. There was much puritanical sniffing and sniping at Truman's personal circle, including insinuations that it was a nest of corruption. But so strict was Truman's own political rectitude that, so far as I know, not even the slightest corrupt act was ever charged against him. That was not, unfortunately, the case with all the personal friends in whom he reposed trust.

2. The fight over the Office of Price Administration (OPA) concerned the sensitive question of whether and, if so, for how long and on what items price controls would be retained after the end of the war—an issue of explosive significance, both fiscally and politically. Henry Wallace, whom Truman had succeeded as vice president, had broken with Truman and become a third-party candidate on the Progressive ticket in 1948. John L. Lewis, the colorful and self-consciously eloquent head of the United Mine Workers, conducted a strike in 1946 that greatly agitated the Truman administration and the nation. Coal was then a far more critical industrial fuel than it is today, and before it was settled, the strike threatened to bring on national economic paralysis. Lewis Schwellenbach (for whom the Alsops reserved a sort of amused contempt) was an old Senate colleague and friend of Harry Truman's (from Washington State) who became his secretary of labor, succeeding Frances Perkins.

3. The secretary of state was John Foster Dulles. The two "brilliant Soviet experts" were the Alsops' friends Chip Bohlen and George F. Kennan. Bohlen's "exile" was the U.S. embassy in Moscow. Kennan had resigned with the change of administration in 1953.

4. The unmistakable echo is of the publican's voice in T. S. Eliot's *The Waste Land.* Joe Alsop's uncertainty suggests, perhaps, that in his innumerable visits to England he had spent very little if any time in pubs.

Bibliographic Essay

In 1964, Joseph and Stewart Alsop began donating their papers, in stages, to the Manuscript Division of the Library of Congress. These materials—manuscripts and drafts, personal and professional correspondence, assorted family mementos—form the documentary backbone of this book. Joe Alsop was a prolific and often argumentative letter-writer. His correspondence often supplements and illuminates what he was writing or planning to write for publication. Stewart Alsop tended to be a more utilitarian letter-writer, or at any rate less personal. In any case, some three-quarters of the nearly 50,000 items in the Alsop Papers are by, or pertain to, Joe Alsop.

As the reader of this book will have noted, however, the narrative line has been reinforced by key memoirs and secondary works on the period. The most useful of these are listed and discussed by categories below. The list is of course far from exhaustive, for one who undertook to master the entire historical literature of the Cold War period would have no time to write about it.

GENERAL STUDIES

For continuity throughout the period, John Lewis Gaddis's *Strategies of Containment: A Critical Appraisal of Postwar American National Security Policy* (New York: Oxford University Press, 1982) is indispensable. It carries the story from the early postwar years to the eve of the Reagan administration. Gaddis, who is currently preparing a biography of George F. Kennan, writes from a centrist point of view that reflects, though not uncritically, a general sympathy with the "cold war liberalism" which was also the animating creed of the Alsops. Robin Edmonds, in *Setting the Mould: The U.S. and Britain, 1945–1950* (New York: Oxford University Press, 1986), is keyed to the perspective from embassies and chanceries. Edmonds, a distinguished British diplomat and historian, shares with the Alsops a deep attachment to the Anglo-American "special relationship." Edmonds, *The Big Three: Churchill, Roosevelt, and Stalin in Peace and War* (New York: Norton, 1991) covers the World War II years but also provides valuable background on the postwar years. Two younger writers, Walter Isaacson and Evan Thomas, both accomplished newsmagazine journalists, collaborated on *The Wise Men: Six Friends and the World They Made* (New York: Simon & Schuster, 1986). Isaacson and Thomas concern themselves in this book with Washington figures—McCloy, Kennan, Bohlen, and others—who were Alsop friends and sources. The authors are sensitive, by personal experience, to the ways in which high officials and reporters who write about them interact. For *Eisenhower: The Inside Story* (New York: Harper, 1956), Robert J. Donovan, then chief Washington correspondent for the *New York Herald Tribune*, was given unique access to behind-the-scenes decision-making in the Eisenhower administration. Although in part superseded by later scholarly studies, Donovan's report is still valuable for its sensitive blend of a contemporary perspective and high-level sourcing. Donovan later wrote a readable two-volume biography of Harry S. Truman. Fred Greenstein's *The Hidden-Hand Presidency: Eisenhower as Leader* (New York: Basic Books, 1982) is the work of a Princeton University political scientist now widely recognized as the bellwether of the revisionist view of the Eisenhower presidency. As a college student in the 1950s, Greenstein had viewed Eisenhower "as a good-natured bumbler, who lacked the leadership qualities to be an effective president," but later, as a scholar, he found that "events, speculations and hard evidence changed my view." Chief among those events was almost certainly the fiasco of U.S. policy in Vietnam, which served to highlight, by contrast, the wisdom of Eisenhower's 1954 decision to avoid United States intervention at Dien Bien Phu. Anyone writing about American life and politics in the 1950s will find William Manchester's *The Glory and the Dream: A Narrative History of America, 1932–1972* (New York: Little, Brown, 1974) vividly written and useful for continuity. Manchester has a keen eye for detail and for revealing social trends. No general bibliography of the period could omit Dean Acheson's *Present at the Creation: My Years in the State Department* (New York: Norton, 1969) or George F. Kennan's *Memoirs, 1950–1963* (Boston and Toronto: Little, Brown, 1972). Acheson and Kennan, Truman administration colleagues and collaborators in many crucial postwar battles, were also men of contrasting temperaments who later clashed over strategic judgment. Both are elegant stylists. Three very original books by one of the finest historians of our day have influenced my own view of the postwar world, which was taking shape when I was still a boy. They are John Lukacs's *A History of the Cold War* (Garden City, N.Y.: Anchor, 1961), *The Last European War* (Garden City, N.Y.: Anchor, 1976), and *1945: Year Zero* (Garden City, N.Y.: Doubleday, 1978).

BOOKS BY THE ALSOPS

Both Joe and Stewart Alsop wrote memorable autobiographies. Stewart Alsop's *Stay of Execution: A Sort of Memoir* (Philadelphia: J. B. Lippincott, 1973) is an entertaining and gallant reminiscence written, as the title indicates, while its author was in remission from a mysterious form of leukemia. Light-hearted remembrance alternates with clinical detail about his illness, told with the flair of a great reporter. Joe Alsop's memoir, *"I've Seen the Best of It"* (New York: Norton, 1992), was ably completed by his collaborator Adam Platt and appeared three years after his death. The book is engagingly written—especially in earlier chapters, where Alsop's own touch is evident—but is almost as notable for its concealments, gaps, and unannounced second thoughts as for its revelations. Stewart Alsop's *The Center: People and Power in Political Washington* (New York: Harper &

Row, 1968) is dated now, a period piece that deals reportorially with figures and events now vanished, a relic of a different era and mood. It is nonetheless written with Stewart Alsop's usual charm and, for the student of his journalism, offers useful sidelights on Alsopian attitudes and the people he and his brother relied on as sources. *The Reporter's Trade* (New York: Reynal & Company, 1958) collects samples from a dozen years of joint columnizing, with commentary by both Alsops. It has been an invaluable source for this study. Joe Alsop's earlier books, *The 168 Days* (with Turner Catledge of the *New York Times*; Garden City, N.Y.: Doubleday, Doran, 1938) and *Men around the President* (Garden City, N.Y.: Doubleday, Doran, 1939) are out of print and difficult to find; they deal with pre–World War II New Deal events and issues. But after more than half a century, both testify to the elder Alsop's brilliance as a reporter and stylist—as does his brief but luminous *FDR: A Centenary Remembrance* (New York: Viking, 1982).

THE KOREAN WAR

Max Hastings's account in *The Korean War* (New York: Simon & Schuster, 1987) is authoritative, balanced, and up to date. In his vivid biography of Douglas MacArthur, *American Caesar* (New York: Little, Brown, 1978), William Manchester is informative on the politics of the war and the developing tension between Tokyo and Washington that ultimately led to President Truman's dismissal of the general. Concerning the MacArthur dismissal and its roots and repercussions, Richard Rovere and Arthur Schlesinger, Jr., in *The General and the President and the Future of American Foreign Policy* (New York: Farrar, Strauss and Young, 1951) collaborated on a lively contemporary evaluation. They wrote rapidly, but the book retains historical value. Both Rovere and Schlesinger were sympathetic to Truman and United Nations policy (which MacArthur had challenged) but are critical of the administration's failure to make the rationale of the then-novel doctrine of "limited war" clear to the American public.

THE CHINA ISSUE

E. J. Kahn, Jr.'s *The China Hands: America's Foreign Service Officers and What Befell Them* (New York: Viking, 1975) is a popular and sympathetic treatment of the ordeal of the State Department's Far East specialists during the McCarran-McCarthy inquisition. Kahn, a *New Yorker* writer, offers reportage, not history, but with diverting particulars about the personalities of figures like John Paton Davies, John Carter Vincent, and others. John King Fairbank's *The Great Chinese Revolution, 1800–1985* (New York: Harper & Row, 1986) provides background on the political and social upheavals that informed the postwar "China issue." In his *The Soong Dynasty* (New York: Harper & Row, 1985), Sterling Seagrave, who spent his boyhood on the China-Burma border, chronicles the rise of the intriguing family whose three sisters—one of whom became Madame Chiang Kai-shek—played guardian angels to the three principal factions in China's civil war. Seagrave is a Stilwell partisan. Robert Barnett, author of *Wandering Knights: China Legacies Lived and Recalled* (Armonk, N.Y.: M. E. Sharpe, 1990), is an Asian scholar and Foreign Service officer, sometime director of the Asia Society, who worked with Joe Alsop in wartime Chungking and recalls his "electric presence" in Chennault's headquarters. Of all those who have considered the Stilwell-Chennault conflict over American strategy, Barbara Tuchman is the most emphatically pro-Stilwell and is consequently caustic on the subject of Joe Alsop. Tuchman's book *Stilwell and the American Experience in China, 1911–1945* (New York: Macmillan, 1971), like many of her other popular works, combines brilliant narrative with an occasional excess of what has been called "Cleopatra's nose" history—the assignment of great causative weight to small, single factors. *Wedemeyer Reports!* (New York: Henry Holt & Company, 1958) is the memoir of Gen. Albert C. Wedemeyer, who assumed command in China after Stilwell's recall. Wedemeyer's equivocal view of the China Hands who advised him, and his suggestion that General Marshall was the "captive" of those advisers, echo his disappointing response, in 1951, to Joe Alsop's call for help in the McCarran interrogations. One who compares Tuchman and Wedemeyer comes away with the impression that the violent and sometimes nasty postwar controversy over American policy in China may be traced more to temperamental and ideological differences between the observers than to objective events. Of all the China Hands, none was more highly qualified, or more controversial, than John Paton Davies. His memoir *Dragon by the Tail* (New York: Norton, 1972) is a delightful behind-the-scenes evocation of wartime Chungking and of the political intrigues whose reverberations were to be so lasting. An ally and sympathizer of Davies and other professionals, Theodore White in his *In Search of History: A Personal Adventure* (New York: Harper & Row, 1978) recalls his heady tour as Henry Luce's ace correspondent in China during his early and mid-twenties. White, one of the premier American journalists of the half century, files an impassioned brief for Marshall and Stilwell and the young men who served and advised them. A more scholarly perspective informs Herbert Feis's *The China Tangle* (Princeton: Princeton University Press, 1965). Feis was a sometime New Deal official who turned historian. Unlike Joe Alsop, who tended to view the China issue as a personal and temperamental struggle of titans, Feis emphasizes such impersonal constraints as limits of supply and manpower.

Richard Rovere's *Senator Joe McCarthy* (New York: Harcourt, Brace, 1959) remains the best journalistic portrait of the century's most noted American demagogue. As Washington correspondent for the *New Yorker*, Rovere, a witty and graceful writer, took a continuing interest in the senator's anticommunist activities from their inception in February 1950 and followed McCarthy to the end. The same writer's *Affairs of State: The Eisenhower Years, 1950–1956* (New York: Farrar, Straus, and Cudahy, 1956), collects Rovere's *New Yorker* dispatches, which remain strikingly readable and shrewd after nearly forty years. A notable book with a specialized perspective, by another close student of McCarthy and his methods, is Edwin R. Bayley's *Joe McCarthy and the Press* (Madison: University of Wisconsin Press, 1981). Bayley was political correspondent for the *Milwaukee Journal*, an excellent and powerful regional newspaper that was emphatically anti-McCarthy. Bayley's book is informative about McCarthy's Wisconsin home base and about the Wisconsin newspapers and journalists who grasped the fraudulence of his charges from the first. In *The Politics of Fear: Joseph R. McCarthy and the Senate* (Lexington: University Press of Kentucky, 1970), Robert Griffin offers a meticulously researched look at the institutional politics of the Senate during McCarthy's ascendancy. Griffin shows how the political fears generated by Korea and the MacArthur controversy inhibited and silenced internal Senate opposition. In the vast McCarthy literature, no book is more absorbing and entertaining than William Bragg Ewell, Jr.'s oddly titled *Who Killed Joe McCarthy?* (New York: Simon & Schuster, 1984). Ewell, a stylish writer, was a staff assistant at the Eisenhower White House and became the first writer to use—to excellent effect—the Fred Seaton papers, an invaluable archive relating to the Army-McCarthy clash. Ewell's earlier *Eisenhower the President: Crucial Days, 1951–1960* (Englewood Cliff, N.J.: Prentice Hall, 1981) provides a sympathetic insider's view of the Eisenhower years. David Eisenhower's *Eisenhower at War, 1943–1945* (New York: Random House, 1986) evaluates his grandfather's role in grand strategy after the Normandy invasion—the so-called "broad front" issue. Joe Alsop believed, for reasons not readily apparent to other readers of the book, that David Eisenhower's account was inspired by a family wish to clear Ike of imputations that his decisions to hold back from drives on Berlin and Prague could be construed as "pro-Russian," a view entertained only by Senator McCarthy and his followers in the 1950s and a few right-wing cranks subsequently. Lillian Hellman's account of her clash with the McCarthyites in *Scoundrel Time* (New York: Little, Brown, 1976) is likewise of tangential interest. She was a close friend of Joe Alsop, Henry A. Wallace, Joseph L. Rauh, and others of the Washington anti-McCarthy camp. This brief memoir was roundly attacked as self-serving and tendentious when it appeared—it was at the root of the Hellman–Mary McCarthy libel action—but, biased or not, it recaptures the flavor of the time.

The Oppenheimer security case has attracted many fine writers, and the literature, which necessarily includes many excellent books about the origins and development of the atomic weapon, is rich. A good starting place is John Major's
The Oppenheimer Hearing (New York: Stein and Day, 1971), a volume in the Historic Trials Series edited by J. P. Kenyon. Major (who is not, by the way, the
prime minister of that name) brings an English perspective to bear in a book
that is incisive and diligently researched. Charles P. Curtis's *The Oppenheimer Case:
The Trial of a Security System* (New York: Simon & Schuster, 1955) is an early
scrutiny of the Gray Board report by a distinguished trial lawyer. Curtis argues
that the AEC proceedings violated basic norms of due process. That view is
echoed and reinforced by Philip M. Stern (with the collaboration of Harold P.
Green) in *The Oppenheimer Case: Security on Trial* (New York: Harper & Row,
1969), an exhaustive account drawing upon interviews and documentary materials. For the student of the Manhattan Project itself, several works stand out.
Pride of place must be given to Richard Rhodes's magnificent *The Making of the
Atomic Bomb* (New York: Simon & Schuster), winner of the National Book
Award for 1987. Rhodes follows the bomb project from start to finish, brilliantly recapturing the climate of urgency, the scientific background, and the personalities. A very different but also magisterial work is McGeorge Bundy's *Danger
and Survival: Choices about the Bomb in the First Fifty Years* (New York: Random
House, 1988). Bundy, a historian by training and sometime national security adviser to Presidents Kennedy and Johnson, examines the strands of debate relating to the development and control of nuclear weapons with the eye of a seasoned player in the making of high national security policy. The book includes a
very negative assessment of the AEC's condemnation of Oppenheimer. For the
lay student of the Manhattan Project, Nuel Pharr Davis's *Lawrence and Oppenheimer* (New York: Simon & Schuster, 1968) is a key book, examining the two
commanding figures of the U.S. bomb project with lucidity, humanity, and evident scientific understanding. In *The Atom Bomb Spies* (New York: Atheneum,
1980), H. Montgomery Hyde offers a readable popular account of atomic espionage—a field sure to be increasingly active and controversial as Soviet intelligence archives are opened. Richard Pfau's *No Sacrifice Too Great* (Charlottesville:
University Press of Virginia, 1984) is a sympathetic biography of Admiral Lewis
Strauss, who emerged as both Oppenheimer's patron and—in the Alsop view, at
least—his principal persecutor. Pfau's view of the Oppenheimer case is naturally partial to Strauss. An older but brilliant popularization of the atomic bomb
story is Robert Jungk's *Brighter Than a Thousand Suns: A Personal History of the
Atomic Scientists*, trans. James Cleugh (New York: Harcourt, Brace, 1958). For
those with an appetite for the detail of the century's most fascinating "national
security" case, the thousand-page transcript of the Gray Board hearing, with relevant documents, was republished as *In the Matter of J. Robert Oppenheimer* (Cam-

bridge: MIT Press, 1971), with a foreword by Philip M. Stern. Finally, the Alsops' own book *We Accuse* (New York: Simon & Schuster, 1954) is one of the key texts of the Oppenheimer story; but as I noted above (chapter 10), the book was largely ignored, never appeared in hard covers, and now seems to be almost unobtainable. *Atoms and the Universe*, by G. O. Jones, J. Rotblat, and G. J. Withrow (New York: Viking Penguin, 1973) is an extremely useful primer on nuclear fission, geared to the lay reader of science.

MISCELLANEOUS SOURCES

As background for the so-called missile-gap controversy, Michael R. Beschloss's *Mayday: Eisenhower, Khrushchev and the U-2 Affair* (New York: Harper & Row, 1986) is readable and dramatic. Jules Witcover's *Crapshoot: Rolling the Dice on the Vice Presidency* (New York: Crown, 1992) and James T. Patterson's *Mr. Republican: A Biography of Robert A. Taft* (Boston: Houghton Mifflin, 1972) throw revealing light on two critical presidential campaigns in which the Alsops were deeply engaged. Bernard B. Fall's *Hell in a Very Small Place: The Siege of Dien Bien Phu* (New York: Random House, 1966) is a classic treatment of the climactic Indochina battle, in which Joe Alsop intrigued to involve the United States (see above, chapter 9). In *Mornings on Horseback* (New York: Simon & Schuster, 1981), David McCullough delightfully evokes the pre-presidential Theodore Roosevelt and the ambience of the family whose heritage explains so much about TR's grand-nephews, the Alsop brothers. Eric Larrabee's *Commander in Chief: Franklin Delano Roosevelt, His Lieutenants, and Their War* (New York: Simon & Schuster, 1987) contains, among other excellent things, the most balanced assessment of the Stilwell controversy that I have encountered. Herbert Agar's *The Unquiet Years: U.S.A. 1945–1955* (London: Rupert Hart-Davis, 1957) is history-as-personal-essay at its best. I first read it as a student at Oxford in the 1950s, and it opened my eyes to the intriguing possibilities of the form, while helping shape my lasting views (and prejudices) on the period. Finally, I wish to acknowledge two valuable unpublished sources: Charles Sergis's master's thesis on the Alsops, written at the University of Missouri in the late 1950s, and Don Oberdorfer's senior honors thesis at Princeton University (1951–52) on the McCarran China hearings.

213
Bibliographic
Essay

Index

Acheson, Dean G., 11, 126, 179; blamed by Alsops for secrecy cult, 20; quoted, 50

Achilles, Theodore, 116

Adams, John G., 103, 105, 109

Adams, Sherman, 105

AEC Advisory Committee, 127–28, 134

Alsop, Corinne Robinson, 36; characterized, 37; seconds Landon nomination, 37

Alsop, John, 83, 84

Alsop, Joseph Wright V, 33; interest in family genealogy, 34, 39

Alsop, Joseph Wright VI: sense of history, 2; character, 5, 7, 31; author's acquaintance with, 6; influence of Theodore Roosevelt on, 8; correspondence with George F. Kennan, 9; Signet Society address, 9; homosexuality, 10; and Vietnam War, 11; education, 13; attacks on Truman administration budget economies, 13; claims to have invented "domino theory," 15; clashes with Art Buchwald over *Sheep on the Runway*, 22; fondness for dinner parties, 28; clothing, 28–29; Georgetown house, 28–29, 34; book buying, 30; as pre–World War II columnist, 30; on Franklin D. Roosevelt, 32; at Groton School, 37; weight problem and interest in diets, 37; and FDR destroyers-for-bases swap, 39; in Korea, 40–48; criticizes Truman administration Korean policy, 41; on "lessons of Korea," 42; reactions to battle, 45–46, 47; advocates Korean unification, 48; and China, 49–63; and Wallace mission to China, 73–79; drafts Wallace messages to FDR, 75; testimony to Internal Security Committee, 76, 79; writes "Strange Case of Louis Budenz," 81; worries about "native fascism," 83; criticizes indeci-

siveness of Adlai Stevenson, 90; second thoughts about Stevenson, 91; defends Wendell Furry, 96–100; takes active role in showdown with McCarthy, 105–10; plots to "force" U.S. hand in Indochina, 114; slow to accept atomic stalemate, 121; writes "We Accuse" article for *Harper's*, 140; decides to shift working base to Paris, 146–47, 151; visits Palestinian refugee camps, 148; corresponds with Hugh Gaitskell about Suez crisis, 149; is entrapped by secret police in Moscow, 154–58; and issue of homosexuality in government, 156; considers announcing sexual orientation, 158; dissolves partnership with Stewart Alsop, 158–63; describes special relationship with John F. Kennedy, 174–75

Alsop, Stewart: influence of Theodore Roosevelt on, 8; as *Newsweek* columnist, 11; education, 13; investigates Soviet atomic bomb explosion, 21; characterized, 31; joins Joe as partner in Matter of Fact column, 31; interviews McCarthy, 64–65; quoted on McCarthy, 67–68; collaborates with Charles Bartlett after Cuban missile crisis, 93; writes columns on "bomber" and "air atomic" gap, 137; protests AEC publicity policy, 141; teases Vichinski about Alsops' hereditary "homicidal" tendency, 151; dissolves partnership with Joe Alsop, 158–63

Alsop, Susan Mary, 167

Alsop, Tish, 161

Amerasia affair, 60

American Legion, 91

Americans for Democratic Action (ADA), 19

America's Retreat from Victory, 101

Arab nationalism, 148

Army-McCarthy clash, 100